ANTHROPOLOGICAL PAPERS

MUSEUM OF ANTHROPOLOGY, UNIVERSITY OF MICHIGAN

NO. 45

# MISCELLANEOUS STUDIES IN MEXICAN PREHISTORY

BY

MICHAEL W. SPENCE
JEFFREY R. PARSONS
MARY HRONES PARSONS

WITH A CONTRIBUTION BY
GEORGE FRAUNFELTER

ANN ARBOR, MICHIGAN

1972

TABLE OF CONTENTS

## LIST OF ILLUSTRATIONS

*(Spence and Parsons)*

### Figures



### Plates
(p.37ff)



*(M. H. Parsons)*

### Figures

Maps



Plates
(p.115ff)

# PREHISPANIC OBSIDIAN EXPLOITATION IN CENTRAL MEXICO A PRELIMINARY SYNTHESIS

*Michael W. Spence*
*Jeffrey R. Parsons*

## GENERAL INTRODUCTION

DURING the past few years both of us have had occasion to become interested in the economics of prehispanic obsidian production and distribution in and around the Valley of Mexico: Spence as a result of his involvement with the Teotihuacán Mapping Project, directed by René Millon, and Parsons through participation in William T. Sanders' Teotihuacán Valley Project and his own subsequent investigations in the Texcoco Region.

The present paper is an attempt to draw together a series of admittedly fragmentary and incomplete data bearing upon aboriginal utilization of obsidian in Central Mexico, focusing upon the rich quarries of Cruz del Milagro and Cerro Piñal in southern Hidalgo and certain aspects of obsidian quarrying and working in the eastern Valley of Mexico. While we recognize the speculative and tentative character of many of our conclusions and observations and the far-from-ideal quality of the information at our disposal, we are hopeful that our efforts to synthesize will be provocative and suggestive of directions in which subsequent investigations might best proceed.

In the course of our fieldwork, we have benefited from the assistance of several institutions and numerous individuals. Both Millon's and Sanders' projects have been primarily supported by National Science Foundation Grants GS23800, GS207, GS614, GS1222. Parsons' fieldwork in 1966 was supported by a faculty research grant awarded by the Horace Rackham Graduate School of the University of Michigan, and his 1967 research in Texcoco was sponsored by National Science Foundation Grant GS1617. In all cases, the Instituto Nacional de Antropología e Historia has been most considerate in facilitating and approving all aspects of our work.

We wish to thank René Millon, James A. Bennyhoff, Matthew Wallrath, Jody Hopkins, José Luis Franco, Thomas Charlton, Warren Barbour, and Darlena Blucher for their assistance with various aspects of the study. Our 1966 visits to the Cruz del Milagro and Cerro Piñal quarries were assisted by several University of Michigan graduate students: Robert Bettarel, Richard Blanton, William

Englebrecht, Mary Hrones, and John Speth. We are likewise greatly indebted to our Mexican guides who led us along the intricate pathways into and out of the rugged Sierra of southern Hidalgo: Señor Jesus Lopez, of San Lorenzo, Hidalgo, who took us to the Cerro Piñal quarry, and Señor Carlos Amador, present owner of the Rancho Guajalote and grandson of Holmes' original guide, who led us to the Cruz del Milagro workings. Both individuals graciously offered us the hospitality and refreshment of their own households in addition to their very capable service as guides.

Thanks are due Robert Flaherty for preparation of photographs and to Jean Spence for drawings and maps.

## THE CRUZ DEL MILAGRO QUARRY

A number of writers have noted the extensive Prehispanic obsidian mines of the Cruz del Milagro, in the state of Hidalgo, Mexico (Fig. 1). Humboldt mentioned them in the report of his late eighteenth century trips (1814, Vol. II:204; 1941, Vol. II:205). Tylor visited the quarry in 1856 and stated that it consisted of

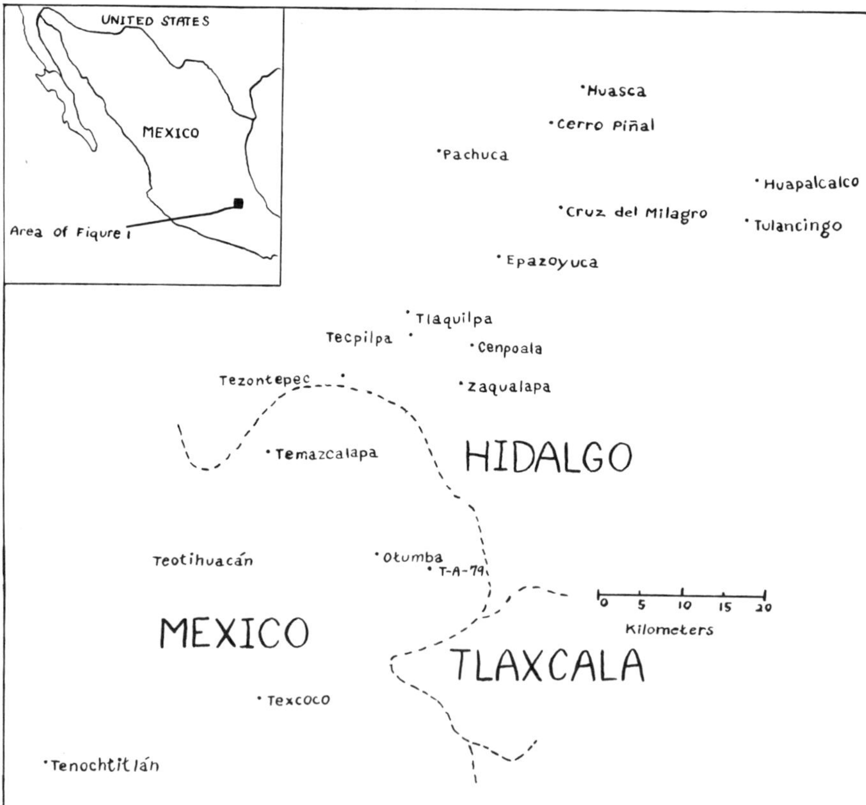


Fig. 1. The Central Mexican Region (after Gibson 1956:Map A).

numerous well-like pits, with some horizontal workings where the obsidian was plentiful (1861:95, 99-100). The most thorough investigation, however, was done by Holmes in the late nineteenth century. He described both the quarry itself and the artifacts he collected there, correctly attributing the operation to the Aztecs (1900; 1919:214, 217-26). Holmes placed the quarry on a long, forested ridge which he considered to be part of the Cerro de las Navajas. This ridge, named the Cruz del Milagro, is actually a distinct feature; so we consider it advisable to drop the old name (Cerro de las Navajas) of the quarry and call it the Cruz del Milagro quarry (see Spence and Parsons, 1967).

Spence, in his first attempt to locate the area, visited the dam spillway north of Huasca, where the surrounding fields are littered with obsidian (Johnson, 1965: 61). The only evidence of human use of the area, however, consisted of a few crude scrapers. Parsons' first trip, in May, 1966, led him to obsidian workings on Cerro Piñal near the village of San Lorenzo, some 11 km north of the Cruz del Milagro deposits. This Cerro Piñal quarry will be described below. In August of 1966 Spence and Parsons together located and surveyed what appeared to be the Cruz del Milagro quarry. Three one-day trips were made, and sites were located on 1:25,000 aerial photographs. The investigations were done very quickly, and no systematic or entirely consistent method was followed in defining or collecting the sites. Also, we examined only a small proportion of the sites in the quarry, and the search for workshops was not very thorough. Thus the conclusions of this report are, in several important aspects, only tentative.

The Cruz del Milagro, now situated on the ejido land of El Nopalillo, can be reached by following a rough, unpaved roadway for about 6 or 7 km north from its junction with the Pachuca-Tulancingo highway somewhat less than 2 km west of the intersection with the main road to Ciudad Sahagún. According to Holmes, the quarry consists of a continuous series of pits and debris mounds running along the south side and base of the Cruz del Milagro, extending 1 or 2 miles (1.6-3.2 km) along the ridge and up to a half mile (0.8 km) in width (1900:409). The present writers surveyed an area 1.75 km long by 0.5 km wide along the south side and base of the ridge. We reached the limits of quarrying only on the southwest. Undoubtedly only a fraction of the total quarry area was seen. Breton states that there are pits and debris mounds also on the north side of the ridge (1902:265).

For the purposes of the survey, complexes of associated pits and debris mounds set slightly apart from other such complexes were collected as separate sites. Because only a few such complexes were examined, and because collections from any one site are often too small to be representative, larger units (quarry areas A and B) were used for the analysis (Fig. 2). The two areas are actually continuous, merging gradually into one another, but certain characteristics allow their distinction. Sites 5 through 14 are in area A, sites 16 through 20 in area B. In both areas the obsidian occurs as chunks and boulders peppering the subsoil, with large masses of waste debris piled up around the mine pits.

Area A is largely on the steeper part of the south side of the Cruz del Milagro. Most of the pits and debris mounds here occur in clusters, though occasional lone

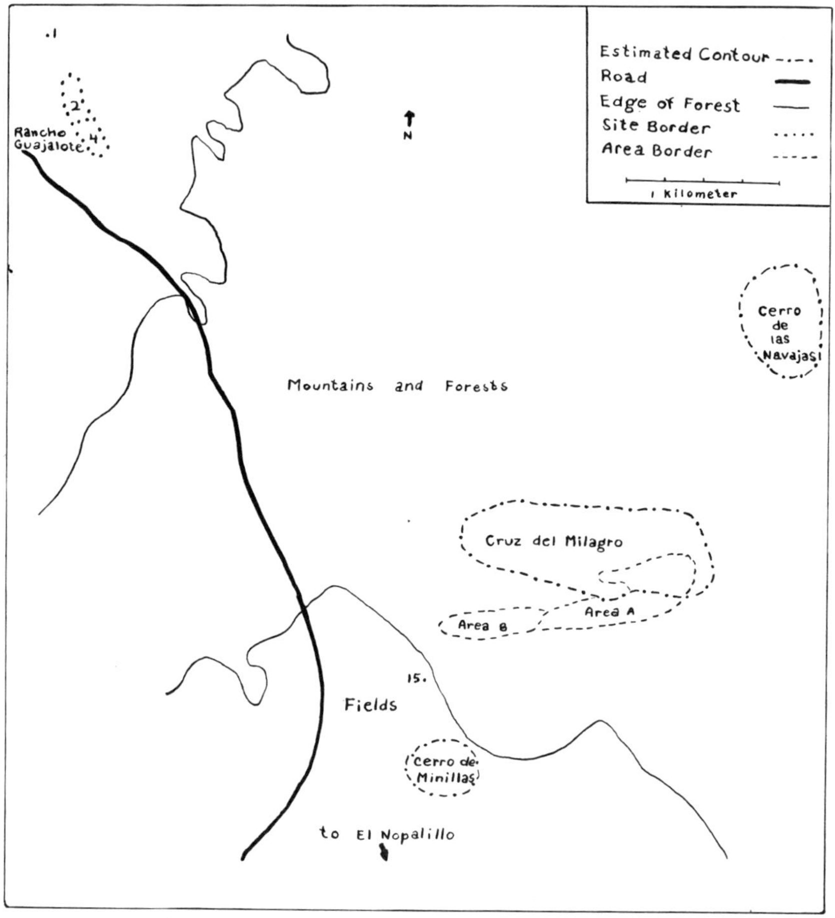


Fig. 2. Quarry Areas and Workshop Sites.

pits were seen. At times the working consists of wide, shallow excavations, one covering an area of about 20 m square but extending only 0.5 m deep. The pits are generally 1 to 2 m in diameter. Depths are about 0.5 to 2.5 m, but there has been partial refilling with soil and debris over the years. Occasionally, larger pits, up to 4 m in diameter and 10 m deep, occur. No side tunnels were seen, but it is probable that they are merely concealed by the partial refilling of pits.

The debris mounds are generally low, under 1 m in height, but measure several square meters in surface area. They occur in clusters between and around pits, and consist of a mixture of soil, some sherds, and large quantities of miscellaneous chips, flakes, and chunks of obsidian. One working described by Holmes has a much larger debris pile than usual (1900:410-11, Pl. XV). One of our sites, number 9, may well be the same complex. The debris there extends over at least

225 m square of the slope (Pl. 7*A*). At the upper end of the debris are 4 pits, about 3-4 m in diameter and up to 4 m deep. They are spaced around an almost vertical central shaft about 1.5 m in diameter by 10 m deep.

Area B is in generally lower and more level land, along the base of the Cruz del Milagro. Sites or complexes here consist of a central pit surrounded by debris piles. The pits are usually 2-3 m in diameter and about 1-2 m deep in their partially refilled state. The area B debris piles are of the same materials, in the same proportions, as those of area A, but now also include some pumice stone. They are larger than those of area A, covering many square meters of ground and averaging 2 m in height (Pl. 7*B*). One pile reaches a height of 12 m. Each such complex of a pit and its associated tailings covers an area between 25 and 40 m in diameter and is about 20 to 60 m distant from other complexes. The small size of the pits, the large size of the associated debris piles, and the occasional presence of a second pit at the outer boundary of the debris mounds suggest that each complex actually encompasses several pits, most of which had become buried by debris with further working.

Though site collections are often too small to be meaningful, enough material was obtained from both areas A and B to allow their comparison (Table 1). Through the courtesy of Dr. Clifford Evans of the Smithsonian Institution, Spence was able to examine Holmes' quarry collection. Not all of his material was seen, but the missing pieces were evidently few. All of the quarry obsidian is green. A relatively translucent green predominates, but cloudy, reddish, and gold-flecked variants also occur. The material is classified (Table 1) in formal categories. All artifacts were examined visually for traces of use, but conclusions based upon such superficial observations are only meant to be suggestive. Microscopic analysis of fracture and use patterns will be necessary for definitive interpretations.

The collections include a large amount of waste (flakes and chunks of irregular form with no signs of retouching or use). Such waste formed the vast bulk of material seen in the quarry areas. Also collected were 27 pieces of irregular form, essentially waste, which seem to have been slightly retouched or used, primarily as scrapers. The retouched edges of three more pieces of waste, all from area A, suggest a spokeshave function. To judge by the width of the spokeshave areas, they would have accommodated shafts of 1.2 to 2.7 cm in diameter.

Two chunks of obsidian, one from each area, show possible use as hammers. The other 3 hammerstones collected are of a hard, greyish, crystalline stone, and all show heavy use. One is oval, one hemispherical, and one cylindrical with rounded ends (see Holmes, 1919:Fig. 96 for other examples).

A total of 40 long, narrow pieces were collected. They are triangular in cross section, usually with two faces straight and flat while the third bears the scars of flaking from one edge. Occasionally two faces bear flake scars while only one is flat. Lengths range from 7 to 21.6 cm, averaging 14 cm. The width of the chipped face is 1.2 to 7.5 cm, averaging 3.1 cm. Holmes illustrates and briefly discusses these items (1900:415, Fig. 48; 1919:Fig. 100). Crabtree (1968:455, 460) identifies them as flakes struck from the corners of obsidian blocks during the process of core blank manufacture. The chipping on one face is the result of straightening the edge of the block. Although not artifacts, these block corners are useful as supplementary indications of core blank production.

Some 28 large end scrapers were found, most formed from chunks of obsidian, although in five cases flake blades had been used. Lengths vary from 5.6 to 17.5 cm, averaging 10.6 cm. Greatest width at the head is 3.1 to 7 cm, averaging 5.1 cm. Most specimens have a teardrop shape, although they range from narrow and elongated to short and nearly rectangular. All taper gradually from head to handle, the head never being clearly set off from the rest of the piece. The specimens are generally rather large and crude, roughly worked on part of the dorsal surface while the flat ventral face is formed by one large percussion scar. Visual inspection shows traces of use on only 7 of the 28 specimens, suggesting that they were primarily intended for export rather than for use at the quarry. Their large size and crudity suggest that they are blanks, rather than completely finished items, and that further refinement at some point beyond the quarry was intended. Some of the more finished specimens are illustrated in Plate 1, D-F (cf. Holmes, 1900:415, Fig. 47; 1919:221, Fig. 99). These items are relatively rare at the quarry and are largely confined to area B. All that were seen were collected, accounting for their relatively high proportion in the collections.

Large blanks for polyhedral cores are numerous, and only a few specimens of those seen were collected. They are generally cylindrical in form, though some are conical or wedge-shaped (Table 1; Holmes, 1900:413-14, Fig. 45; 1919: Fig. 97). The blades removed from them were usually irregularly edged flake blades, rather than the smaller fine blades characteristic of Mesoamerican occupation sites. Usually the blades had been removed from only one end of the blank. The striking platform is generally level, and in most cases is faceted (several flake scars), although a few of the platforms were formed by a single flake scar. Lengths range from 4.3 to 13 cm, averaging 9.3 cm. Platform widths, measured at the widest point, are 4.2 to 8 cm, averaging 5.9 cm. These items are undoubtedly blanks, meant to be further refined elsewhere into the well known polyhedral cores. Their abundance in the quarry refuse suggests a principal orientation toward core blank production at the quarry. This orientation is particularly marked in area A, core blanks being noticeably less frequent in area B. Even in the latter area, however, their presence and the frequency of flake blades and block corners suggest that core blank production was still a major concern.

Only two finished cores, one from each quarry area, were found. Both are comparatively small and produced fine blades. They were probably used by the miners for tasks not directly related to quarry or core blank production. The area A specimen is conical, 6.6 cm long by 3.2 cm wide at the striking platform, which is formed by one large percussion scar. It was found near a mine complex, but not directly associated with mine debris. The area B specimen, found in mine debris, is cylindrical, 6.7 cm long, and has a ground striking platform 5 cm in diameter.

Only one fine blade, the striking platform not ground, was found. A total of 157 flake blades were collected, however, and these represent only a small fraction of the number seen. They have roughly parallel edges with one or two central ridges on the dorsal surface. Lengths range from 4.2 to 19.4 cm, averaging 11.1 cm. Widths are 1 to 7.7 cm, averaging 3.4 cm. Thickness, measured at its maximum point (on a dorsal ridge), ranges from 0.3 to 2.5 cm, averaging 1.1 cm. The vast majority of flake blades are evidently only waste by-products of the roughing out of core blanks. Only 19 of the collected specimens show traces of use.

Holmes noted the puzzling absence of items that would be suitable blanks for projectile points and knives (1919:225). We found several artifacts designated "retouched flake blades" that might be considered point-knife blanks (Pl. 1, G-H) Large flake blades had been broken at a point between 7.6 and 13.3 cm (averaging 11.1 cm) from the proximal (bulb) end. They had been worked on the dorsal face. Of 10 specimens, 2 were worked on the edges only, 3 were retouched on the sides from the edges to the dorsal ridges, and 5 were worked over most or all of the dorsal face. All specimens narrow from the break to the proximal end. Width at the break is 4.6 to 8.4 cm, averaging 6.8 cm. Thickness ranges from 1.4 to 2.5 cm, averaging 1.9 cm. Only 2 of the 10 specimens show signs of use, suggesting that these artifacts were destined for export rather than for use by the miners. They may be blanks for side scrapers, but the dorsal working is frequently much more extensive than is necessary or usual for such an artifact. We feel that the size, form, and working of these specimens suggest their suitability as point-knife blanks.

It has been suggested that unaltered flake blades are point-knife blanks (Coe and Flannery, 1964:48). It is true that many of them are suitable in size and form for this purpose, but, on the other hand, many are not. At the Cruz del Milagro quarry it is more probable that they are merely by-products of core blank production, and that those of suitable size and form were selected for further working into point-knife blanks. This further working reduced the size of the pieces, strengthened them against possible damage in transit, and also produced a blank considerably closer to what the finished form would be. This accords with what seems to be a tendency of the miners, as expressed in the core blanks and end scrapers, to prepare an approximation of the final form when working material for export. Certainly some of the unaltered flake blades could have been exported as point-knife blanks and in fact probably were, but the presence of large numbers of suitable ones in the quarry refuse piles suggests that they are essentially waste, not desired products of working. Retouched flake blades are quite rare and are largely concentrated in area B. All those seen were collected.

Holmes' collection from the quarry, while not included in the above artifact descriptions, fits into our categories well enough. Some pieces, however, deserve special mention. One is a conical core blank, 11.1 cm long by 8.5 cm wide at the platform. It produced large flake blades, somewhat cruder than those of most of the core blanks. At one point a small special striking platform had been prepared on the edge of the core platform by retouching. This, plus the crudity of the blades and the conical form, makes the specimen very similar to pieces from early in the Tehuacán sequence and from the El Chayal quarry in Guatemala (Kent V. Flannery, personal communication; Coe and Flannery, 1964:43; MacNeish et al. 1967:28). The Cruz del Milagro specimen, however, is probably Late Postclassic, implying a long and conservative tradition of core preparation in Mesoamerica.

The two finished cores in the Holmes collection were producing fine blades. The striking platform of one is ground, the other lacks such grinding. Holmes' sample also includes a large, thin, roughly rectangular chunk of obsidian, 10 cm wide by 12 cm high by 4 cm thick, which produced flake blades but does not seem similar to anything else from the quarry. Another unusual item is a roughly circular piece, 5.2 cm in diameter by 2.1 cm thick, which has been roughly worked bifacially to a lenticular cross section. Finally, there is the basal part of a large knife with a rounded base, crudely chipped on both faces with some retouching on the edges. It measures 10.4 cm wide by 3.2 cm thick. The last three items discussed here are included in the "other" category in Table 1.

The ceramics recovered from the quarry area were examined by Parsons and by Dr. James A. Bennyhoff. The small size of the sample, its surface provenience, and the lack of published ceramic studies in the region make it advisable to discuss the material only in general terms.

Most undecorated sherds from both quarry areas seem to represent a local ceramic tradition. While apparently dating to Late Postclassic times, this plainware differs too greatly in several respects from Valley of Mexico Aztec wares to be considered a part of the Aztec ceramic tradition. Generally, these sherds are more poorly fired than Aztec wares and have a coarser, more friable paste. Vessel forms of this utilitarian pottery include bowls, poorly finished basins, and burnished brown ollas and jars.

Some undecorated sherds and nearly all decorated material are virtually indistinguishable from standard Valley of Mexico Aztec ceramics, although minor differences in paste, finish, and decoration suggest that some may have been locally produced. The Aztec wares include, among others, burnished orange, Black-on-Orange, and Black-on-Red. Vessel forms represented are jars, ollas, dishes, molcajetes, bowls, hollow tubular handles (possibly for ladle censers), basins, a possible comal, one serpent effigy support or handle, and one censer. The latter vessel is an Aztec III hourglass form with an encircling band which bears what seem to be alternating ilhuitl and butterfly designs (Fig. 3). It was found within a few meters of the edge of the refuse pile at site 9 (described above) and may have been utilized in some ceremonial context related to quarrying.

Five sherds, almost certainly imports, deserve special mention. Three of these are from area A: a small sherd of Texcoco Fabric marked and two sherds of Texcoco Filleted – one with a small nubbin handle (Tolstoy, 1958:51, 49). The two specimens from area B include a sherd of a fine paste, polished, light orange bowl of unknown origin and one piece of red and black on brown Chalco-Cholula polychrome. One sherd, from an area A refuse heap, is possibly a Classic period handled cover of Teotihuacán style, but this identification is very uncertain.

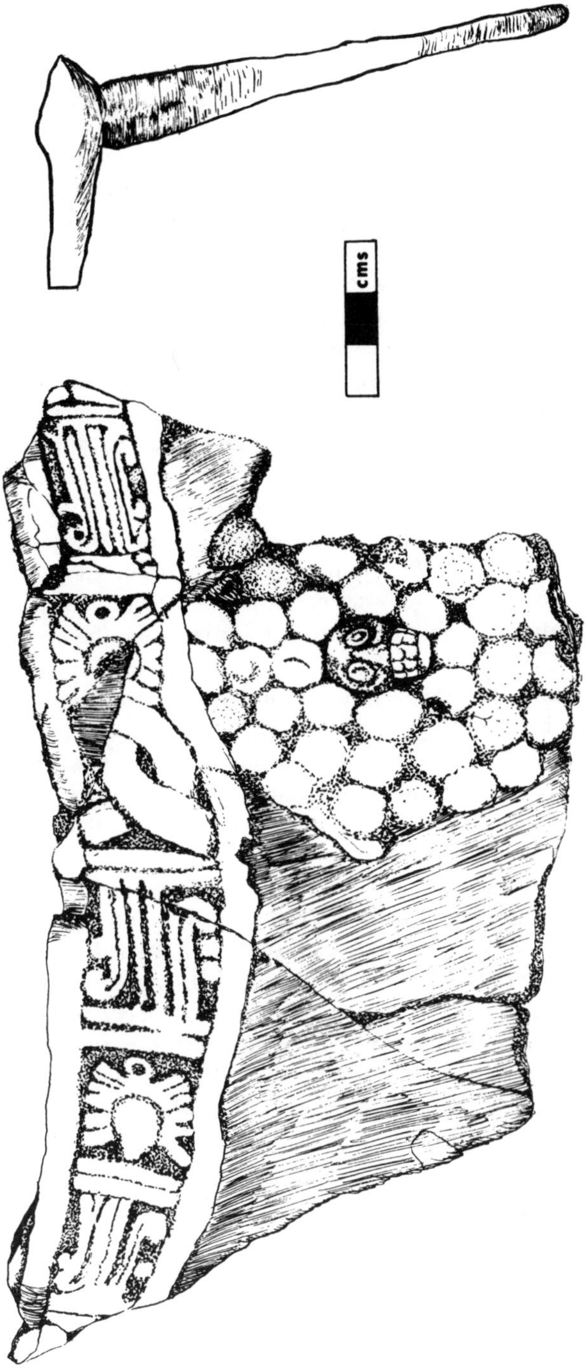


Fig. 3. Late Postclassic censer.

Holmes' collection from the quarry includes several Aztec sherds. The forms represented are jars, ollas, molcajetes, a comal, and a ladle censer. One sherd, however, is of a smoothed but unburnished black flaring-wall basin with a fine, white-speckled paste. It is not an Aztec ware and does not resemble any of the quarry ceramics we recovered.

Many of the distinctly Aztec sherds can be placed in the Valley of Mexico sequence. All such sherds in area A are Aztec III, while in area B Aztec III and IV are about equal, and there is one possible Aztec II sherd. The mining operations and the collected material, then, may safely be considered of Aztec III date in area A and Aztec III through IV in area B.

The quarry is very extensive and rich, suggesting well organized, large-scale exploitation. The primary purpose of this exploitation was evidently, as Holmes noted, the production of core blanks (1919:220). There is a suggestion in the areal distribution of material that Aztec IV times saw an increased emphasis on the production of end scrapers and point-knife blanks, but the number of flake blades and block corners in area B and the continued presence of core blanks imply that core blanks continued to be a major item. Many of these conclusions must of course remain tentative, resting as they do upon the unproven assumption that retouched flake blades are point-knife blanks, upon a dependence on only visual examination for use and wear patterns, and upon the inference of temporal change from surface distributions in something less than the total quarry area.

Holmes (1900:411) saw the remains of walled structures in the quarry area, but we found no evidence of construction. The lack of any substantial occupational debris and structural remains in our Cruz del Milagro survey area suggests that the quarry was exploited by persons whose permanent residences were elsewhere. Judging from the indication that our sample of utilitarian ware is largely locally produced, it seems reasonable to postulate that obsidian mining and core blank preparation here were being performed by people who resided permanently in communities adjacent to prime agricultural land at lower, less sloping locations in the local area. Residence near the quarry itself was probably limited at most to small, temporary camps, lacking any substantial architecture, where sizable concentrations of occupational refuse never accumulated.

Since at least a portion of the Late Postclassic decorated pottery used in the Cruz del Milagro area is apparently coming directly from the Valley of Mexico, we can postulate close economic ties between the Cruz del Milagro area and major Aztec urban communities to the southwest. The obsidian core blanks produced at the Cruz del Milagro quarry may have been channeled into the market and tribute system focusing on Tenochtitlán, Texcoco, and other principal power centers. Decorated pottery, among other items, comprised part of the flow of finished products outward from urban markets in the Valley of Mexico.

Another possibility would be that some quarrying and core blank manufacture were carried out by workers who resided permanently in the Valley of Mexico and who came to the rich quarry as corvee laborers or mining specialists for short periods. The non-Valley nature of plainwares found in the quarry area, however, make this possibility the less plausible of the two.

TABLE 1

CRUZ DEL MILAGRO MINE MATERIAL

| | Area A | Area B | Cerro Piñal | Holmes Collection |
|---|---|---|---|---|
| Waste | 118 | 14 | 29 | 7 |
| Waste, retouched or used | 20 | 7 | 5 | 5 |
| Spokeshaves | 3 | 0 | 0 | 0 |
| Core blanks, total | 16 | 6 | 0 | 6 |
| - conical | 2 | 2 | 0 | 1 |
| - wedge | 2 | 1 | 0 | 1 |
| - cylindrical | 10 | 1 | 0 | 4 |
| - other | 2 | 2 | 0 | 0 |
| Finished cores | 1 | 1 | 0 | 2 |
| Fine blades | 1 | 0 | 0 | 1 |
| Flake blades | 101 | 56 | 1 | 3 |
| Retouched flake blades | 2 | 8 | 0 | 0 |
| Block corners | 23 | 17 | 0 | 7 |
| End scrapers | 3 | 25 | 1 | 5 |
| Obsidian hammers | 1 | 1 | 0 | 0 |
| Other obsidian | 0 | 0 | 0 | 3 |
| Total obsidian | 289 | 135 | 36 | 39* |
| Hammerstones | 2 | 1 | 0 | 5 |
| Sherds | 40 | 40 | 19 | 8 |

* Not all specimens examined.

## THE NOPALILLO-GUAJALOTE WORKSHOPS

It is evident that obsidian working at the quarry was limited to the rough processing of blanks for export and the preparation of some tools for immediate use in quarry activities. Rapid survey of the lower ground to the west and south of the quarry, around the Rancho Guajalote and between El Nopalillo and the quarry area, turned up only a few small workshops, all of which were thoroughly collected. Because of small sample size, no attempt has been made to designate projectile point types in our descriptions of material from these workshop sites.

Workshop site 1 is located on a low ridge about 5 km northwest of the quarry (Fig. 2). Obsidian waste and artifacts are scattered over an area about 50 by 40 m, where erosion has removed topsoil. The artifact cover is light, and no evidence of structures appears. The obsidian here is all green, but probably came from a source closer than the Cruz del Milagro quarry area (possibly from the same source used by the artisans of workshop sites 2 and 4). The ceramics collected are 1 glazed and 13 unglazed sherds. The latter cannot be temporally defined. They include 1 polished, brownish-orange, incised, simple-bowl sherd; 6 olla sherds; 2 polished brown pieces; 2 red-on-brown bowl sherds; 1 red-on-brown jar sherd; and 1 polished, reddish-brown jar sherd.

The collected obsidian amounted to 71 pieces, including:

50 pieces of waste

4 amorphous pieces retouched as end scrapers

4 fine blades

3 small flake blades

1 fragment of a cylindrical core which seems to have been finished and in use, producing fine blades

1 end scraper, crudely worked, with edges expanding slightly toward the proximal ("handle") end

2 tip fragments of knives, evidently unfinished

1 finished knife base, sharply convex (almost pointed), 4.4 cm wide by 1.1 cm thick

1 finished knife base, convex, 6.4 cm wide by 1 cm thick

2 finely worked projectile point tips

1 reject, probably intended to be a stemmed point

1 finished point with a diamond shape and straight, serrated blade edges. The serration might suggest a Preclassic position (Tolstoy, n.d.:13). The point is very similar to the Pelona type of the Tehuacán area, dated from the Coxcatlán phase to about AD 1 (MacNeish et al., 1967:70, Fig. 54).

Workshop sites 2 and 4 (Fig. 2) are actually one continuous area of obsidian debris extending along the west side of a long, low hill about 350 m east of the Rancho Guajalote buildings. The area as a whole is about 575 m north-south by 100 m wide (from top to bottom of the hill). Obsidian chunks of varying size are embedded in tepetate in a stream bed running along the west base of the hill, and also seem to be eroding out onto the site surface from a subsoil stratum. These chunks undoubtedly provided the raw material for the workers. No signs of construction were seen, and sherds are sparse. The obsidian debris is denser in the northern 300 m of the area, and this section was designated site 2. The southern 275 m, site 4, reveals less debris, though still enough to show that it had functioned as a workshop.

This obsidian area as a whole is the richest workshop discovered in the survey, but nonetheless is still comparatively small. As will be evident from descriptions of the collected material, its size and richness are probably more a factor of the area's use over a long period of time than of the presence of large numbers of obsidian workers at any one time.

Site 2 ceramics include 40 sherds, 25 of which are modern and probably associated with a modern threshing floor on top of the hill. Four sherds cannot be identified, while 8 others are probably Late Postclassic. These include 4 olla sherds of a non-Aztec tradition and 4 sherds of Aztec orange ware. Three sherds are probably of the Classic period. One of these is a red-on-brown bowl, while the other 2 are olla fragments.

A total of 145 pieces of green obsidian and 2 pieces of grey obsidian (projectile points) were collected from site 2, including:

81 pieces of waste

11 retouched amorphous pieces – 8 scrapers, 1 knife, 1 graver, and 1 spokeshave

6 flake blades, averaging 8 cm long by 2.5 cm wide

2 small end scrapers (Pl. 3, D-E), differing from quarry specimens in their smaller size and roughly parallel edges. Dorsal faces are high (1.8 and 1.9 cm), reaching greatest height near the scraping end, and roughly worked

8 knife fragments, 6 tips and 2 center pieces

5 knife bases, convex, from 4.5 to 7 cm wide and 1.2 to 1.8 cm thick (Pl. 2, A-B). This form is common at Teotihuacán, but may well have existed through a very long period of time

3 sharply convex, almost pointed, knife bases (Pl. 2, E-F). Width is 4.2 to 5.5 cm, thickness 0.9 to 1.7 cm. This also is a common Teotihuacán form, but again may have had a long temporal existence

3 broadly oval (almost circular in one case) knives (Pl. 3, G-I). They average 6.1 cm long, 4.4 cm wide, and 1.3 cm thick.

Probably the roughly circular bifacial item in Holmes' collection from the quarry falls in this class, too, suggesting that they are Late Postclassic. García Cook found similar items, his "cuchillos ovalados," in Classic and Postclassic levels at Nopalera (1967:Lám. III, 2).

1 complete knife with edges irregular but generally expanding to a straight base (Pl. 2, D). It is probably related to the "rectangular apuntado" type appearing throughout the Nopalera sequence (García Cook, 1967:Lám. IV, 2; Cuadro 7).

1 base of a narrow knife with edges contracting slightly to a straight base (Pl. 2, H).

3 specimens too unfinished for form definition, although points or knives were probably intended (Pl. 3, C).

3 projectile point tips

1 point, too unfinished to identify form

4 points with slightly concave to straight blade edges and parallel-sided to contracting stems (Pl. 5, A-C). One is of grey obsidian. The two complete bases are straight, and shoulders are small and generally horizontal. The four specimens are so similar in form and workmanship that they may be the products of one man. They are probably related to the Tlatilco type, largely Middle Preclassic (Lorenzo, 1965:28-31; Tolstoy, n.d. 17, Fig. 2v).

2 points with straight blade edges, horizontal or slightly down-sloping shoulders, and stems contracting slightly to a rounded base. The one complete specimen (Pl. 5, D) has one blade edge serrated. Tolstoy places similar specimens, designated Gary Typical, largely in Middle Preclassic to Classic times (n.d. 16, Table 2). Müller (n.d.) places this form in her type 12, which she feels dates from the Tlamimilolpa to the Metepec phase (Teotihuacán II-III to IV) in Teotihuacán. García Cook, calling them Gary B, gives this form a Late Preclassic to Classic date at Nopalera (1967:64, Lám. XI, 3-4).

2 points with straight blade edges, slightly barbed shoulders, and a stem contracting markedly to a rounded, almost pointed, base. Both are badly broken, but seem generally related to some Gary horizon variants and so may date from somewhere in the Middle Preclassic to Classic period span. Müller (n.d.) designated similar specimens type 13a, Tlamimilolpa to Metepec phases in Teotihuacán.

2 points with straight blade edges, barbed shoulders, and large stems contracting to the bases. One specimen of this variety was also found in site 4 (Pl. 5, M – shoulders are broken).

1 point with a short, squat blade, small and slightly outflaring shoulders, and a very large stem contracting to a rounded base (Pl. 5, L). It is thin and well worked. MacNeish's Garyito type, extending from the Coxcatlán to the Palo Blanco phase in the Tehuacán Valley, is probably related to this specimen (MacNeish et al, 1967:66-67, Fig. 51).

2 points with straight blade edges and small shoulders, horizontal to slightly barbed, in line with the blade edges (Pl. 5, E-F). Stems are slightly concave-edged with slightly convex bases. One is of grey obsidian. These may be related to the Palmillas type of Tolstoy and MacNeish, lasting to Postclassic times in the Tehuacán Valley, but predominantly Late Preclassic in the Valley of Mexico and at Nopalera (MacNeish et al, 1967:72, Fig. 57; Tolstoy, n.d.:15, Fig. 2K; García Cook, 1967:64, Lám. XI, 7-8).

2 points with straight blade edges, horizontal shoulders, and a parallel-edged to slightly contracting stem with a straight to slightly convex base (Pl. 5, G-H). MacNeish's La Mina type, which he places as 5000 to 3000 BC in Hidalgo, is very similar (MacNeish et al, 1967:62, Fig. 44).

2 points with concave blade edges, widely flaring shoulders, and stems contracting to straight bases (Pl. 5, I-J). In both specimens, the blade portion is displaced markedly to one side, rather than being directly in line with the stem.

1 point of a bipointed eliptical form, crudely worked (Pl. 5, K). This seems to be a Lerma variant, placed by Tolstoy in the Pre-classic and Classic periods in the Valley of Mexico but extending back to the Ajuereado phase in the Tehuacán Valley (Tolstoy, n.d.: Table 2; MacNeish et al, 1967:56-57, Fig. 35).

1 point which seems to have been finished and possibly in use (Pl. 4). It is 6.8 cm long, from the tip to a level with the basal extremities, and 4.6 cm from the tip to a level with the shoulders. Width at the shoulders is 3.7 cm, and maximum thickness is 1.3 cm. Both edges, from the shoulders to the basal extremities, have been ground. The small lateral projections here termed shoulders were formed by the grinding on the basal edge and by the contraction of the blade edges above these shoulders. There is no evidence that the point owes its form to reworking, and abrasions on the basal concavity suggest that it may have been hafted at one time. The specimen is very similar to the Meserve type, differing primarily in its greater width and the lack of blade beveling (cf. Suhm and Jelks, 1962:217). Other possible Meserve-related points from Mexico seem much less similar to the Meserve type (cf. Müller, n.d.; Aveleyra Arroyo de Anda, 1964:392-93; Tolstoy, n.d.:13-14). However, MacNeish's Flacco type is probably more closely related to the site 2 specimen and is said to date from the El Riego, Coxcatlán, and Abejas phases, lasting until about 2000 BC (MacNeish et al, 1967:58-59, Table 10, Fig. 39). Whether the specimen is considered a Meserve-related point or a Flacco point, it definitely is an early form.

The ceramics of site 4 include 1 post-Conquest glazed sherd, 3 plain orange sherds which may be modern, and one sherd that is possibly a Classic period comal fragment.

The workshop site 4 obsidian includes 43 pieces, all green obsidian:

14 waste

4 amorphous pieces retouched, 3 as scrapers and 1 as a spokeshave

1 small flake blade

1 unfinished item, intended to be either a core or a turtleback scraper.

1 oval side scraper, retouched around the edges

2 large oval chunks, roughly worked bifacially, showing use as choppers (Pl. 1, I-J). They measure 11.1 and 11.7 cm long, 6.8 and 8.5 cm wide, and 2.9 and 4.8 cm thick.

5 knife tips

1 narrow knife, edges contracting slightly to a roughly straight base (Pl. 2, G). This specimen is probably related to a similar one from site 2 (Pl. 2, H).

1 piece with convex edges that was apparently stemmed at one time (Pl. 2, C). It may actually be an unfinished point.

2 knives with convex edges expanding to a convex base (Pl. 2, L). These are very similar to García Cook's "ojival alargado" type, predominantly of Classic and Early Postclassic date (1967: Lám. III, 8; cuadro 7).

2 knives, unfinished, but possibly intended to be large with relatively straight bases (Pl. 2, J-K).

1 nearly finished knife with a slightly concave base and possibly a curved blade (Pl. 2, I).

1 projectile point tip

1 unfinished point of indeterminate form

3 points with parallel blade edges and narrow, shallow side notches, below which the lateral edges of the blade contract to a base notched in the center (Pl. 5, N-P). A similar point, termed Frio, came from a Late Postclassic level at Nopalera (García Cook, 1967: Lám. XV, 7; cuadro 9).

1 point with straight blade edges and shallow side notches, below which the blade edges contract to a concave base (Pl. 5, Q). The specimen is of Tolstoy's Late Postclassic period Texcoco type (n.d.:18-19, Fig. 3p).

1 point with straight blade edges, barbed shoulders (broken), and a large stem contracting to a straight base (Pl. 5, M). As mentioned earlier, 2 site 2 specimens seem related.

1 large unfinished point with horizontal shoulders and a contracting, round-based stem (Pl. 5, R). Tolstoy terms

similar items Gary Large, and places them predominantly in the Classic period (n.d.:16, Fig. 2u) Müller (n.d.) places them in her type 9, Miçcaotli phase (Teotihuacán II) to Metepec phase (Teotihuacán IV).

Workshop site 15 (Fig. 2), on lower ground to the south of the mines, is an area about 70 m in diameter with a sparse scattering of obsidian waste and a few artifacts. No sherds or structures were seen. Chunks of obsidian eroded down from the higher land to the north pepper the soil here, providing the raw material. The site is so small, and the material so sparse, that it must represent only temporary working by one or a very few individuals.

Some 20 pieces, all green, were collected:

12 waste

4 flake blades, averaging 8.3 cm long by 3.4 cm wide.

2 unfinished knife fragments

1 point with a long narrow blade portion, very small horizontal shoulders, and a stem which has been broken off (Pl. 5, T). The chipping is in the "pennado" type described by Lorenzo (1965:30), causing the blade edges to be slightly serrated. The specimen is probably a variant of the Tlatilco type (see Lorenzo, 1965:foto 1).

1 point with straight blade edges, corner notches, and a short, broad, expanding stem (Pl. 5, S). The base has been partially broken, preventing determination of its form. Corner notching seems generally to be a Late Preclassic period trait (Tolstoy, n.d.:16; Spence, 1967:509-10).

Workshop site 21 is located on the dirt road to El Nopalillo, about 4 km southwest of the village, near a hacienda marker where the road forks. Sparse workshop debris and some sherds are eroding out of the topsoil on both sides of the road and extend over an area about 80 by 35 m. No signs of construction were seen, and almost certainly the site represents working by only a few individuals. No immediate source for the obsidian could be seen, but sources closer than the quarry were probably utilized. Certainly the grey obsidian on the site did not come from the quarry we surveyed.

Ceramic finds at workshop site 21 include 2 late Aztec Black-on-Red sherds indistinguishable from Valley of Mexico material, 4 orange ware sherds (probably Late Postclassic but evidently produced locally), 1 modern glazed sherd, 1 unidentifiable sherd, and 2 possible Classic sherds.

A total of 87 pieces of obsidian (including 6 grey pieces) were collected at workshop site 21. One basalt scraper was also found. The obsidian includes:

45 pieces of waste (3 of them grey)

13 amorphous pieces retouched to form scraping edges

4 flake blades averaging 3.7 cm in width. One had been retouched to form a spokeshave.

4 fragments of fine blades, only one of which still retains its striking platform (which shows grinding).

2 tapering end scrapers, similar to but smaller than the quarry specimens (Pl. 3, A-B).

10 unfinished and unidentifiable knife or point fragments

1 small knife, made by bifacial retouching on the edges of a thin, flat piece of obsidian (Pl. 3, F). The form is rectangular with rounded corners and a small projection on the left side at each end (the lower one has broken off).

1 sharply convex, almost pointed, knife base of grey obsidian, 3.9 cm wide by 0.8 cm thick.

2 thick, crudely worked, narrow knives with straight bases, averaging 2.7 cm wide by 1.5 cm thick.

1 well-worked projectile point, broken but probably once shouldered and stemmed.

1 well-worked, diamond-shaped point of grey obsidian, with straight edges and a narrow, diagonal base (Pl. 5, V – in the illustration the point is placed diagonally instead of vertically; the tip, upper left, is broken).

1 small point made on a waste flake by unifacial chipping and edge retouching (Pl. 5, W). The edges and base are convex. The specimen is similar to Tolstoy's "short uniface" type of the Classic period (n.d.:20, Fig. 3n).

1 small broad point with slightly convex blade edges, barbed shoulders, and a broad, quadrangular stem (Pl. 5, U). The specimen is of grey obsidian. It is very similar to García Cook's Carrollton variety, a Late Preclassic form at Nopalera (1967:Lám. X, 11-12; cuadro 9).

1 upper part of a small point made from a fine blade. Blade-derived small points are usually Classic or Postclassic period.

Workshop site 1, then, is probably Preclassic. Ceramics and obsidian artifacts suggest that workshop site 2 was utilized in the Middle Preclassic, Late Preclassic, Classic, and Late Postclassic periods. The Flacco point and the La Mina-like points suggest a preceramic occupation also. Workshop site 4 seems to be Classic and Late Postclassic, differing from site 2 particularly in its concentration of Aztec style projectile points. Workshop site 15 is evidently Middle or Late Preclassic, while workshop site 21 appears largely Classic and Late Postclassic but has one possible Late Preclassic point.

The ground striking platform of the workshop site 21 blade is apparently a Postclassic trait (cf. Tolstoy, n.d.:7; MacNeish et al, 1967:28). We have noted this treatment on a fair proportion of cores and blades from Aztec residential sites in the Valley of Mexico. The absence of grinding on the core blanks from the quarry suggests that this was done elsewhere and was not part of the quarry processing of blanks. Workshop sites 2 and 4 are unique in their lack of fine blades or definite cores. This might suggest that these locations were concerned solely with knife, point, and scraper production. The presence of flake blades and a possible unfinished core, however, might indicate otherwise.

Any interpretation of the relationships between workshop and quarry sites in our survey area is severely hampered by the restricted size of the region examined and the small number of localities from which collections were made. However, several salient points may be suggestive of the general economic and political framework within which the rich obsidian resources of southern Hidalgo were exploited in prehispanic times.

Quite clearly, all localities we have designated as workshops are quite small and not representative of any intensive use. Furthermore, raw material utilized at our workshops does not clearly derive from any of the quarry areas we sampled. This dichotemy might indicate local populations utilizing marginal sources of obsidian for local uses, with most or all of the produce from the main rich mines reserved for export to large urban centers in the Valley of Mexico. Aztec pottery from workshop sites 2 and 21 suggests some direct ties between the Nopalillo-Guajalote area and the Valley of Mexico in Late Postclassic times.

## THE CERRO PIÑAL QUARRY

On May 9, 1966 Parsons, together with several University of Michigan students, reconnoitered an extensive obsidian quarry on the slopes of Cerro Piñal a few km south of the village of San Lorenzo (Fig. 1). This heavily forested. region is covered with numerous pits and piles of obsidian refuse and artifacts in much the same fashion as the Cruz del Milagro survey area. Such pits usually range between 2 and 5 m in diameter, and from 1 to 2 m deep. Several deeper features were noted, and one shaft was seen which measured roughly 8 m deep and 1 m in diameter, cut into a hillside at an angle of about 30 degrees from the horizontal. In the area of their densest concentration, pits are distributed almost continuously over the hillslopes at intervals of 5 to 10 m. In such areas dense concentrations of quarry tailings and refuse litter the ground surface between the pits to depths of 10 to 30 cm.

Interestingly enough, our guide informed us that several pits near the base of the hill had been quarried in 1964 by a group of men from San Francisco Mazapan in the Valley of Mexico, who carried out some 200 kilos of obsidian. Today, this village and several others in the immediate vicinity of the archaeological zone of Teotihuacán produce large quantities of obsidian souvenirs for sale to tourists. They especially favor a gold-sheen variety, which they apparently obtain in large quantities from the Cerro Piñal quarry area.

A small collection of obsidian was taken from over the entire hillslope, with no attempt at systematic sampling of specific areas (Table 1). There was no attempt made to locate or sample workshop areas in the general area, although scattered obsidian debris was noted in many sections of the piedmont slopes below the quarry area.

We noted no surface pottery in the general quarry area. A few sherds were collected from the floor of a large cave on the steep northwest side of the hill. These included 9 fragments of utilitarian ollas, each with one burnished black surface, and 6 sherds that are probably Aztec III wares (4 comal fragments, 1 bodysherd, and 1 Black-on-Red sherd).

The Cerro Piñal and Cruz del Milagro quarries are very probably only two isolated examples of prehispanic (and some post-Conquest) exploitation of the rich obsidian resources of this large section of southern Hidalgo. Further exploration and testing should reveal large quarries of similar character wherever accessible sources of abundant, high-quality obsidian occur.

## THE T. A. 79 QUARRY

In 1964 Parsons, working with the Teotihuacán Valley Project, surveyed a large obsidian quarry area about 2 km east of San Marcos, a small town some 5 km east of Otumba in the southeastern Valley of Teotihuacán (Fig. 1). The quarry and associated residential site were designated T. A. 79 (Sanders, 1965: Fig. 11). Spence later spent a day collecting the site in 1965. A wide, deep barranca, running south toward Cerro de Campanario (mentioned for its obsidian by Gamio [1922:Vol. II:48-49]), passes on the east side of two moderate-sized hills. There is a gravel mine on top of the southernmost hill, and a fair amount of obsidian on its northern side. The northernmost hill has a dense obsidian cover over its whole surface. Sherds, all Late Postclassic, were generally very sparse, but there was a light-to-moderate concentration of late Aztec ceramics on the upper south end of the hill. Small boulders and chunks of obsidian occur throughout the shallow soil cover and embedded in the tepetate subsoil where they show clearly on the erosion-scarred surface. Shallow digging would have provided large quantities of raw material here. At one point on the south side of the hill there is a pit about 2 m deep with a side tunnel roughly 1 m high extending horizontally for about 3 m. Large chunks of obsidian occur throughout the pit's profile. Other scattered pits, generally filled with debris, were seen in the vicinity. No evidence of definite structures was seen on the quarry hill itself, but remains of three Late Postclassic walled buildings with heavy ceramic debris were located at the south end of the hill, adjacent to the barranca.

At a wide point in the barranca east of the quarry hill there are a number of easily accessible caves in the cut's western wall. These caves were apparently partially formed by mining activities. Their walls are thickly embedded with obsidian chunks. Traces of digging show that these chunks were being extracted from the loose conglomerate matrix of the cave walls. Near one cave entrance there is a vein of the distinctive red and black spotted "meca" obsidian. All the rest of the obsidian, both in the caves and on the adjoining hill, is grey-black in color.

Fifteen possible mining tools, all heavy chunks of obsidian worked to shape by a few strong blows, were collected within the caves. They fall into two general types. Eight are elongated tools, averaging about 10.5 cm long by 5.5 cm wide and 3 cm thick. They are bluntly pointed at one end, which shows traces of heavy use. The other 7 items are roughly circular or hemispherical with a slightly concave ventral surface. They average 5.7 cm in diameter by 3.2 cm high. Both types of tools, to judge by their sizes and traces of use, were utilized to knock obsidian chunks free of their matrix in the cave walls.

A total of 178 pieces were collected from the hill area in general. As at the Cruz del Milagro quarry, no systematic nor entirely consistent method was followed, but an attempt was made to obtain a sample of the various artifact types present. Of the 178 pieces, 107 were waste, some of which show traces of utilization. Two are small chunks showing heavy battering use – possibly to break up other obsidian pieces. Another chunk had been retouched as a side scraper. There are also 20 flake blades, like those of the Cruz del Milagro quarry but slightly smaller, averaging 7.6 cm long by 2.8 cm wide and 1.1 cm thick.

Cores are not common in the hill area, and the 7 seen were all collected. Five of these, 4 cylindrical and 1 conical, seem to have been finished and in use, producing fine blades for the most part. Striking platforms were formed by one large percussion scar, and in one core the platform had been ground. They average 6.8 cm long and 2.9 cm wide at the platform, similar in size to the finished cores of the Cruz del Milagro quarry and considerably smaller than the blanks from there. The other two T. A. 79 cores average 11 cm in length and 4.4 cm wide, falling much closer to the dimensions of the Cruz del Milagro core blanks. They produced flake blades, rather than fine blades. Both are cylindrical, their striking platforms being formed by one large percussion scar.

Four block corners are identical to the Cruz del Milagro ones in all respects but size. The T. A. 79 specimens are slightly smaller, averaging 10.5 cm long by 2.4 cm wide (on the worked face).

Fifteen crudely worked end scrapers, or end scraper blanks, were collected from the hill (Pl. 1, A-C). They average 8.1 cm long by 3.7 cm wide at the head, thus being slightly smaller than the Cruz del Milagro quarry specimens. In all other respects, however, they fit the description given for the Cruz del Milagro end scrapers. Visual inspection suggests traces of use on 5 of the 15 specimens. End scrapers seemed to be a fairly common item at T. A. 79, and only part of those seen were collected.

Two scrapers are of roughly humped (crudely hemispherical) form with steep sides. The dorsal surfaces were formed by crude percussion blows, the flat ventral faces by one large percussion scar. They average 6.4 cm in diameter by 3.5 cm high. Nothing similar was seen at the Cruz del Milagro quarry.

Nineteen pieces collected from the hill seem to be point-knife blanks, although different from those of the Cruz del Milagro quarry. These items appeared to be quite common at T. A. 79, and only some of those seen were collected. All are bifacially worked, generally very crudely. There is not much edge retouching, and in many cases the edges are much too blunt and irregular to be effective in cutting or scraping. Only two of the specimens show clear traces of use. The blanks are generally very thick, and in some cases working is more extensive on one face than on the other. They seem to have been made from chunks, rather than from large flake blades. Two general divisions of these specimens can be defined: narrow (point blanks?) and broad (knife blanks?). The narrow forms include:

> 2 fragments, 1 tip and 1 midsection
>
> 2 blunt-ended laurel-leaf forms averaging 8.5 cm long, 4.3 cm wide, and 1.8 cm thick (Pl. 6, H-I). They resemble the "cuchillos elipticos," possibly also blanks, which are found predominantly in Late Postclassic levels at Nopalera (García Cook, 1967:Lám. III, 3; cuadro 7).
>
> 3 longer pieces, with roughly straight to slightly convex bases, averaging 10.7 cm long, 4.5 cm wide, and 2 cm thick (Pl. 6, E-G).

The broad forms include:

> 6 fragments, 5 tips and 1 midsection
>
> 3 with sharply convex bases (Pl. 6, A-C). They average 5.9 cm wide by 1.6 cm thick. One, to judge by cortex at its upper end, is complete (Pl. 6, A). The other two are broken, so length cannot be estimated.
>
> 3 with roughly straight bases (Pl. 6, J-L). Widths average 6.1 cm, thickness 1.4 cm. Lengths are all incomplete, but must have been over 7 cm.

Finally, there is one nearly circular piece (Pl. 6, D), 6.8 cm long, 5.8 cm wide, and 1.5 cm thick. This specimen is similar to pieces from workshop site 2 in the Nopalillo-Guajalote area (Pl. 3, G-I), and lends some further support to the Late Postclassic date suggested for the latter items. The T. A. 79 specimen is probably a finished item rather than a blank.

Surface surveys conducted over the southeastern Teotihuacán Valley in 1964 turned up an abundance of Late Postclassic sites with extraordinarily heavy concentrations of obsidian debris (Sanders, 1965:83, 190). Fragments of obsidian tools are common at all sites of this period throughout the whole eastern Valley of Mexico, but the relative abundance of tools and working debris is generally far greater in the Otumba-San Marcos area than elsewhere. Tolstoy's earlier survey had likewise encountered two locations south of Otumba (his sites 15 and 16) where obsidian debris was relatively abundant (1958:72). After several seasons of intensive reconnaissance over the entire Teotihuacán Valley and much of the adjacent Texcoco Region to the south, no additional quarry locations have been found. These considerations strongly suggest that the relatively dense Late Postclassic population of the agriculturally marginal southeastern Teotihuacán Valley was to some extent specialized in obsidian quarrying and tool production, and that much of the obsidian used in the workshops came from the T. A. 79 quarry.

Spence located one Late Postclassic workshop of moderate size very near the southwest edge of the T. A. 79 quarry hill. A rapid and partial collection of the site produced 22 pieces of obsidian, 4 of which are of green obsidian foreign to the area. The collection includes:

13 waste pieces, all grey

5 fine blades. Three are of grey obsidian, and in two cases their striking platforms are present (one is ground, one not). The other two blades are of green obsidian, one with the striking platform missing and the other with a ground platform.

2 end scrapers of green obsidian. One, of teardrop shape, had been made from a flake blade. It shows no use marks, and measures 6.7 cm long by 3.2 cm wide at the head. The other, of short rectangular form, had been made from a chunk. It too shows no traces of use and measures 6 cm long by 4.4 cm wide at the head.

1 incomplete reject of grey obsidian, probably intended to be a point or knife.

1 long, narrow, crudely worked point, with a roughly rounded base (Pl. 6, M), of grey obsidian.

The smaller number of cores at the quarry, plus the fact that most of them were evidently finished and in use by the miners, suggests that core production was probably not the primary purpose of the T. A. 79 exploitation. Some cores, as seen by the two blanks, were undoubtedly made for use beyond the quarry, but our observations and collections suggest that the exploitation of the quarry was more oriented toward the production of end scrapers and, even more so, point-knife blanks.

The T. A. 79 quarry, like the Cruz del Milagro quarry, was clearly involved in the extraction and rough processing of material which was then passed to workshops beyond the quarries for further refinement. In comparing the Cruz del Milagro quarry with the T. A. 79 one, we are first of all impressed with the considerable difference in the scale of mining operations at the two locations. The Hidalgo source is much larger, with a correspondingly greater intensity of extraction. Another sharp contrast is the relative proximity of T. A. 79 to major consuming centers in the Late Postclassic Valley of Mexico. Virtually nothing is known of prehispanic settlement patterning in southern Hidalgo, but population in the Valley of Mexico in Late Postclassic times had clearly reached its peak pre-Conquest size and overall density. The Valley of Mexico was certainly the major demographic focus of the Mexican Central Highlands, as it had been since the beginning of Classic times.

We require considerably more information on the characteristics of obsidian in residential communities of both the Cruz de Milagro and T. A. 79 areas, but there is already some suggestion that much of the T. A. 79 obsidian was locally consumed by workshops in the Otumba-San Marcos area, while most of the Cruz del Milagro material was exported and not worked or utilized locally. This might imply local community control of the restricted T. A. 79 source, opposed to more highly organized state-oriented exploitation of the rich Cruz del Milagro resource.

## CONCLUSIONS AND SPECULATIONS

Coe and Flannery (1964:48) have pointed out that the obsidian quarry at El Chayal, Guatemala, shares several traits with the Cruz del Milagro quarry. Also, the crude bifacial items of El Chayal may be related to the point-knife blanks of T. A. 79 (see Coe and Flannery, 1964:44, 46, Fig. 3 e-f, i-1). If the early date for El Chayal is accepted, these similarities suggest considerable spatial and temporal continuity in quarrying and processing techniques. However, it should be noted that El Chayal lacks the retouched flake blades and end scrapers of the central Mexican quarries, while these latter in turn lack the celts, picks, scraper forms, and finished points and knives of El Chayal. The Ixtepeque quarry of Guatemala is similar to the Cruz del Milagro workings in that large core blanks were roughed out at the quarry and then taken elsewhere for further refinement (including treatment of the striking platform). At Ixtepeque, however, the large flake blades produced during core blank preparation were used as knife blanks (Graham and Heizer, 1968).

Although published material dealing with the subject is scanty, there is enough information available to permit a somewhat speculative reconstruction of the Late Postclassic obsidian industry in the central Mexican region. The three Late Postclassic period obsidian workshops found to date in Aztec Teotihuacán employed green obsidian and were specialized toward the production of cores and blades. No point or knife workshops of this period have yet been found in Teotihuacán, but the scattered Late Postclassic points discovered there are predominantly of grey obsidian. Probably the Aztec population of Teotihuacán obtained points and knives in finished form from the workshops of the Otumba-San Marcos area, but relied upon imported green obsidian, worked locally, for cores and blades (Spence, 1967:511).

In 1967 Parsons surveyed two small Late Postclassic workshops near Texcoco. Both lacked the subspecialization evident in the three Teotihuacán workshops, were rather producing the full range of obsidian items: cores, blades, points, knives, and scrapers. One, Tx-A-27 and 28, is about five miles north of Texcoco, on the southwest flank of Cerro Patlachique. Grey obsidian was utilized for the most part, even for cores and blades. The other workshop site,

Tx-A-10, on the Tepexpan-Texcoco highway about two miles north of Texcoco, has points of grey obsidian, scrapers of both grey and green obsidian, and blades and a core fragment of green obsidian.

Müllerried and von Winning (1943:138-39) analyzed the obsidian of a predominantly Late Postclassic period site (not a workshop) near Tepotzotlán, in the northwest Valley of Mexico. The blades are largely of green obsidian but non-blade material is too poorly represented to be sure of its significance. Obsidian from the Postclassic site of Tenayuca proved to be about 80 percent green and 20 percent grey (Noguera, 1935:162). Unfortunately no information is given on the relationship of color proportions to various types of items, but probably most blades (usually the most numerous obsidian artifacts on Late Postclassic sites) are green while the points, which occur in some abundance, account for most of the grey obsidian (Noguera, 1935:161).

In general, green obsidian seems to have been the preferred material for core-blade production, at least in all but some of the smaller sites. This is supported by the presence of green obsidian blades even in sites such as Aztec Teotihuacán and the workshop near T. A. 79, which lie very near sources of grey obsidian. Points and knives were probably made of green obsidian if it was plentifully available, but are for the most part of grey obsidian (it must be remembered that some of the smaller Late Postclassic points were made from fine blades, and so would usually be of green obsidian).

The green obsidian used for blades in the Late Postclassic period is generally a fine, translucent variety visually identical to the Cruz del Milagro material. Analysis by a method more sophisticated than visual examination will be necessary to establish firmly the source of this material, but the only natural sources of green obsidian in central Mexico known to us are those of southern Hidalgo – specifically, Cruz del Milagro, Cerro Piñal, and the Huapalcalco area. The green obsidian of the Huapalcalco source is opaque and of a considerably poorer quality than that of the other two sites (Fraunfelter, Appendix A; Aveleyra Arroyo de Anda, 1955:48-49). In view of this, and of the great size of the Cruz del Milagro quarry in comparison with that of Cerro Piñal, it seems reasonable to conclude that at least a major proportion of the green obsidian used for cores and blades of the Late Postclassic period in the central Mexican region came from the Cruz del Milagro quarry (Holmes, 1900:414). The x-ray fluorescence analyses of green obsidian blades from two Aztec burials at Tlatelolco show that the obsidian was of the Cruz del Milagro-Cerro de las Navajas area (Jack and Heizer, 1968:87, 90-91). Green obsidian specimens surface collected from Mitla and Texcoco also proved to be from that area (Stross et al., 1968:61, 69).

The basis for the grey-green distinction lies in the different physical qualities of these obsidians. Aveleyra Arroyo de Anda (1955:45, 48) has pointed out that the green obsidian used in blades has a fine grain and uniform texture, allowing the extraordinarily long and straight fractures necessary for the consistent production of fine cores and blades. In an appendix to this work, Dr. George Fraunfelter points out that samples of obsidian from the T. A. 79 and Huapalcalco areas have a secondary fracture pattern oblique to the conchoidal pattern, rendering these obsidians generally less suitable for blade manufacture than the Cruz del Milagro material, which lacks this secondary pattern. The obsidians of T. A. 79 and Huapalcalco, however, were still quite suitable for the production of points and knives, which did not demand such long and straight fracture as did blade production.

Variations in the physical properties of different obsidians and the consequent preferences for certain obsidians in the manufacture of certain items were thus the basic factors in the development of the complementary specialization noted at the Cruz del Milagro and T. A. 79 quarries. This specialization was of course not absolute. Both quarries produced end scrapers, grey obsidian was used by some smaller sites for cores and blades, and where extra Cruz del Milagro material was available it was probably funneled into point and knife production. Complementary specialization was, however, well enough developed to determine the general orientation of quarry production.

The green obsidian of the Cruz del Milagro was probably also an important article of long-distance trade. Sahagún stated that the pochteca carried obsidian in the form of earplugs, blades, and points to Xicalango and, probably, Soconusco (1959:8, 17-18, 31). Soconusco must have had contact with the Guatemalan highlands, and so would have had available an adequate supply of grey obsidian (cf. Chapman, 1959:54). Tabasco and the Yucatan peninsula probably also received grey obsidian from the Guatemalan highlands (cf. Kidder, 1947:10; Thompson, 1964:30; Stross et al, 1968:61). In view of this, there would have been very little demand for central Mexico grey obsidian in these parts of Mesoamerica. Thus the obsidian carried by the Aztec pochteca was most probably green obsidian. This suggestion is supported by several finds of green obsidian in Late Postclassic period contexts in the Maya area. These include three blades and a waste (core) fragment at Mayapan (Proskouriakoff, 1962:369, 371), a bifacially worked leaf-shaped knife and possibly some blades in the Xinabahul phase of Zaculeu (Woodbury and Trik, 1953: Vol. 2, pp. 228-31), and a pair of earplugs of the Chipal 3 period in the Alta Verapaz (Butler, 1962:256, Pl. XIa; Kidder, 1947:10). Kidder notes that most, if not all, Mesoamerican obsidian earplugs are of green obsidian (1947:32), although those of Tarascan manufacture may be of local grey obsidians. The most significant find of green obsidian with reference to pochteca trade, however, is a number of green obsidian blades in graves at Atasta, a site very near the location of Xicalango in Campeche (Berlin, 1956:140, 142, 148, 149). The material is from the latter part of the Late Postclassic Cintla horizon, and consists of 45 green obsidian blades and only 14 black-grey blades.

Material from the Cruz del Milagro quarry seems also to have been involved in the Aztec tribute or taxation system. Barlow notes a number of towns, in northern Estado de México and southern Hidalgo, which paid a tribute of blades to Texcoco and, later, also to Tenochtitlán (1949:71, ff81 and 82). The towns were Cenpoala, Tlaquilpa, Tecpilpa, Tzaquala (Zaqualapa?), Epazoyuca, Pachuca,

Tezontepec, and Temazcalapa (Fig. 1). The Relaciones Históricas Estadísticas state that the tax was of "nabajas con que hazian macanas" (quoted in Barlow, 1949:ff81-82). Since macanas were swords edged with large obsidian blades (Kidder, 1947:29), the document evidently refers to a tax of blades or, possibly, core blanks. The towns involved are all geographically clustered and in some cases (Pachuca and Epazoyuca) lie quite near the Cruz del Milagro quarry. The only other known source they might have drawn upon would be T. A. 79, and indeed a few of the towns are closer to T. A. 79 than to the Cruz del Milagro quarry. Several factors, however, indicate that the Cruz del Milagro quarry was the source. For one, the towns are geographically clustered and thus presumably politically interrelated and drawing upon the same source. Also, Epazoyuca, nearest to the Cruz del Milagro source, seems to have been most heavily involved in this tax, supplying both Texcoco and Tenochtitlán with blades. Finally, T. A. 79 was not oriented toward core-blade production, and in any case would have paid tax through Otumba, its cabecera, rather than through the towns mentioned in the document.

The importance of this tax to the main Aztec centers is evident in Tenochtitlán's demand, in Itzcoatl's reign, that Texcoco share with it the towns involved (Barlow, 1949:71, ff81 and 82). Probably the exploitation of the Cruz del Milagro quarry was done by local people subject to the tributary towns. The material was carried in blank form to these towns and then redistributed in regional trade and as tribute to Texcoco and Tenochtitlán. The regional trade aspect of this redistribution probably involved both itinerant traders and the well developed market system of the central Mexican region. Sahagún noted the presence of obsidian sellers in markets (1954:68; 1961:85). The large demand for green obsidian in core-blade production throughout the central Mexican region, and its involvement in taxation and long-distance trade, adequately account for the large scale and intensity of the Cruz del Milagro exploitation and the absence of evidence for local consumption of its produce.

There were other sources, producing obsidian of poorer quality, also being exploited in the central Mexican region. Huapalcalco and T. A. 79, utilized in the Late Postclassic period, have been mentioned. Deposits at Calixtlahuaca, near Toluca, may also have been quarried at that time (Aveleyra Arroyo de Anda, 1955:50). We have heard of still other deposits, but have not yet been able to confirm the reports (the workings near Zinapécuaro, Michoacán, were within another socio-political realm – the Tarascan – and so are here excluded from consideration). To judge by T. A. 79 and Huapalcalco, the produce of these quarries was in large part consumed locally, and not disseminated in quantity throughout the central Mexican region as was that of the Cruz del Milagro quarry. There is no evidence to suggest that these obsidian sources were involved in state taxation or long distance trade, certainly not to the extent that the Cruz del Milagro produce was. Areas exploiting these lesser workings were, however, probably firmly tied into the larger pattern by their dependence on the Cruz del Milagro obsidian for core-blade material, as seems certainly to have been the case with the Valley of Teotihuacán.

In sum, the evidence suggests several closely interrelated characteristics of the Late Postclassic obsidian industry in central Mexico: (1) a dependence upon the Cruz del Milagro obsidian for core-blade material and the use of other, local, obsidian sources for points and knives; (2) the resulting complementary quarry specialization; (3) workshop sub-specialization in some cases; and (4) the use of Cruz del Milagro obsidian in state taxation and long-distance trade. The historical development of this pattern can be traced to some extent, although direct information on pre-Aztec quarrying practices is lacking (cf. Vaillant, 1935: 240-43; Kidder, 1947:10; Aveleyra Arroyo de Anda, 1955:48-49). A blade of green obsidian was found with the first Santa Isabel Iztapán mammoth (Aveleyra Arroyo de Anda and Maldonado-Koerdell, 1952:24-25, Fig. 6, no. 5). Blades of the Cruz del Milagro-Cerro de las Navajas area green obsidian were being traded as far as La Venta, Tabasco, in the Middle Preclassic (Jack and Heizer, 1968: 88-89). At El Arbolillo most of the green obsidian found had been utilized in blade manufacture (Vaillant, 1935: Table 20), showing that the superior qualities of this green obsidian for core-blade production had been recognized by the Middle Preclassic period, if not before.

In Classic Teotihuacán this preference had become well entrenched, most of the blades and cores being of green obsidian while points and knives were predominantly of grey obsidian (Séjourné, 1966:217, 222; Spence, 1967:510). There was strong sub-specialization of some Classic Teotihuacán workshops in core-blade manufacture, with green obsidian being used for 84 percent of these items (Spence, 1967:510-11). Long-distance trade was practiced, and green obsidian of this period found in the Mayan area had undoubtedly been traded there from Teotihuacán. Dr. Robert F. Heizer, through x-ray fluorescence examinations, has identified some of this Early Classic period green obsidian from the Mayan area as derived from the Cruz del Milagro-Cerro de las Navajas region (Spence, 1967:513; Stross et al., 1968:61, 72). This suggests that Teotihuacán was getting its green obsidian from somewhere in that region. Neutron activation studies currently being undertaken by Dr. James B. Griffin and his associates should provide further information on this point.

It is thus evident that at least some of the basic characteristics of the Late Postclassic Aztec obsidian industry were already developed in Classic Teotihuacán: dependence on green obsidian for cores and blades, workshop sub-specialization, and the long-distance trade of green obsidian items. Probably most of the green obsidian came from somewhere in the Cruz del Milagro-Cerro de las Navajas region, while most of the grey obsidian came from the Otumba-San Marcos area (Stross et al., 1968:61).

The very large quantities of both grey and green obsidian used in Classic Teotihuacán suggest exploitation of sources on a considerable scale, and probable control over the source areas (Millon, 1967:39; Spence, 1967:512). Certainly the area around San Marcos and T. A. 79 is close enough to have been under Teotihuacán control. There are no Classic sites or quarries known in the area, but possibly these lie in unsurveyed sectors south of T. A. 79, around Cerro de

Campanario. Again, no Classic period quarries have yet been located in the Cruz del Milagro region, but our brief survey merely touched on a part of the obsidian-rich region. The scale of Teotihuacán's obsidian use certainly implies quarry operations of considerable intensity and extent, and the strong grey-green distinction in the manufacture of items suggests that complementary specialization may well be a feature of such quarries.

Unfortunately, we have very little information on obsidian for the period between the fall of Teotihuacán and the Late Postclassic exploitation of the Cruz del Milagro. Green obsidian continued to be traded to the Mayan area. There are three green obsidian blades from a Magdalena phase tomb (Late Classic period) in the Montagua Valley of Guatemala, and some Early Postclassic finds of a green obsidian blade at the Temple of Phalli, Chichén Itzá, and of a few green obsidian pieces at Tajumulco, Guatemala (Smith and Kidder, 1943:163, 164; Kidder, 1947:10; Dutton and Hobbs, 1943:45). Heizer, through x-ray fluorescence, has identified an obsidian bead from the Cenote of Chichén Itzá as derived from the Cruz del Milagro-Cerro de las Navajas region (Robert F. Heizer, personal communication to René Millon). Our only central Mexican data, however, is Kidder's observation that green obsidian is common at Tula (1947:10) and the identification of a Tula surface artifact as of Cruz del Milagro-Cerro de las Navajas area obsidian (Stross et al., 1968:61, 70). Probably further investigation will show that the basic characteristics of the Teotihuacán obsidian industry continued through the Early Postclassic period and eventually (as described above) formed the basis of the Aztec obsidian industry.

## APPENDIX

## OBSIDIAN SPECIMENS

*by Dr. George Fraunfelter*

With the exception of the "shiny" specimens, the material from all three sites, Huapalcalco, Cruz del Milagro and T. A. 79, shows some degree of devitrification, the greatest degree of which imparts a coarse-grained appearance to the specimens. Obsidian often exhibits a secondary set of fine fractures at an angle to the conchoidal fracture pattern. The specimens of obsidian from Huapalcalco and T. A. 79 possess a secondary strain or flow structure oblique to the conchoidal fracture pattern and to the original banding due to flow. The surface of this secondary flow structure is uneven and contains strain "blobs" here and there, indicating that the lava was partially solidified and then subjected to stress prior to final solidification. These surfaces of secondary flow structure produce a secondary set of planes of weakness or fracture pattern oblique to the normal conchoidal fracture pattern. The degree to which this secondary fracture pattern is developed would largely determine how useful, if at all, the obsidian from the two above listed sites would be for the manufacture of blades. Some of the specimens of obsidian were also spherulitic. The presence or absence of spherulites would have little affect, in this case, on the quality of the material for blade manufacture.

# BIBLIOGRAPHY


Aveleyra Arroyo de Anda, Luis

1955 Productos Geológicos del Valle de México. Revista Mexicana de Estudios Antropológicos Vol. 14, Pt. 1:41-52. Mexico City.

1964 The Primitive Hunters. Handbook of Middle American Indians Vol. 1: 384-412. University of Texas Press, Austin.

Aveleyra Arroyo de Anda, Luis and Manuel Maldonado-Koerdell

1952 Asociación de Artefactos con Mamut en el Pleistoceno Superior de la Cuenca de México. Revista Mexicana de Estudios Antropológicos Vol. 13, Pt. 1:3-30. Mexico City.

Barlow, R. H.

1949 The Extent of the Empire of the Culhua Mexica. Ibero-Americana No. 28. Berkeley.

Berlin, Heinrich

1956 Late Pottery Horizons of Tabasco, Mexico. Carnegie Institution of Washington, Publication 606. Contributions to American Anthropology and History No. 59. Washington.

Breton, Adela

1902 Some Obsidian Workings in Mexico. Proceedings of the Thirteenth International Congress of Americanists, pp. 265-68.

Butler, Mary

1962 A Pottery Sequence from the Alta Verapaz, Guatemala. The Maya and their Neighbors, second edition, pp. 250-67. D. Appleton-Century Co., New York.

Chapman, Anne M.

1959 Puertos de Intercambio en Mesoamérica Prehispánica. Instituto Nacional de Antropología e Historia, Serie Historia III. Mexico City.

Coe, Michael D. and Kent V. Flannery

1964 The pre-Columbian Obsidian Industry of El Chayal, Guatemala. American Antiquity Vol. 30, No. 1:43-49. Salt Lake City.

Crabtree, Don E.

1968 Mesoamerican Polyhedral Cores and Prismatic Blades. American Antiquity Vol. 33, No. 4:446-78. Salt Lake City.

Dutton, Bertha P. and Hilda Hobbs

1943 Excavations at Tajumulco, Guatemala. Monographs of the School of American Research No. 9. Santa Fe.

Gamio, Manuel

1922 La Población del Valle de Teotihuacán. Dirección de Talleres Gráficos, Secretaria de Educación Pública. Mexico City.

García Cook, Angel

1967 Análisis Tipológico de Artefactos, Instituto Nacional de Antropología e Historia Investigaciones No. 12. Mexico City.

Gibson, Charles

1956 Llamamiento General, Repartimiento, and the Empire of Acolhuacan. Hispanic American Historical Review Vol. 36:1-27. Durham.

Graham, John A. and Robert F. Heizer

1968 Notes on the Papalhuapa Site, Guatemala. Contributions of the University of California Archaeological Research Facility No. 5:101-25.

Holmes, W. H.

1900 The Obsidian Mines of Hidalgo, Mexico. American Anthropologist, n.s., Vol. 2, No. 3:405-16. New York.

1919 Handbook of Aboriginal American Antiquities. Part I, Introductory: the Lithic Industries. Bureau of American Ethnology, Bulletin 60. Washington.

Humboldt, Alexander de

1814 Researches Concerning the Institutions and Monuments of the Ancient Inhabitants of America, with Descriptions and Views of Some of the Most Striking Scenes of the Cordilleras. Longman, Hurst, Rees, Orme and Brown, J. Murray, and H. Colburn. London.

1941 Ensayo Político sobre el Reino de la Nueva España. Editorial Pedro Robredo. Mexico City.

Jack, Robert N. and Robert F. Heizer

1968 "Finger-Printing" of some Mesoamerican Obsidian Artifacts. Contributions of the University of California Archaeological Research Facility No. 5: 81-100.

Johnson, Paul Willard

1965 Field Guide to the Gems and Minerals of Mexico. Gembooks. Mentone.

Kidder, A. V.

1947 The Artifacts of Uaxactún, Guatemala. Carnegie Institution of Washington Publication 576. Washington.

Linné, S.

1942 Mexican Highland Culture. The Ethnographical Museum of Sweden, n.s., No. 7. Stockholm.

Lorenzo, José Luis

1965 Tlatilco, Los Artefactos. Instituto Nacional de Antropología e Historia Investigaciones No. 7. Mexico City.

MacNeish, R. S., Antoinette Nelken-Terner, and Irmgard W. Johnson

1967 The Prehistory of the Tehuacán Valley Vol. 2: Nonceramic Artifacts. University of Texas Press, Austin.

Millon, René

1967 Teotihuacán. Scientific American, Vol. 216, No. 6:38-48. New York.

Müller, E. F. Jacobs

1961 Tres Objetos de Piedra de Huapalcalco, Estado de Hidalgo. Homenaje a Pablo Martínez del Río, pp. 319-22. Instituto Nacional de Antropología e Historia. Mexico City.

n.d. El Material Lítico de Teotihuacán. MS, to be published by the Instituto Nacional de Antropología e Historia. Mexico City.

Müllerried, F. K. G. and H. VonWinning
1943 El "Cerrito" al Este de Tepotzotlán, México, en el Valle de México. El México Antiguo, Vol. 6:131-39. Mexico City.

Noguera, Eduardo
1935 La Cerámica de Tenayuca y las Excavaciones Estratigráficas. *In:* Tenayuca, pp. 141-201. Talleres Gráficos del Museo Nacional de Arqueología, Historia, y Etnografía. Mexico City.

Proskouriakoff, Tatiana
1962 The Artifacts of Mayapan. Carnegie Institution of Washington Publication 619, Pt. 4. Washington.

Sahagún, Fray Bernardino de
1954 General History of the Things of New Spain, Book 8: Kings and Lords. Translated by A. J. O. Anderson and Charles E. Dibble. Monographs of the School of American Research No. 14, Pt. IX. Sante Fe.
1959 General History of the Things of New Spain, Book 9: The Merchants. Translated by Charles E. Dibble and A. J. O. Anderson. Monographs of the School of American Research No. 14, Pt. X. Sante Fe.
1961 General History of the Things of New Spain, Book 10: The People. Translated by Charles E. Dibble and A. J. O. Anderson. Monographs of the School of American Research No. 14, Pt. XI. Sante Fe.

Sanders, William T.
1965 The Cultural Ecology of the Teotihuacán Valley. Department of Sociology and Anthropology, the Pennsylvania State University, University Park.

Séjourné, Laurette
1966 Arquitectura y Pintura en Teotihuacán. Siglo XXI Editores. Mexico City.

Smith, A. L. and A. V. Kidder
1943 Explorations in the Montagua Valley, Guatemala. Carnegie Institution of Washington Publication 546, Contributions to American Anthropology and History No. 41. Washington.

Spence, Michael W.
1967 The Obsidian Industry of Teotihuacán. American Antiquity, Vol. 32, No. 4: 507-14. Salt Lake City.

Spence, Michael W. and Jeffrey Parsons
1967 Prehispanic Obsidian Mines in Southern Hidalgo. American Antiquity, Vol. 32, No. 4:542-43. Salt Lake City.

Stross, F. H., J. R. Weaver, G. E. A. Wyld, R. F. Heizer, and J. A. Graham
1968 Analysis of American Obsidians by X-ray Fluorescence and Neutron Activation Analysis. Contributions of the University of California Archaeological Research Facility No. 5:59-79.

Suhm, Dee Ann and Edward B. Jelks
1962 Handbook of Texas Archeology: Type Descriptions. The Texas Archeological Society and the Texas Memorial Museum. Austin.

Thompson, J. Eric S.
1964 Trade Relations between the Maya Highlands and Lowlands. Estudios de Cultura Maya Vol. IV:13-50. Mexico City.

Tolstoy, Paul
1958 Surface Survey of the Northern Valley of Mexico: The Classic and Post-classic Periods. Transactions of the American Philosophical Society, n.s., Vol. 48, Pt. 5. Philadelphia.

n. d. Stone, Bone and Antler Tools of Central Mexico from Preclassic to Aztec Times. MS, to be published in Handbook of Middle American Indians, edited by Robert Wauchope. University of Texas Press. Austin.

Tylor, Edward B.
1861 Anahuac: Mexico and the Mexicans, Ancient and Modern. Longman, Green, Longman, and Roberts. London.

Vaillant, George C.
1935 Excavations at El Arbolillo. Anthropological Papers of the American Museum of Natural History, Vol. 35, Pt. 2. New York.

Woodbury, Richard B. and Aubrey S. Trik
1953 The Ruins of Zaculeu, Guatemala. William Byrd Press, Inc. Richmond.

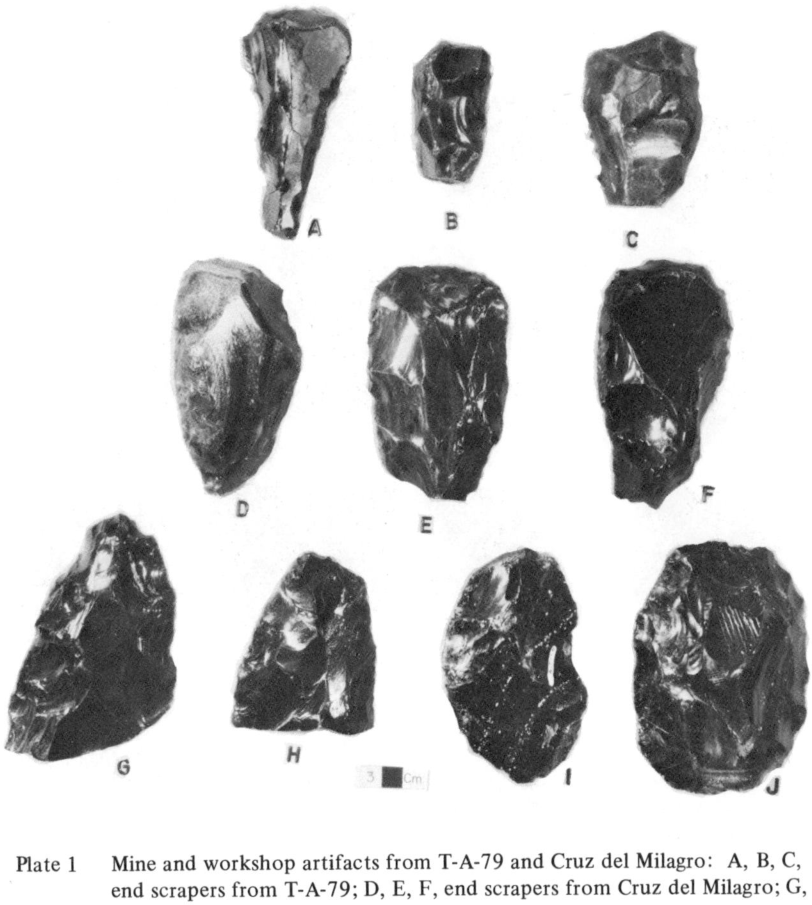


Plate 1 Mine and workshop artifacts from T-A-79 and Cruz del Milagro: A, B, C, end scrapers from T-A-79; D, E, F, end scrapers from Cruz del Milagro; G, H, retouched flake blades from Cruz del Milagro I, J, choppers, Cruz del Milagro site 4.

# PLATE 2

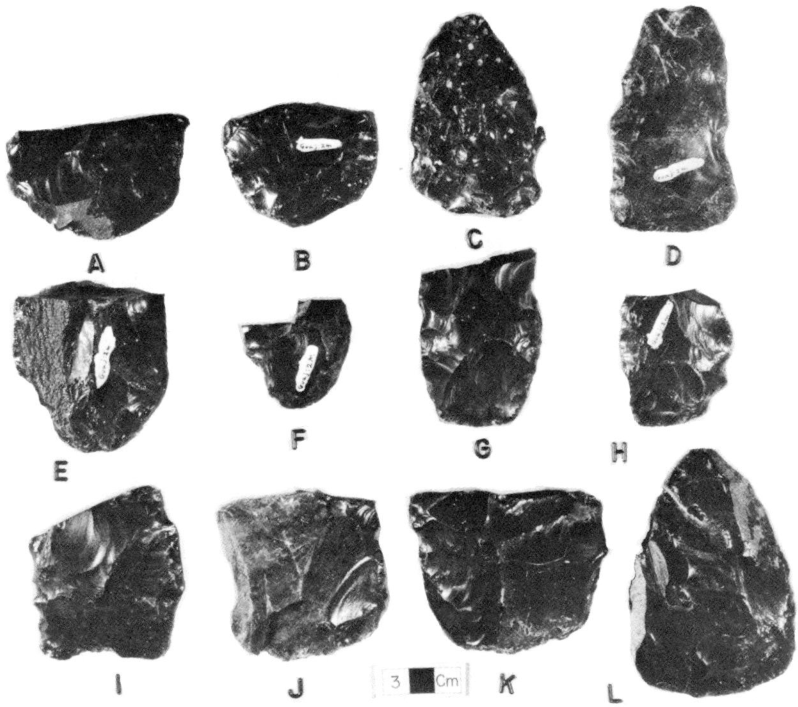


Plate 2 Workshop site artifacts: A, B, convex base knives from Cruz del Milagro site 2; C, stemmed knife from Cruz del Milagro site 4; D, straight base knife from Cruz del Milagro site 2; E, F, sharply convex base knives from Cruz del Milagro site 2; G, narrow knife from Cruz del Milagro site 4; H, narrow knife from Cruz del Milagro site 2; I, concave base knife from Cruz del Milagro site 4; J, K, unfinished knives from Cruz del Milagro site 4; L, ovate knife from Cruz del Milagro site 4.

Plate 3 Workshop site artifacts: A, B, end scrapers from Cruz del Milagro site 21; C, unfinished specimen from Cruz del Milagro site 2; D, E, small end scrapers from Cruz del Milagro site 2; F, small knife from Cruz del Milagro site 21; G, H, I, oval knives from Cruz del Milagro site 2.

Plate 4 Flacco-like point from Cruz del Milagro site 2.

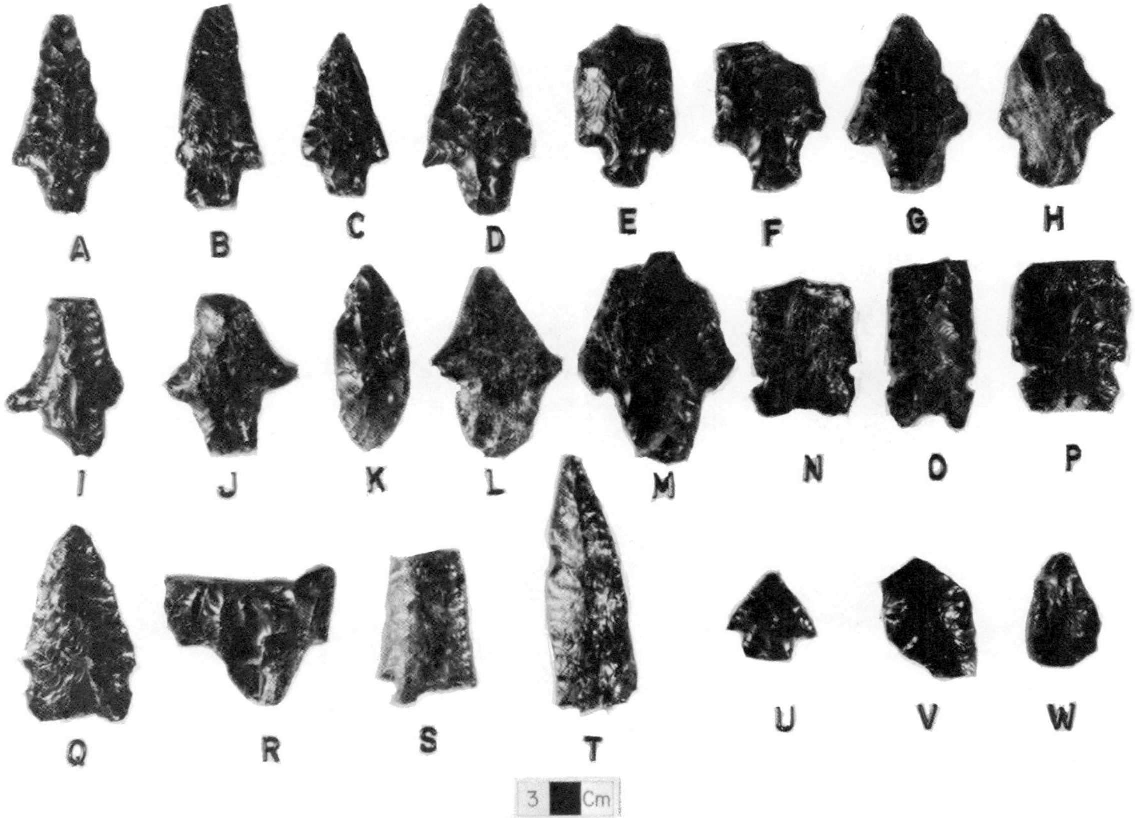


Plate 5 Projectile points from workshop sites: A-L, points from Cruz del Milagro site 2; M-R, points from Cruz del Milagro site 4; S, T, points from Cruz del Milagro site 15; U, V, W, points from Cruz del Milagro site 21.

# PLATE 6

Plate 6 T-A-79 artifacts: A, B, C, broad convex base blanks; D, oval knife; E, F, G, narrow long blanks; H, I, narrow short blanks; J, K. L, broad straight base blanks; M, projectile point.

Plate 7A Debris of site 9, Area A, Cruz del Milagro

Plate 7B Area B mine complex debris pile, Cruz del Milagro

# SPINDLE WHORLS FROM THE TEOTIHUACÁN VALLEY, MEXICO

*Mary Hrones Parsons*

## PREFACE

THE figurines and spindle whorls studied in these papers were collected during a five-year program of surface survey and excavations in the Teotihuacán Valley, Mexico. This Teotihuacán Valley Project was directed by W. T. Sanders of Pennsylvania State University between 1960 and 1965.

I would like to thank my husband, J. R. Parsons, of the University of Michigan Museum of Anthropology, who made most of the Aztec surface collections for the Teotihuacán Valley Project, and who suggested that I work with the Teotihuacán collections. He has read this manuscript and made many helpful suggestions. I would also like to thank Dr. Gordon Ekholm who kindly informed me of the Kaplan and Parker theses, and helped me to obtain them. He also gave me access to the figurine collections at the American Museum of Natural History. The Museo Nacional de Antropología in Mexico City kindly allowed me to study its large figurine collection. Both Mrs. Kaplan and Mr. Parker have generously allowed me to use their thesis data and photographs. Mr. George Stuber took many of the photographs used in this paper. My thanks also go to Mady Hirning who drew Figures 5-7 and Plate 37.

The research for both this paper and the following one on Aztec figurines was done while I was a research assistant at the University of Michigan Museum of Anthropology.

## TEOTIHUACÁN SPINDLE WHORL TYPES

A sample of 92 spindle whorls was obtained during surface survey of rural "Aztec" sites in the Teotihuacán Valley. No particular effort was made to look for spindle whorls, but they were picked up when seen. An additional 136 were recovered from the excavation of Aztec and mixed component sites in which there was, unfortunately, a lack of stratigraphy. Cultural affiliation cannot be ascertained from surface finds alone until we have stratified excavated data to back it up, but it is likely that most of the whorls in our collection are Postclassic. See Table 1 and Map 1 for provenience of whorls. Only 87 complete whorls were found, but it was possible to reconstruct the total diameter and hole diameter of most of the broken whorls. The weight could be approximated with reasonable accuracy in most cases.

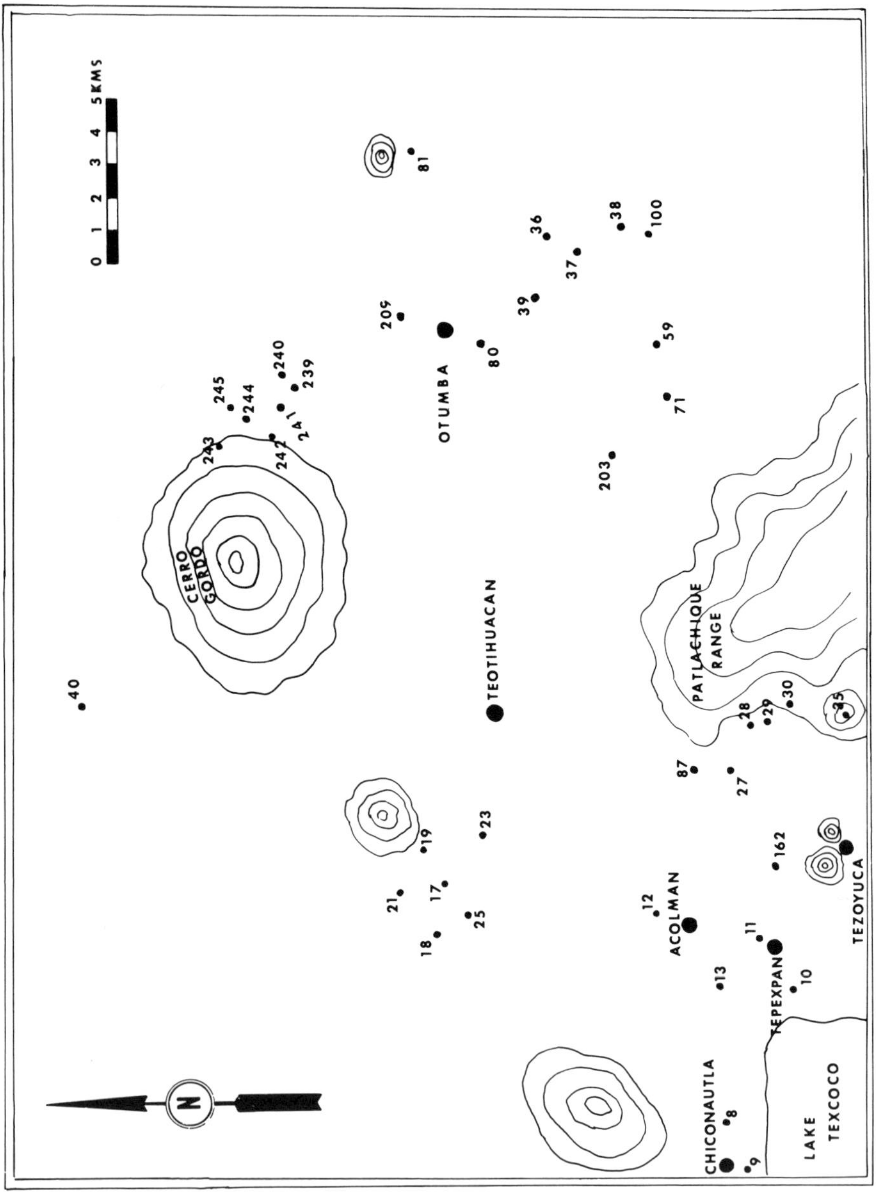


Map 1. The Teotihuacán Valley, showing Aztec period sites mentioned in the text.

The spindle whorls fall into a number of different categories, but three major types emerge, and will be described in some detail below.

Type I (82 examples)

This type is usually hemispherical in shape, but several specimens are truncated conical. The surface is highly polished but unslipped, ranging from black to buff in color. The whorls are relatively large, 35-61 mm in diameter (most falling between 40-52 mm). The temper is quite fine, consisting of splinter-shaped pieces of obsidian and tiny quartz crystals. All the whorls are decorated on the sides only (not on the "top" or "bottom").[1] All of them have one or two horizontal concentric circles incised around the top and the base of the whorls, delineating a panel in which a geometric design is incised (Fig. 1). In some cases the design zone is further divided into sections by vertical lines. Parts of the incised geometric pattern are filled in with a small square-shaped check stamp, a tiny diamond-shaped stamp, finely incised parallel lines, a dentate stamp, or tiny punctates. Several whorls had incised imitations of the check stamp. In many cases the grooves of the concentric circles almost appeared to be polished, perhaps indicating that they were cut into the whorl while it was still relatively moist. The incisions of the geometric design within the design zone lack this smooth groove, perhaps indicating that they were cut into the whorls after they were drier. This would make sense. First a decorative zone was delineated by concentric lines; later a design was outlined by deep incisions or sometimes horseshoe-shaped (reed?) impressions. Then the check stamp or

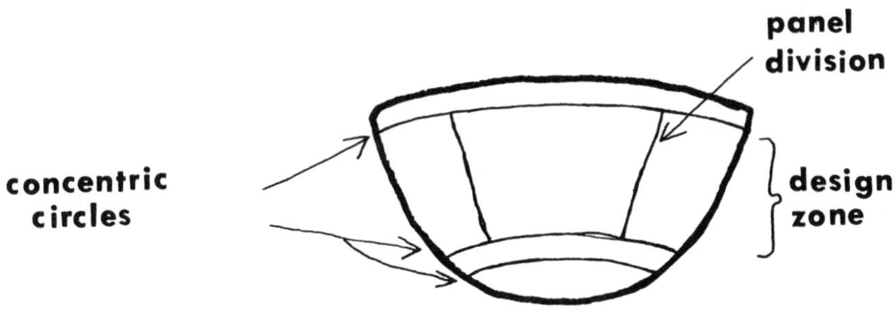


Fig. 1. Type I spindle whorl. Drawn to scale.

1 As Franco (1956) has pointed out, spindle whorls have commonly been illustrated upside down in publications. About ninety-nine percent of all spindle whorls have one plain surface and one convex surface taking a number of different forms. The flat, plain surface is functional -- the thread wound on the spindle rests on it during the spinning process. Using ethnographic data and illustrations from the codices, Franco shows that the spindle whorl is clearly used with the plain surface facing upward.

some other filler was applied to certain enclosed areas, and the entire whorl was polished, often obscuring the stamped filler.

On the basis of the decorative technique used in the design zone defined by the concentric rings, the Type I whorls can be divided into five groups.

*Group A* (33 examples). A check or dentate stamp was used to fill in areas of the geometric design. The stamping is extremely fine and small. A tiny stamped pattern, usually about 3 mm wide by 10-15 mm long, was cut into a small (probably wooden) dowel. The dowel stamp was impressed onto certain areas of the whorl, and then deep incisions were cut to outline these stamped areas in a geometric form. The most common stamp pattern was that composed of tiny squares, resembling the pattern of metal screening. We have 24 examples of this (Pl. 1*b, g*). There are two examples of a diamond or rhomboidal stamp pattern (Pl. 1*a, f*), and one example of definite dentate stamping (Pl. 1*h*). Six examples had incised imitations of the check stamp (Pl. 1*c, d*). Stamping in many cases was obscured by subsequent polishing. All whorls in this group were hemispherical except three, two of which were truncated conical, and one which was plain conical (Figs. 2 and 3).

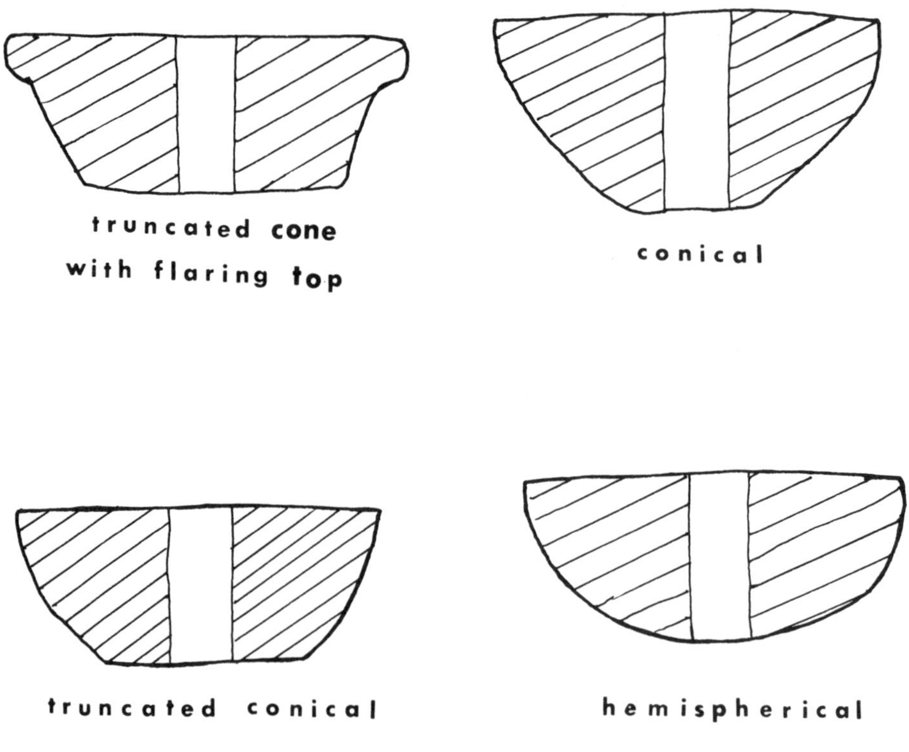


Fig. 2. Various spindle whorl shapes. Drawn to scale.

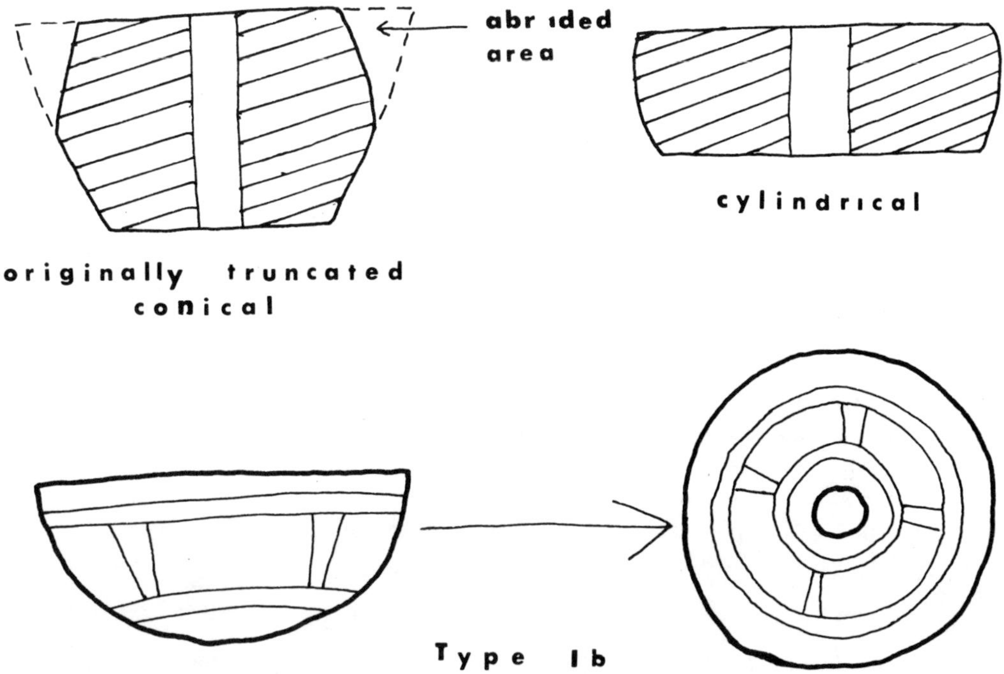


Fig. 3. Various spindle whorl shapes. Drawn to scale.

The most predominant design pattern was that of a spiral with a stepped-fret tail (20 examples) (Pl. 1*f* and Pl. 2*a*). The stepped-fret can be angular or composed of small curvilinear (reed?) impressions (Pl. 2*b*). In one case the spiral itself has been angularized (Pl. 2*c*). A second design motif in this group (6 examples) consists of merely the dividing of the design zone into from four to six panels by pairs of parallel vertical (or single vertical) lines. Every other panel or every two adjacent panels are then filled in solidly with check stamping (Pl. 2*d*). A third design group (7 examples) consists of miscellaneous geometric patterns filled with check stamping. One pattern of enclosing half loops forms what may be a flower, the only naturalistic example among the Type I whorls.

*Group B* (10 examples). Except for the lack of stamping (the panels are left completely empty), this group is exactly like the second form of Group A (Fig. 3). Seven are hemispherical, and three are truncated conical. Two whorls are heavily abraded around the top (Fig. 3*a* and Pl. 3*b*). The concentric circles and panel divisions on one specimen were crudely scratched on after firing.

*Group C* (5 examples). In this group a series of tiny punctates is used to fill in the angular geometric forms in the design zone (Pl. 3*a, b*). Four examples are truncated conical, and one is hemispherical. Three specimens show evidence of white paint in the punctates, and one had been heavily abraded at the top. (Pl. 3*b*).

*Group D* (8 examples). Fine incised parallel lines are used to fill the triangles, circles, and half loops in the design zone (Pl. 3*c*). Four of the whorls show traces of white paint in the incisions. Seven were hemispherical, one truncated conical.

*Group E* (13 examples). A small geometric stamp was made in the shape of a circle, a radiating sun, or an S-curve, and this was impressed upon the whorl at intervals (Pl. 4*a, b*). No large geometric areas are outlined, and there is *no* use of a filler (punctate, fine parallel lines, or check stamping). Seven of the whorls are hemispherical and six are truncated conical. One has been heavily abraded around the top.

*Group F* (7 examples). These whorls are completely plain (Pl. 4*c*). Four are hemispherical, two are truncated conical, and one is cylindrical.

*Group G* (6 examples). All these have an incised decoration of some sort or another, but not filled geometric areas as in Groups A, C, and D. One has four concentric incised circles within the two concentric circles defining the design zone (Pl. 4*f*). Another has curvilinear incisions and punctates in a single line (not used as a filler) (Pl. 4*d*). Others have sets of approximately parallel diagonal lines spaced at intervals within the design zone. Four whorls are truncated conical, two are hemispherical, and one is conical. The firing process has left one whorl polished half black and half buff.

*Group H* (no examples in this collection, but several in the Texcoco collection). In this type, wide areas are cut out in relief in a geometric stepped-fret pattern much like that in Group A. These tend to be quite large whorls (66-71 grams). See Figure 4.

Type II (34 examples)

These whorls are larger, 45-73 mm in diameter, and are covered with a deep polished red slip. The temper, if present, is very fine (finer than Type I) and

Fig. 4. Type I-H spindle whorl (UMMA-Texcoco Region, Strip II, no provenience). Drawn to scale.

difficult to see. The predominant shape is the truncated cone either with or without a flaring top. We have 8 examples of the former and 7 of the latter. See Figure 2. There are 12 examples of hemispherical whorls, 9 with a flaring top. Three specimens are conical; 4 others were so fragmentary as to be of undeterminable form.

*Group A* (21 examples). The decoration is a good deal more complex than in Type I. Deep, broad incisions of a complex geometric nature are made and then badly smeared by subsequent polishing (Pl. 5*a-f*). The initial design was cut into the whorl by an instrument 1-2 mm wide, leaving a deep clear impression. (Two specimens have a finer size incision – one-half to three-fourths mm wide.) The incision appears to have been cut after the red slip was applied, but prior to the final polishing. This final polishing has in many cases blurred and partially obliterated the original design so that it is difficult to make out the design motif (Pl. 5*a*, Fig. 5*b*). On some of the whorls the decoration is retouched by secondary incision, so that the original pattern is made somewhat more discernible (Pl. 5*d*).

*Group B* (11 examples). These whorls contain no other decoration than the polished red slip (Pl. 6*a*). Seven are truncated conical, four with a flaring top, three are hemispherical, and one is a flattened disk.

*Group C* (2 examples). This is an easily recognizable type. The entire whorl is given a red slip, and then an additional black slip is applied to the sides of the whorl only. With a thin-pointed instrument a fine geometric line pattern (zigzags and short parallel lines) is scratched through the black slip to the red slip below (Pl. 6*b-d*). Both our examples are truncated conical, as are similar specimens I have seen.

*Group D* (no examples in this collection, but several in the Texcoco collection). In this type the decorative motif is mold-made as in Group A, but it is

A

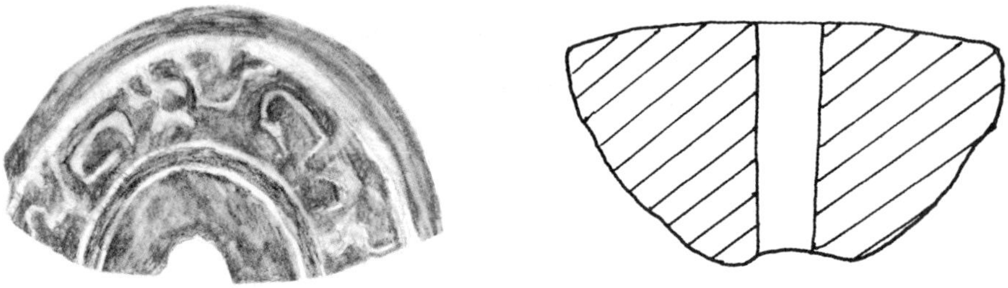

B

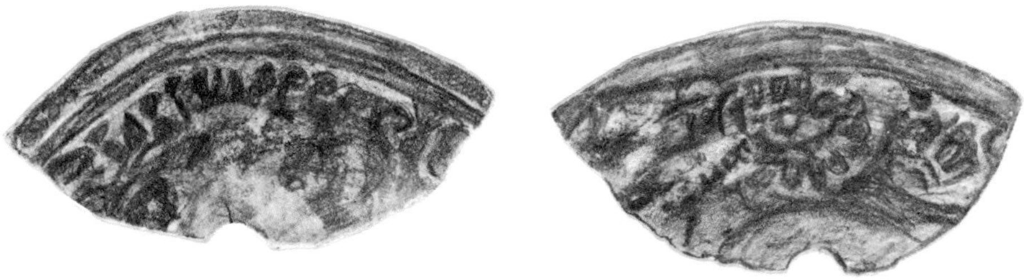

Fig. 5. Rubbings made from spindle whorls. Drawn to scale. A, Type II-A whorl, PSUDA Cat. No. T-A-246; B, Type II-A whorl, PSUDA Cat. No. T-A-245; C, Type VII-B whorl, PSUDA Cat. No. T-A-246.

not obscured by polishing. The motif is naturalistic: a jaguar or frog or human figure (Pl. 7).

### Type III (78 examples)

This type of whorl is much smaller than the other two types, ranging from 15-31 mm in diameter, with 88 percent in the 18-28 mm category. It comes in a wide variety of shapes. There are thin flat disks, hemispherical ones, and the whole range between. There are truncated cones and a variety of exotic "compound" whorls consisting of a basic disk with additive elements – cones, hemispheres, cylinders, and combinations of these elements (Pl. 8). Although some of the whorls are too badly weathered to tell, 38 are polished, and the others are at least finely manually smoothed. One has traces of red paint, but the color of the others appears to be the natural result of the firing conditions. Two are black, one is white, and the others range from buff to orange and red. The temper, like that of Type II, is extremely fine.

*Group A* (74 examples). These whorls have no decoration such as incision or stamping (Pl. 8). They are by far the most common of Type III whorls.

*Group B* (1 example). This type has an incised design. Our single example has parallel slanted incisions around the sides cut after the polishing (Pl. 9*a, b*).

*Group C* (1 example). This type has a series of stamped impressions much like those found in Type I-E.

*Group D* (2 examples). These have elaborate mold-made designs (Pl. 9*c*).

### Type IV (2 examples)

These whorls are polished buff in color and cylindrical in shape. The sides are decorated with a series of short parallel lines and an occasional looped figure incised when the clay was partially dry. As in Group II-A, the design has been blurred by the final polishing (Pl. 10*a*). The whorl diameters were about 53 mm and the approximated weight was 51 grams. The temper is composed of quartz and obsidian fragments.

### Type V (9 examples)

Except for the fact that these are polished buff (lacking a red slip), they are just like Group II-A. The design technique, motifs, and smearing are the same, as is the range of shapes (4 hemispherical, 5 truncated conical). The size range (39-56 mm diameter, weight 26-62 grams) is smaller than Type II-A, but this may be a function of our smaller sample (Pl. 10*b-d*).

### Type VI (2 examples)

These are manually polished buff-colored whorls, truncated conical in shape, with very crude and sloppy deep incision on the sides. The design pattern (parallel vertical lines and hook figures) has been blurred by final polishing. One whorl has a diameter of 42 mm and the other of 47 mm. They weigh approximately 44 grams each. The temper is extremely fine (Pl. 11*a*).

### Type VII (2 examples)

This category is composed of two large whorls decorated with mold-impressed, naturalistic, but highly stylized images. They are polished, but unslipped.

A) A hemispherical, polished black whorl 51 mm in diameter and weighing 47.8 grams. The mold-impressed decoration is very clearly and sharply cut and portrays a monkey and a plumed serpent (Fig. 6).

B) A truncated conical, polished buff whorl 52 mm in diameter and weighing approximately 55.8 grams. The molded decoration is that of a highly stylized plumed serpent. Its contours have been blurred some by final polishing as in Type II-A (Fig. 5C).

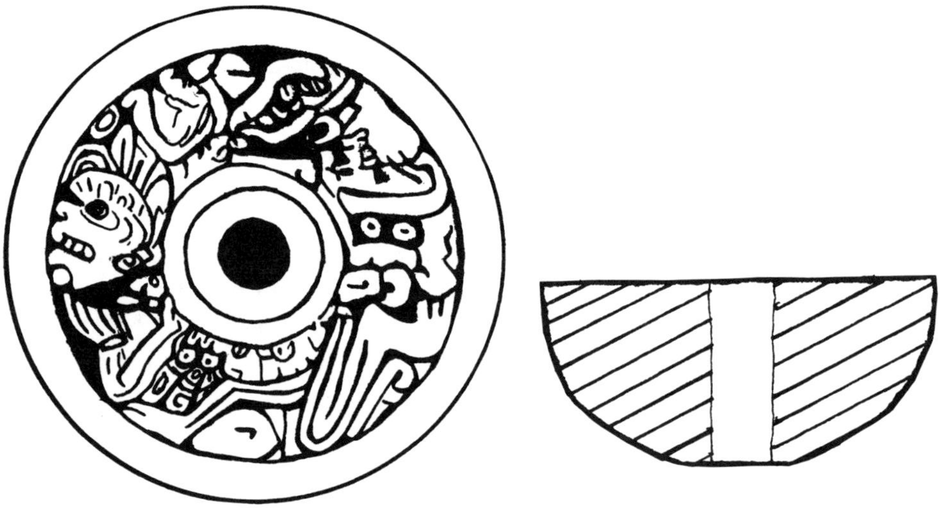

Fig. 6. Type VII-A whorl. Drawn to scale (PSUDA Cat. No. 8173).

Type VIII (2 examples)

Both are small, polished buff, mold-decorated whorls. They are low hemispherical in form and have a very sharp molded decoration of a highly stylized nature. One is a very complex plumed serpent, illustrated by Franco (1955). See Plate 11*b*. The other has a more naturalistic motif but is less readily understood (Fig. 7). It is perhaps a profile of a head surrounded by a tailed serpent. One whorl has a 36 mm diameter and weighs 10.4 grams, and the other has a 29 mm diameter and weighs 7.4 grams.

Type IX (2 examples)

Both examples are only small fragments, but would have been about 44 mm in diameter and would have weighed about 31 grams. They are polished buff,

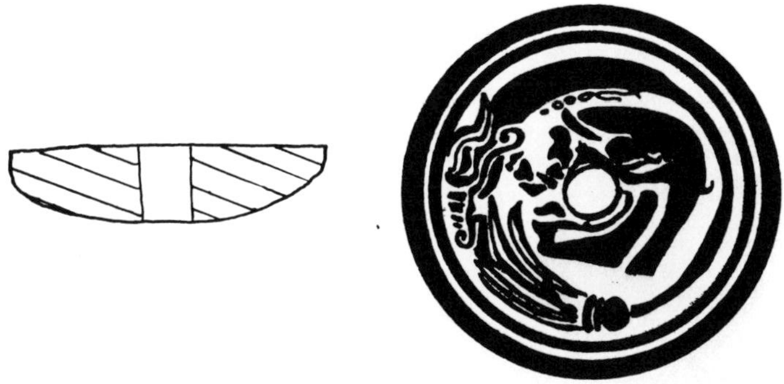

Fig. 7. Type VIII whorl. Drawn to scale (PSUDA Cat. No. 3533).

truncated conical whorls. The geometric motif is concentric spirals (Pl. 11*c*). The temper is of quartz and obsidian fragments, as in Type I.

Miscellaneous (6 examples)

A) A polished buff hemispherical whorl with a flaring top and a geometric design (Pl. 12*a*). The same motif is repeated four times. It is 46 mm in diameter and weighs 24.9 grams.

B) This is a large, badly weathered whorl – 50.5 mm in diameter and weighing 38 grams. It was at least manually smoothed and perhaps polished or slipped, although weathering has destroyed all evidence of this. It is truncated conical with a very elaborate mold-made sunburst decoration on the base and sides. Despite intensive weathering, the pattern is clear and deeply cut (Pl. 12*b*).

C) This is a large, buff, badly-weathered whorl which was smoothed but probably not polished. It has a 48 mm diameter and weighs 38 grams. It is hemispherical with a molded design in extremely high relief, consisting of lines, triangles, and looped figures (Pl. 12*c*). The Yale Peabody Museum has a collection of 33 whorls of this type, 27 of which are from Cholula. See Map 2.

D) A small, gray, polished whorl which is truncated conical in shape. It weighs 15.4 grams and has a diameter of 36 mm. There is some extremely sloppy deep incision in line and stepped-fret decoration (Pl. 13*a*).

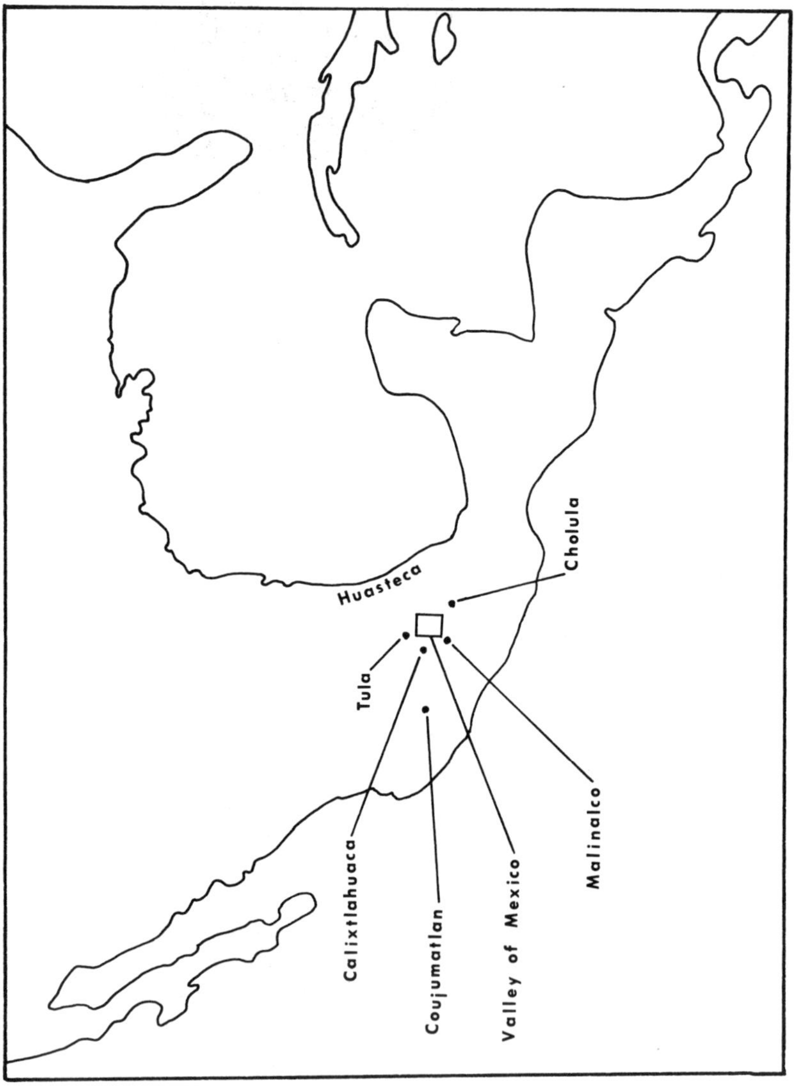


Map 2. Map of Mexico showing locations of spindle whorl from outside the Valley of Mexico mentioned in the text.

E) A small, polished, black whorl, 33 mm in diameter and weighing 11 grams. It is truncated conical in shape with a flaring top. The molded design is composed of four petals symmetrically arranged around the central hole of the whorl (Pl. 13*b*). A whorl just like this was found by Franco at Tula. He places it in his miscellaneous mold-made Type A-3 category.

## TRADE WHORLS

There are five whorls that appear to be of definite "foreign" origin, i.e., they are from outside the Teotihuacán Valley area (Map 2). Three asphalt decorated Huasteca whorls are present, probably good evidence of trade contacts with the coastal lowlands. We have one each of Ekholm's Type 2, Type 6, and Type 7 Huasteca whorls (Pl. 14*a-c*).[2] Our sample also included three whorls probably from the Toluca Basin area of Mexico. This type of whorl is a polished buff color and truncated conical in shape with decoration on the sides and on one or both flat surfaces. Our unbroken example has a diameter of 59 mm and weighs 62.3 grams. Parker (1952) has studied a number of these whorls which he calls "Type 2." Those in his sample were unpolished. Some were decorated on both the top and bottom surface in addition to the sides. The decoration is either stamped or grooved and of a symmetrical geometric nature (Pl. 15*a-c*, 16). Parker's "Type 2" whorls differ from his "Type 3" whorls only in the nature of the geometric motif (Pl. 15*d-g*). Parker, who studied 373 of these "Type 2 and 3" whorls from Yale's Peabody Museum collection, found that 206 of them were from Calixtlahuaca and 115 from Tenango del Valle. Lister (1949) mentions 57 whorls from Coujumatlán which appear to be of this type, and I have seen examples of them at Malinalco. The third possible example of a trade whorl is example C under the miscellaneous whorls which, as I mentioned earlier, may be a Cholula variety.

## CULTURAL IMPLICATIONS

The importance of certain variables (whorl diameter, weight, and hole diameter) in relation to the kind of spinning being done is an interesting problem. When these three variables are plotted against each other for our Teotihuacán Valley Types I, II, and III there is a clear bimodal distribution with no zone of overlap, and a significant gap between the two (Figs. 8-10). Types I and II are

2 Other sites outside of the Huasteca area reported to have Ekholm's Type 2 whorls are Texcoco (3), Culhuacán (3), Coatlinchán (2), Tenayuca (1), Tlaxcala (1), Cholula (1), Calixtlahuaca (1), Azcapotzalco (1) (Parker, 1952); Coatlatlán and Monte Albán (Ekholm, 1944*b*). Ekholm's Type 7 whorls are found at Tula (Franco, 1956) and at Culhuacán (Parker, 1952).

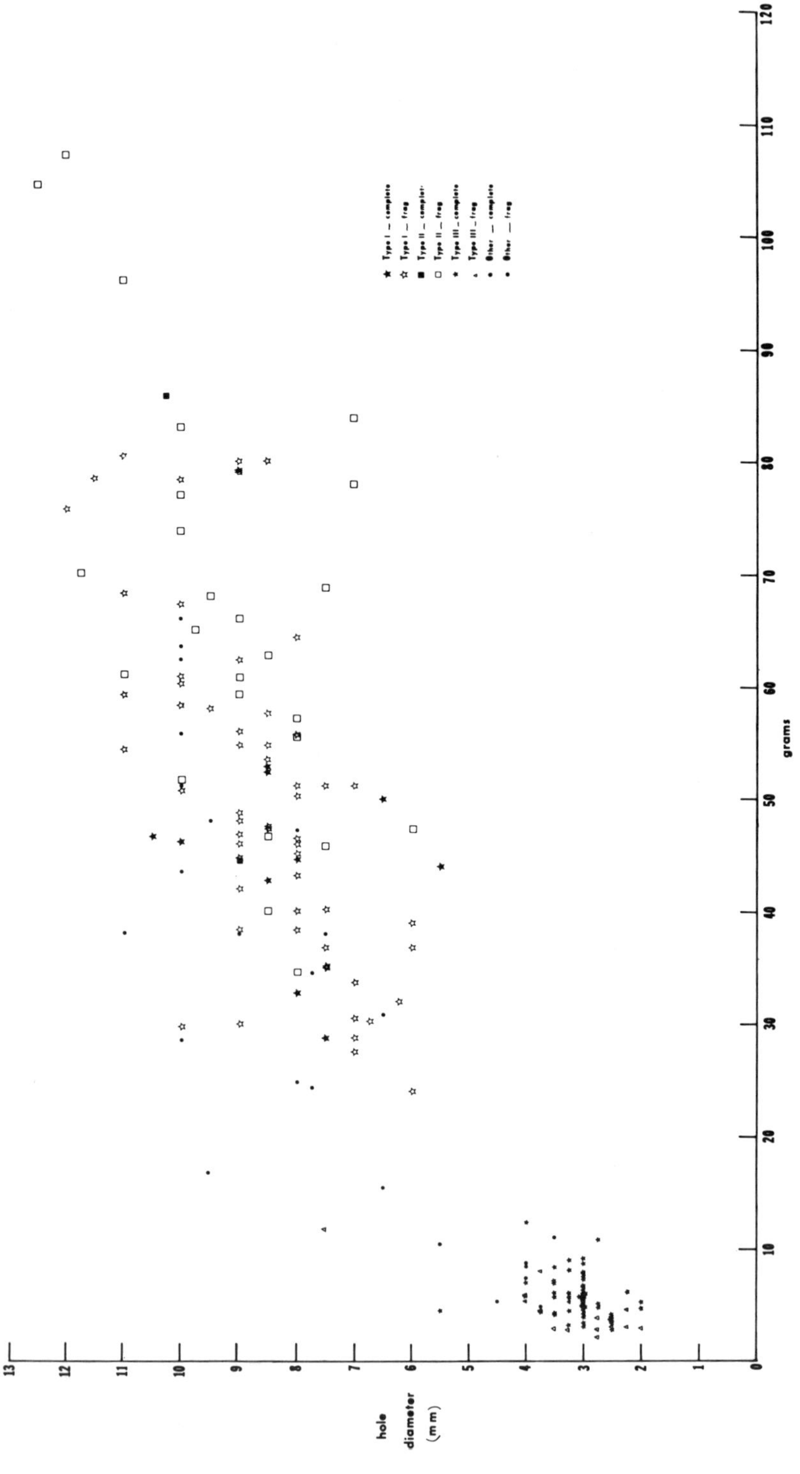


Fig. 8. Relationship between the hole diameter and weight of the major spindle whorl types.

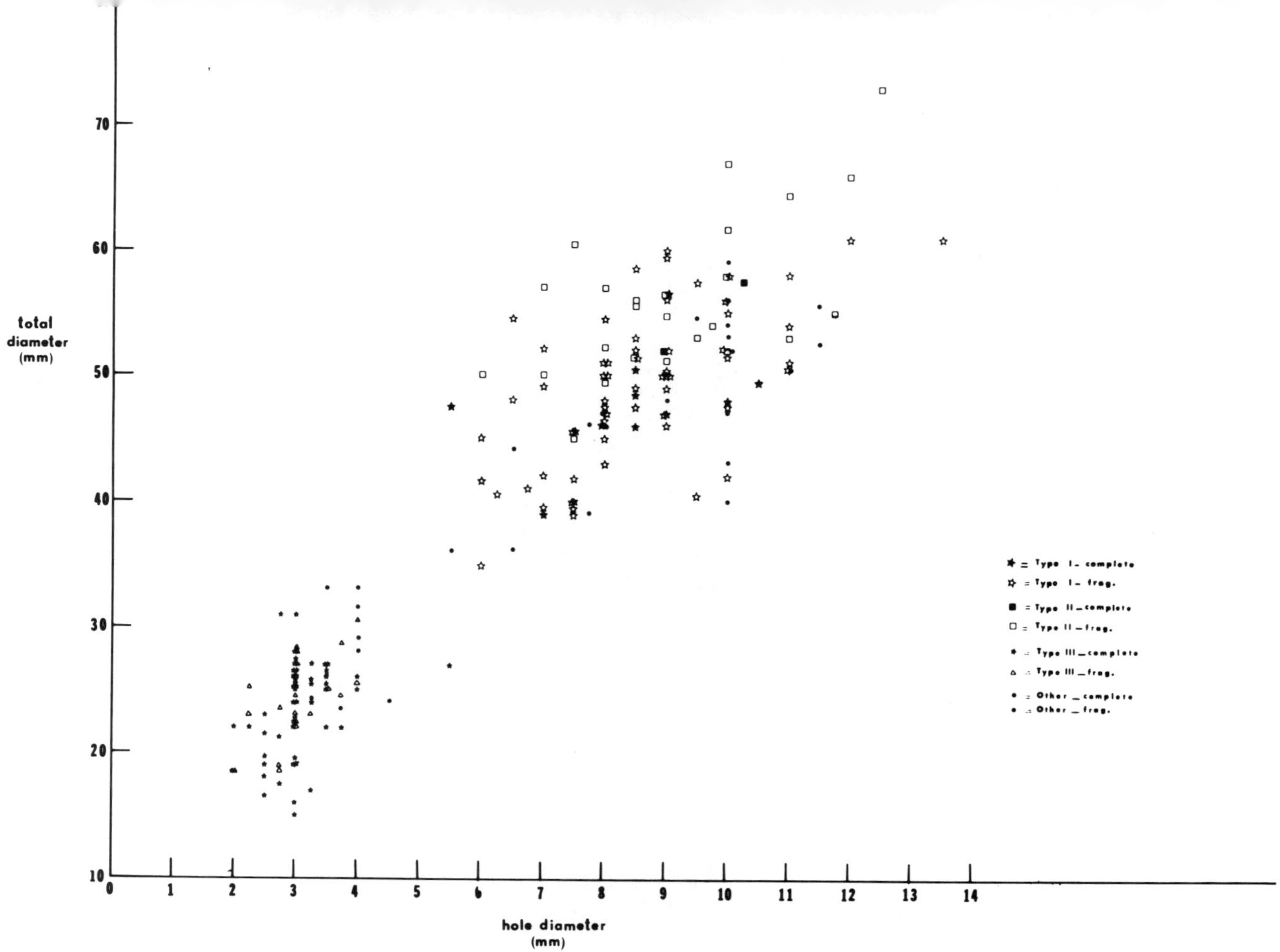


Fig. 9. Relationship between the total diameter and the hole diameter of the major spindle whorl types.

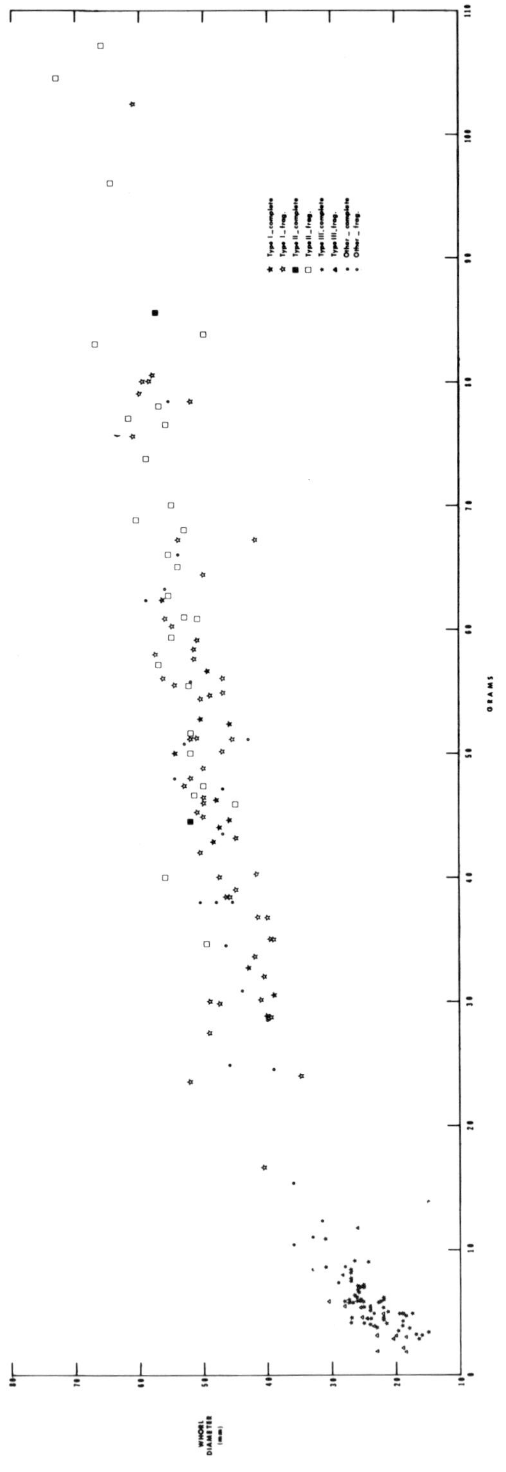


Fig. 10. Relationship between the total whorl diameter and the weight of the major spindle whorl types.

clearly distinct from Type III in all cases. This may substantiate the idea that we are dealing here with whorls used on two different and distinct types of fiber. O'Neale (1945) and Kent (1957) state that in present-day Guatemala the spinning of woolen yarn is done on large disk whorls, while cotton is spun on small bead whorls. O'Neale tells us that larger and heavier spindles are needed for spinning wool because wool yarn is much thicker than cotton yarn. Before the Spanish Conquest wool was unknown in Mesoamerica, but another heavy fiber, maguey, was in common use. As Linné has stated, light whorls are best suited for spinning cotton thread: "Heavy whorls are most suitable for the spinning of *ixtli*, the strong fibre obtainable from the maguey plant" (1934:128). Linné has also said that the whorl size (and by this he means the weight) is related both to the material being spun and to the quality of the thread. But the weight factor is not a simple one. Weight can be added by increasing the diameter of the whorl, or by holding the whorl diameter constant and increasing the height. When weight alone is plotted against hole diameter in the small Type III whorls, there is a wide range of variation in weight while the hole diameter measurements remain basically constant (Fig. 8). This indicates that for the type of fiber being spun (cotton) a small spindle was required (indicated by the small hole diameter on the whorl). The noticeable difference in the weight of these whorls may be the factor determining the fineness of the particular cotton thread – a lighter whorl producing a finer thread.

Since most of the Type III whorls were complete or almost complete, the weight figures on these whorls are quite accurate. But in the case of Type I and II whorls, we seldom had even half of the whorl, and the weight estimates cannot be regarded as wholely reliable. For the Type I and II whorls (the large whorls), when approximated weight is plotted against hole diameter, there is a rather vague general trend for both to increase together (Fig. 8).

When total whorl diameter is plotted against hole diameter, there is a tendency in all three types for the variables to increase proportionally (Fig. 9). When total whorl diameter is plotted against weight, again both variables increased proportionally in all types (Fig. 10).

In all these graphs it is important to note that though Type I and II whorls overlap in range, the Type III whorl (for cotton) remains functionally distinct (Figs. 11-13). The hole diameter, which is a function of spindle size, and the overall size of the whorl seem to corrolate directly with the type of fiber being spun (probably cotton with Type III whorls and maguey with Types I and II whorls). The whorl diameter and weight together determine the moment of inertia, or angular velocity with which the spindle rotates. The moment of inertia is probably the basic factor involved in determining the fineness of the thread spun, be it cotton or maguey. Bernal Diaz tells us that the maguey worn by the Tlaxcalan nobility was extremely fine and beautiful. One would expect that the smaller Type I and II whorls would be used to make this extremely fine maguey cloth.

Whether the different whorl types (I, II, and III) represent different chronological periods cannot be determined without well-controlled excavations covering

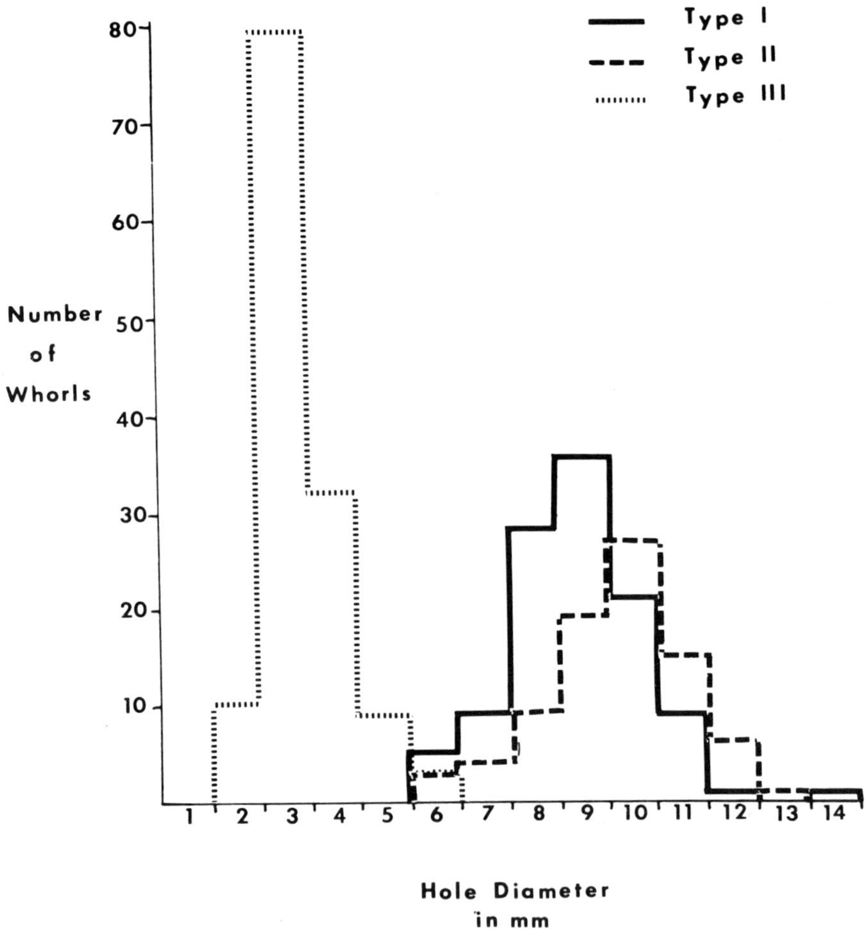


Fig. 11. Comparison of the hole diameters of the three major spindle whorl types.

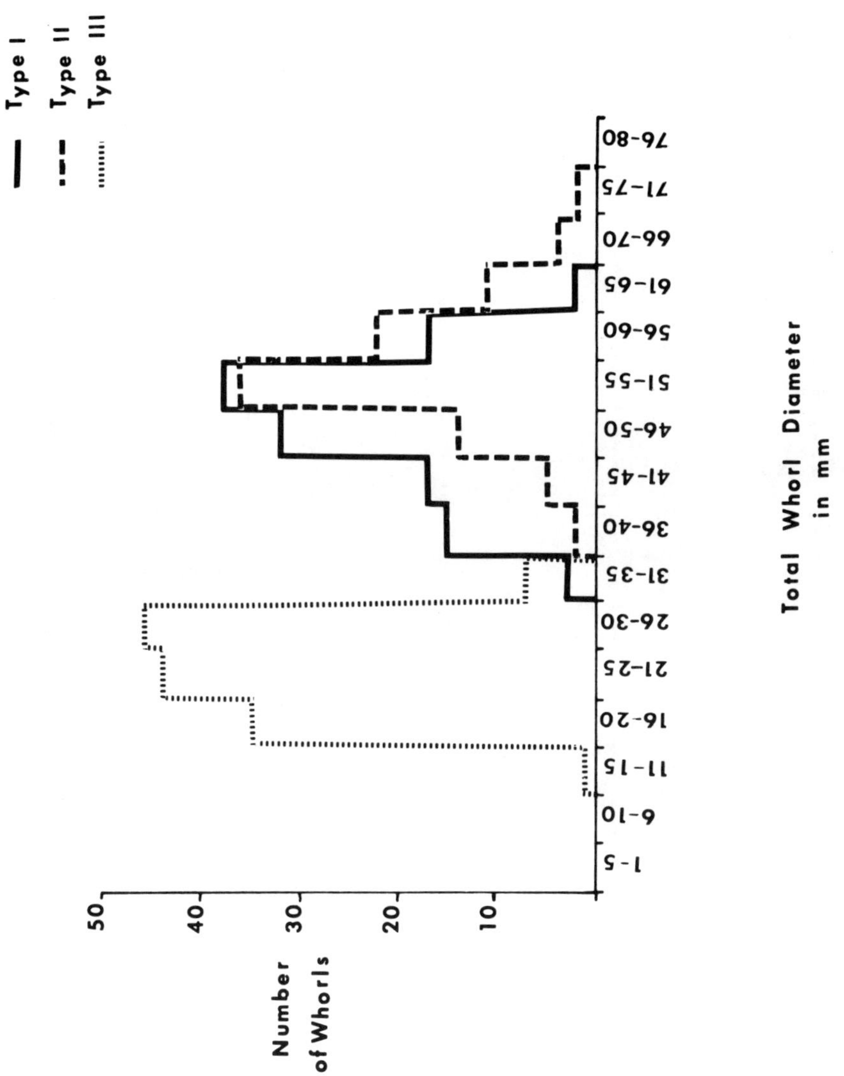


Fig. 12. Comparison of the total whorl diameters of the three major spindle whorl types.

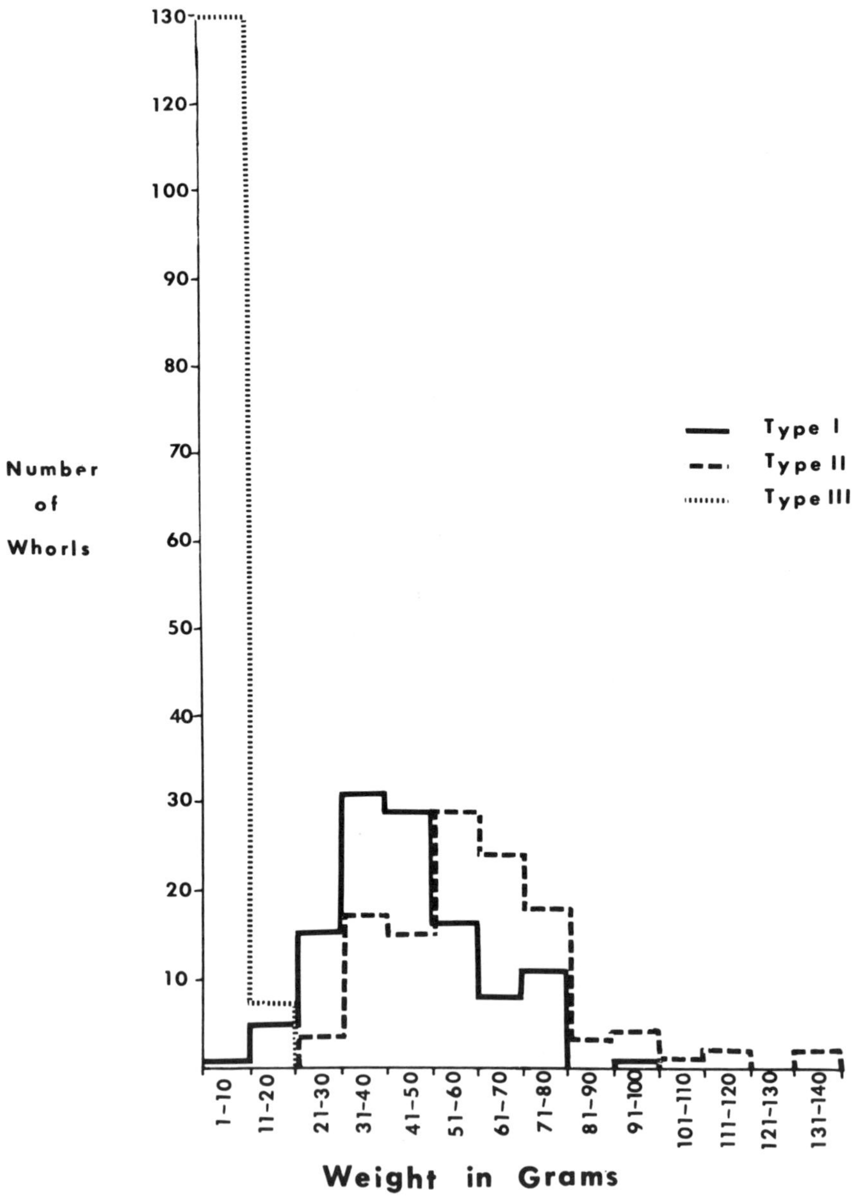


Fig. 13. Comparison of the weights of the three major spindle whorl types.

the total cultural sequence. Vaillant (1950:152-53) says that in the fifteenth century spindle whorls became much smaller, indicating the spinning of more delicate cotton threads. He feels that the heavily burnished black or red whorls with incised or stamped designs and with large central holes (our Types I and II) belong to the fourteenth century.

The importance of spindle whorls lies in their great variability in size, shape, and decoration from area to area. Distinctive types emerge which can be corrolated with specific regions. Only preliminary work has been done, but it is evident that spindle whorls can be important indicators of interregional trade and perhaps chronology. For example, Franco (1956), using his own data from Tula, Hidalgo, and Ekholm's data from the Huasteca, has tried to show that Tula was importing cotton cloth from the Huasteca (see Map 2). Tula has many large maguey whorls, but only a few small cotton whorls. These small whorls appear to be crude imitations of Huasteca whorls. The Huasteca lacked large maguey whorls but had many small cotton whorls. Cotton could not be grown on the Altiplano; thus local manufacture could take place for only the rough maguey fiber – the finer-spun cotton being imported from the Huasteca region. Franco concludes that Tula's contact with the Huasteca fostered some local attempts in the highlands to spin imported cotton. It was only natural that they should imitate the small asphalt whorls used in the coastal area, their source of cotton.

Our data shows that 34 percent of our whorls from the Teotihuacán Valley are Type III, or cotton spinning whorls. This clearly indicates that there was a considerable amount of cotton spun in the Teotihuacán Valley, an area which could not have grown the cotton it was spinning. Tribute lists and early documentary sources indicate that cotton was coming into Tenochtitlán and Texcoco from the Huasteca area and the Valley of Morelos. In many cases, the cotton came in as finished cloth, but there are a few references to raw cotton. Perhaps others, however, have been lost or omitted in the Spanish copies of tribute lists (Barlow, 1949). The Teotihuacán Valley is on the direct trade route from the Huasteca to Tenochtitlán or Texcoco. One could not use a route farther south because Tlaxcala, an area never incorporated into the Aztec "empire," blocked the way. A route farther north would have made the trip unnecessarily longer. It appears that raw cotton was shipped from the coast to Texcoco via the Teotihuacán Valley where some of it was spun, and perhaps woven into cloth, before it was sent on to Texcoco for the use of a privileged few. Duran tells us that starting in Moctezuma I's time, "The common people [were] not allowed to wear cotton clothing, under pain of death, but only garments of maguey fiber" (1964:131). He also tells us that after losing a battle to Tlaxcala, the Aztec officers were forbidden to wear cotton mantles. "From now on these officers were to wear cloaks of maguey fiber like those of the common man" (1964: 244-45). We know that the Teotihuacán Valley was politically marginal in Aztec times, so that very few of the people living there would have been entitled to or could have afforded to wear cotton cloth. The cotton was probably spun by part-time specialists who never used what they made but sent it on to Texcoco. It is conceivable that the Teotihuacán Valley's tribute to Texcoco consisted, at least in part, of the personal services rendered by these cotton spinners. Alva Ixtlilxochitl says that in the fourteenth century certain towns that were tributary to Texcoco specialized in spinning and weaving cotton (1952:1:146-147). Nuttall (1926) tells us that in 1580 the town of Tequisistlán specialized in spinning and weaving cotton obtained from Morelos (p. 80). See Map 3. Zorita speaks of areas that "did not grow cotton but worked it into a very good cloth. This excellent cloth was made by the people of the tierra fria, who are better workers than those of the tierra caliente. Thus some towns gave cotton and others turned it into cloth" (1963:187). The Teotihuacán Valley was very likely one of those cotton-spinning areas.

## SUMMARY

In this paper I have tried to show how spindle whorl data can be used to reflect trade patterns and the local production of two fibers – one native to the area and the other imported.

Working independently and on different spindle whorl collections, Dr. Leo P. Biese (1960) and I arrived at the same working premises: (1) spindle whorls differ in shape, decoration, material of construction, and size from area to area; (2) variation in spindle whorl size may indicate that "either two different weights of thread were spun for different use or that two different fibers were used to make cloth" (Biese, 1960:37). Dr. Biese's sample consisted of twelve whorls picked up after heavy rains on the Panama Viejo site. He worked with the following variables – surface color and finish, decoration, maximum whorl diameter, and weight. Although he does not give information on the hole diameter, judging from the small overall whorl size (2.0-3.1 cm maximum whorl diameter) the hole diameter range was probably no more than 1-2 mm. This would mean that spindle size remained the same, but spindle whorl weight varied, indicating that different finenesses of the same fiber were being spun. In the Teotihuacán Valley case, where maximum whorl diameter, weight, and hole diameter form a clear binomial distribution, we are almost surely dealing with the spinning of two different fibers, cotton and maguey. Maguey is native to the area, but cotton is not. Using sixteenth century Spanish sources, we find that cotton cloth was worn only by the elite segment of Aztec society. Since the Teotihuacán Valley was politically marginal in Aztec times, it is suggested that cotton was spun in the Teotihuacán Valley as a tribute service for the large Aztec center of Texcoco. Documentary sources seem to support this idea.

## FRAMEWORK FOR FUTURE RESEARCH

Chronology remains a problem. Were cotton whorls used in the Early Aztec period (*ca.* A.D. 1150-1350) in the Valley of Mexico, or do they date from the Late Aztec period (*ca.* A.D. 1350-1520) when trade and tribute networks had greatly expanded? Were certain communities or sections of communities involved

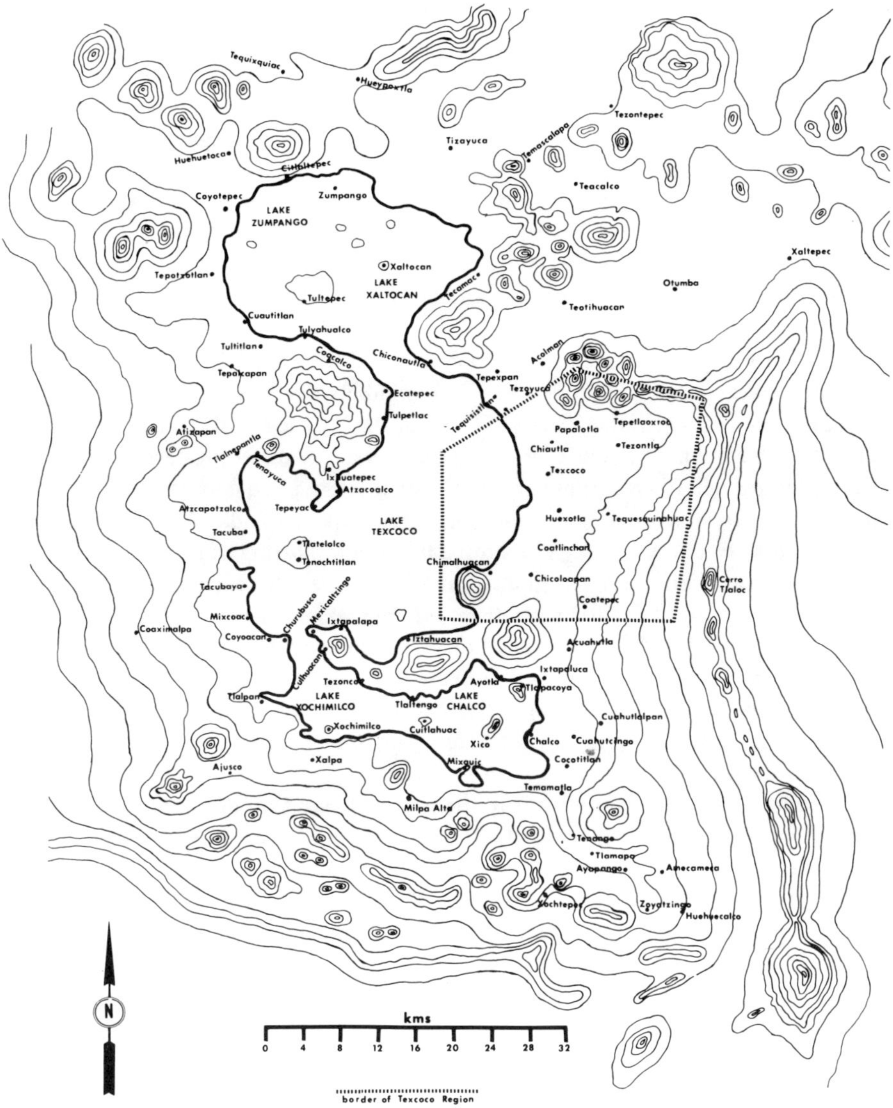


Map 3. The Valley of Mexico.

in spinning cotton as several documentary sources have indicated? If so, is this valid evidence of functional specialization among Aztec communities? To answer these questions, we need good stratigraphic excavations of several sites and carefully controlled surface sampling. We should definitely be able to place the three major spindle whorl types mentioned in this paper into a chronological framework and settle the problem of the presence or absence of cotton whorls in the Valley of Mexico in the Early Aztec period. Perhaps Type I and II maguey whorls are not chronologically different, but simply were produced in different centers in the Valley of Mexico, as the Texcoco data in the appendix of this paper suggest.

The problem of functional specialization of cotton or maguey spinning could be approached through the study of differential distribution of cotton and maguey whorls both within sites and between different sites. If a certain community or certain households within a community specialized in spinning a single fiber (cotton or maguey), we would expect to find a higher proportion of this type of spindle whorl on that site or portion of the site where this specialized activity took place.

Up to this point I have only been concerned with the Valley of Mexico. It would be very interesting to see whether spindle whorl data from other areas (Tlaxcala, the Huasteca, the Valley of Toluca, the Pacific Coast) can be used to determine the spinning of either two different fibers or different degrees of fineness of a single fiber in these areas. Unfortunately good comparative data are lacking. Provenience and accurate measurements of spindle whorl variables are necessary for comparison. The simple bar graph plotting of each of three variables (total whorl diameter, hole diameter, and weight) is useful in determining whether one is dealing with different degrees of fineness of a single fiber or two different fibers. Clear bimodal distribution as with Types I and III or Types II and III in Figure 11 would indicate the presence of two different fibers. A normal distribution as with Types I and II in Figure 11 would indicate a single fiber of different weights. A scattergram, as in Figures 8-10, may be helpful in showing the interrelation of two variables.

It would be interesting to study the range of variation in cotton whorls and the corresponding fineness of the thread spun in cotton-growing areas such as the Huasteca. Ethnographic data on spinning and actual observations of hand spinning would be essential in determining this. Published descriptions of spindle whorls from the various prehispanic cotton-producing areas might aid in determining cotton trade and tribute networks, as Franco (1956) has indicated.

Tlaxcala would probably be the best place to study the range of variation in maguey whorls. In concluding this paper, I would like to pose a hypothesis about spindle whorls in the Tlaxcala area that should be testable archaeologically. Bernal Diaz (1908:274) and others (Cortes, 1962:46; Anghiera, 1628:28) state that the Aztecs in the Valley of Mexico had so effectively shut Tlaxcala off from the coast, that the Tlaxcalans could not obtain any cotton. They compensated for this, Bernal Diaz tells us, by developing a method for spinning extremely fine maguey cloth for high status individuals. If this is true, we would expect there to be a striking absence of the small cotton whorls, at least in late Postclassic sites in Tlaxcala. We would also expect to find a wide range of maguey whorls, some noticeably smaller than our Type I and II whorls. These would have been used to spin the fine quality maguey cloth worn by the Tlaxcalan nobility. The production of fine maguey cloth would have been a difficult process, involving the beating of the maguey fibers until the natural bundling was broken apart, and would, therefore, only have been undertaken in areas lacking access to cotton.

# APPENDIX

## A COMPARISON WITH SPINDLE WHORLS FROM THE TEXCOCO REGION SURVEY, 1967

During the summer and fall of 1967, 245 spindle whorls were recovered during a surface survey of the Texcoco Region under the direction of J. R. Parsons of the University of Michigan Museum of Anthropology (see Maps 3 and 4). Whorls were picked up when seen by members of the survey crews; provenience was noted, and the whorls were returned to the laboratory for study. With the exception of three specimens, the spindle whorls came from Aztec or predominantly Aztec sites (Tables 2-4). The Huexotla site (Tx-A-87) produced by far the largest number of spindle whorls for a single site – 50 whorls (see Map 4). Thirteen whorls were found at the Texcoco site (Tx-A-56), eight whorls at the large Chimalhuacán Aztec site (Tx-A-109), and five whorls at three other large sites (Tx-A-17, Tx-A-28, Tx-A-33). But on the average Aztec site very few whorls are present.

In addition to the Texcoco Survey whorls, I also examined a collection of 271 complete whorls in the local Chimalhuacán museum. These whorls were probably recovered from excavations recently undertaken in Chimalhuacán during the restoration of Aztec ruins there. The Chimalhuacán collection was valuable because none of the whorls were broken, and it was possible to obtain accurate weight, hole diameter, and total whorl diameter measurements from them. Most of the whorls picked up on surface survey are broken or at least chipped, so that the weight measurement must often be estimated.

Work on spindle whorls from the Teotihuacán Valley leads me to define three major spindle whorl types there. These are: Type I whorls, large buff to black whorls with distinctive design patterns; Type II whorls, red slipped whorls as large or larger than Type I whorls; and Type III whorls, small buff to brown whorls often in exotic shapes. Type I and II are maguey whorls, and Type III is a cotton whorl. These same three types of spindle whorls are also found in the Texcoco Region, but in different proportions (Table 5).

The samples from the two surveys are comparable – 245 from Texcoco and 223 from Teotihuacán. Both valleys produced a large number of cotton whorls (24.9% in Texcoco, 33.6% in Teotihuacán) for areas that could not have grown the cotton they were spinning. It seems clear that cotton imported from the Gulf Coast and the valley of Morelos was, at least in part, spun into cloth here. The Chimalhuacán museum collection contains 119 or 57.8%

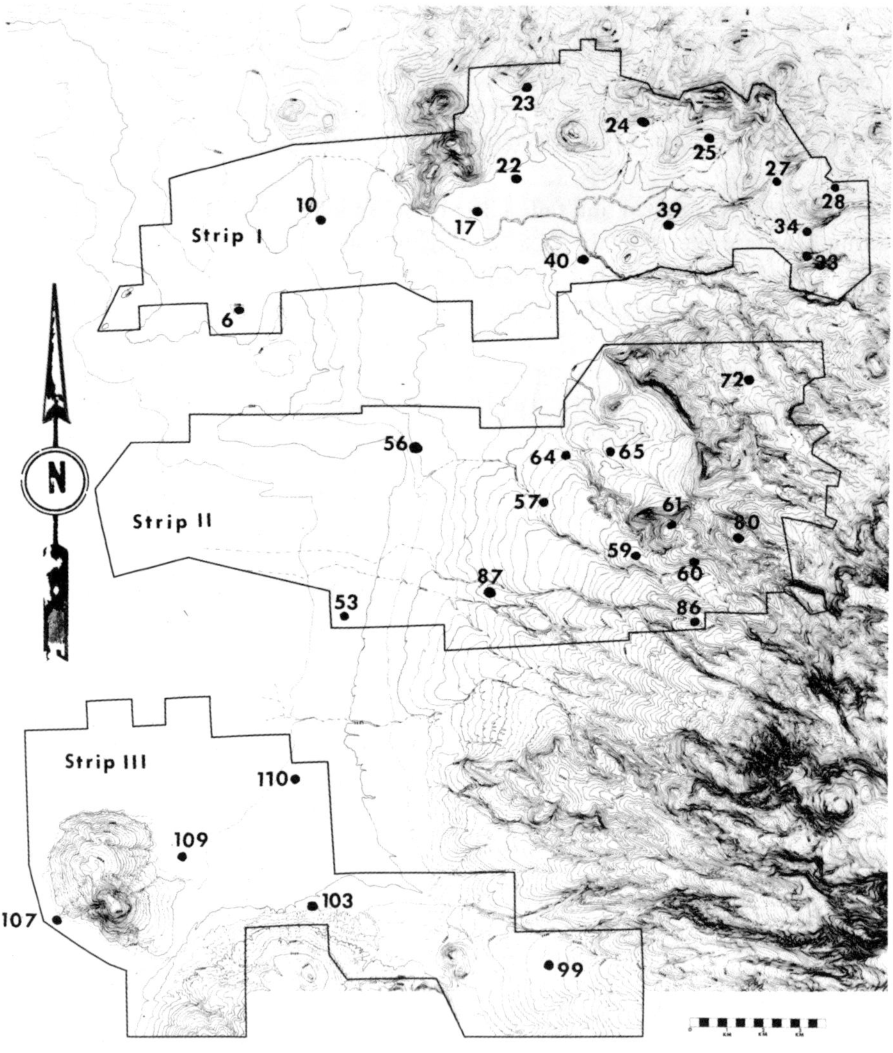


Map 4. The Texcoco Region, showing Aztec period sites mentioned in the text.

TABLE 2
THE SITE PROVENIENCE OF SPINDLE WHORLS FROM STRIP I
TEXCOCO REGION SURVEY

| Site Number | Type I | Type II | Type III | Other |
|---|---|---|---|---|
| Tx-A-6 | | | 2 | |
| Tx-A-10 | | | | 1 Mis. A<br>1 Huaxteca |
| Tx-A-17 | 3 | 1 | | 1 Type V |
| Tx-A-22 | | | 1 | |
| Tx-A-23 | 1 | 1 | | |
| Tx-A-24 | 1 | | 1 | 1 Unclassified |
| Tx-A-25 | 1 | 1 | | |
| Tx-A-27 | | 1 | | |
| Tx-A-28 | 4 | | 1 | |
| Tx-A-33 | 3 | 2 | | |
| Tx-A-34 | 2 | | | |
| Tx-A-39 | | | | 1 Calix. |
| Tx-A-40 | 2 | | | |
| No Provenience | 1 | 2 | 3 | 1 Toltec |
| Total - 40 whorls | 18 | 8 | 8 | 6 |

TABLE 3
THE SITE PROVENIENCE OF SPINDLE WHORLS FROM STRIP II
TEXCOCO REGION SURVEY

| Site Number | Type I | Type II | Type III | Other |
|---|---|---|---|---|
| Tx-A-53 | | | 1 | |
| Tx-A-56 (Texcoco) | 1 | 5 | 6 | 1 Calix.<br>1 Type V |
| Tx-A-57 | 1 | | 2 | |
| Tx-A-59 | 2 | 1 | | 1 Mis. C<br>(Cholula)<br>1 Type V |
| Tx-A-60 | | 1 | | |
| Tx-A-61 | | 1 | | |
| Tx-A-64 | | 1 | | |
| Tx-A-65 | | 1 | | |
| Tx-A-72 | 6 | 4 | | 1 Type V |
| Tx-A-80 | 2 | | | |
| Tx-A-86 | 1 | | | |
| Tx-A-87 (Huexotla) | 3 | 29 | 17 | 1 Calix. |
| Tx-TF-28 | | 1 | | |
| No Provenience | 6 | 30 | 15 | 6 |
| Total - 149 whorls | 22 | 74 | 41 | 12 |

TABLE 4
THE SITE PROVENIENCE OF SPINDLE WHORLS FROM STRIP III AND THOSE WHORLS LACKING SITE PROVENIENCE, TEXCOCO REGION SURVEY

| Site Number | Type I | Type II | Type III | Other |
|---|---|---|---|---|
| Tx-A-99 | 1 | 2 | | |
| Tx-A-103 | | | | 1 Mis. A<br>1 Mis. B |
| Tx-A-107 | | | 1 | |
| Tx-A-109 (Chimalhuacán) | 1 | 1 | 1 | 1 Mis. A<br>3 Type V<br>1 Calix. |
| Tx-A-110 | | | 1 | |
| Tx-LT-59 | | 2 | | |
| No Provenience | | 5 | 2 | 1 Calix. |
| Total - 25 whorls | 2 | 10 | 5 | 8 |
| No Strip Designation | 13 | 5 | 7 | 6 |

TABLE 5
A COMPARISON OF SPINDLE WHORLS FROM THE TEXCOCO AND TEOTIHUACÁN SURVEYS

| Whorls | Texcoco Survey | Teotihuacán Survey |
|---|---|---|
| Type I | 22.2%<br>(55 whorls) | 36.2%<br>(82 whorls) |
| Type II | 39.6%<br>(97 whorls) | 15.1%<br>(34 whorls) |
| Type III | 24.9%<br>(61 whorls) | 33.6%<br>(76 whorls) |
| Trade Whorls | 3.3%<br>( 8 whorls) | 2.7%<br>( 6 whorls) |
| Other Types | 9.8%<br>(24 whorls) | 11.0%<br>(25 whorls) |
| Total | 245 whorls | 223 whorls |

Type III cotton whorls, which would at first seem to indicate a specialization of spinning in Aztec Chimalhuacán. However, one must be careful in using the Chimalhuacán data. The museum contains only complete whorls; the broken ones seem to have been discarded. Since the maguey whorls are a good deal larger than cotton whorls, they break more easily, and many of them must have been discarded as broken fragments. In surface survey collections in both the Teotihuacán Valley and Texcoco Region many complete cotton whorls were found, but it was quite rare to find an unbroken maguey whorl. If in our collections, as in the Chimalhuacán one, only the unbroken whorls were kept, then Type III cotton whorls would be far more numerous than maguey whorls (Types I and II).

In comparing the number of Type I and II whorls in the Texcoco and Teotihuacán samples, one notes an interesting difference. In the Teotihuacán sample, Type I whorls clearly predominated over any other single type (36.2% Type I), with only a small proportion of Type II whorls (15.1%). In the Texcoco sample the situation was just the opposite. Type II whorls clearly predominated (39.6%), with only 22.2% Type I whorls. Because the Texcoco survey consisted of three major survey strips or units running approximately parallel from the old lakebed to the eastern sierras with a gap between each of the strips, it was possible to consider the spindle whorls from each strip separately (Map 4 and Table 6). In doing this, we notice an interesting difference in the Types I and II whorls. Strip I, the northern strip which ran adjacent to the southern border of the Teotihuacán Valley, produced the highest proportion of Type I whorls (45%), with the percentage of Type I whorls decreasing in the central strip (14.8%) and in the southern strip (8%), as the distance from the Teotihuacán Valley increased. On the other hand, while Type II whorls compose only 20% of the whorls found in the northern strip, they make up 49.5% of those found in the central strip (and 76% of all Type II whorls from the Texcoco survey). A second look at Table 2 shows us that Huexotla site alone produced 29 of these Type II whorls, over a third of all those found in Strip II. It is clear from this that the center of manufacture, or at least use of the Type II whorls was located in the central area of the Texcoco Region, and more precisely at the Huexotla and Texcoco sites (Tx-A-87, Tx-A-56). In the case of Type I whorls, the frequency increases in the Texcoco sample as we move northward towards the Teotihuacán Valley, where we find over twice as many Type I as Type II whorls. The center of use of Type I whorls may be in the Teotihuacán Valley, or perhaps to the north-northwest in the Zumpango Region.

By comparing the Texcoco, Chimalhuacán, and Teotihuacán samples, we can define more carefully the weight and size range of each of the three major types (see Tables 7-9). A total of 176 Type I whorls were measured, 144 Type II whorls, and 256 Type III whorls. While Types I and II both clearly fall in the maguey whorl category, Type II whorls have a tendency to be slightly larger than Type I whorls (see Table 10). There is a slight overlap in the size range of the smallest Type I whorls (probably used to spin very fine maguey thread) and the largest Type III whorls (used to make a coarse cotton thread). These small maguey whorls came mostly from the Chimalhuacán museum collection, and were too few to make any study statistically meaningful.

TABLE 6
A COMPARISON OF THE DIFFERENT SPINDLE WHORL TYPES FOUND IN THE TEXCOCO REGION SURVEY

| Whorl Types | Strip I | | Strip II | | Strip III | |
|---|---|---|---|---|---|---|
| | Number | Percent | Number | Percent | Number | Percent |
| Type I | 18 | 45 | 22 | 14.8 | 2 | 8 |
| Type II | 8 | 20 | 74 | 49.5 | 10 | 40 |
| Type III | 8 | 20 | 41 | 27.2 | 5 | 20 |
| Type V | 1 | 2.5 | 5 | 3.4 | 3 | 12 |
| Mis. A | 1 | 2.5 | 1 | 0.7 | 2 | 8 |
| Mis. B | | | | | 1 | 4 |
| Mis. C | | | 1 | 0.7 | | |
| Calixtlahuaca type whorls | 1 | 2.5 | 3 | 2.1 | 2 | 8 |
| Huaxteca asphalt whorls | 1 | 2.5 | | | | |
| Toltec red disk whorls | 1 | 2.5 | | | | |
| New Types | 1 | 2.5 | 2 | 1.3 | | |
| Totals | 40 | 100 | 149 | 99.7 | 25 | 100 |

TABLE 7

TYPE I SPINDLE WHORL MEASUREMENTS

| Provenience | Weight | Total Whorl Diameter | Hole Diameter |
|---|---|---|---|
| Texcoco Region Survey<br>(55 whorls) | 26-78 grams<br>(1 under 30 grams) | 31-61 mm | 7-11 mm<br>(4 over 10 mm) |
| Chimalhuacán Museum Collection<br>(39 whorls) | 11-91 grams<br>(16 under 30 grams)<br>(1 over 78 grams) | 23-70 mm<br>(6 under 31 mm)<br>(1 over 61 mm) | 5-11 mm<br>(6 under 6 mm)<br>(1 over 10 mm) |
| Teotihuacán Valley Survey<br>(82 whorls) | 24-103 grams<br>(3 under 30 grams)<br>(6 over 78 grams) | 35-61 mm | 6-12 mm<br>(1 under 6 mm)<br>(5 over 10 mm) |
| Total of 176 whorls | 11-103 grams<br>(20 under 30 grams)<br>(7 over 78 grams) | 23-70 mm<br>(6 under 31 mm)<br>(1 over 61 mm) | 5-12 mm<br>(7 under 6 mm)<br>(10 over 10 mm) |

TABLE 8

TYPE II SPINDLE WHORL MEASUREMENTS

| Provenience | Weight | Total Whorl Diameter | Hole Diameter |
|---|---|---|---|
| Texcoco Region Survey<br>(97 whorls) | 18-140 grams<br>(5 under 34 grams)<br>(9 over 80 grams) | 30-71 mm<br>(3 under 43 mm)<br>(3 over 64 mm) | 6-12 mm<br>(4 under 8 mm)<br>(4 over 11 mm) |
| Chimalhuacán Museum Survey<br>(13 whorls) | 35-67 grams | 43-56 mm | 7-11 mm<br>(1 under 8 mm) |
| Teotihuacán Valley Survey<br>(34 whorls) | 34-108 grams<br>(6 over 80 grams) | 45-73 mm<br>(1 over 64 mm) | 6-12 mm<br>(3 under 8 mm)<br>(3 over 11 mm) |
| Total of 144 whorls | 18-140 grams<br>(5 under 34 grams)<br>(15 over 80 grams) | 30-73 mm<br>(3 under 43 mm)<br>(4 over 64 mm) | 6-12 mm<br>(8 under 8 mm)<br>(7 over 11 mm) |

TABLE 9

TYPE III SPINDLE WHORL MEASUREMENTS

| Provenience | Weight | Total Whorl Diameter | Hole Diameter |
|---|---|---|---|
| Texcoco Region Survey (61 whorls) | 1-13 grams (5 over 10 grams) | 15-38 mm (2 over 33 mm) | 2-6 mm (2 over 5 mm) |
| Chimalhuacán Museum Collection (119 whorls) | 1-11 grams (1 over 10 grams) | 15-34 mm (1 over 33 mm) | 2-5 mm |
| Teotihuacán Valley Survey (76 whorls) | 2-11 grams (1 over 10 grams) | 18-28 mm | 2-6 mm (1 over 5 mm) |
| Total of 256 whorls | 1-13 grams (7 over 10 grams) | 15-38 mm (3 over 33 mm) | 2-6 mm (3 over 5 mm) |

TABLE 10

SUMMARY OF SPINDLE WHORL MEASUREMENTS *

| | Weight | Total Diameter | Hole Diameter |
|---|---|---|---|
| Type I | 11-103 grams (30-78 grams) | 23-70 mm (31-61 mm) | 5-12 mm (6-10 mm) |
| Type II | 18-140 grams (34-80 grams) | 30-73 mm (43-64 mm) | 6-12 mm (8-11 mm) |
| Type III | 1-13 grams (1-10 grams) | 15-38 mm (15-33 mm) | 2-6 mm (2-5 mm) |

* The figures in parentheses show the range within which most of the whorls of a type will fall. The figures without parentheses show the actual range limits.

There were a few whorls in all three samples that appeared to be imports from another area. In the Texcoco sample there was one asphalt-covered cotton whorl, probably from the Huasteca area, six large maguey whorls (Caliztlahuaca Type) probably from the Toluca Valley, and one whorl that may have been from the Cholula area (Parker, 1952). The Chimalhuacán collection had three Huasteca whorls, ten Caliztlahuaca Type, and three that look very much like Kelly's whorls from Michoacán and western Mexico (Kelly, 1938, 1945*a* and *b*, 1947). The Teotihuacán sample had three Huasteca whorls, two Caliztlahuaca Type, and one of the possible Cholula whorls. Some of the whorls designated as Types IV-IX and Miscellaneous A-F in my Teotihuacán study may also be imports from other regions, for there are seldom more than one or two of them found in our surveys.

# AZTEC FIGURINES FROM THE TEOTIHUACÁN VALLEY, MEXICO

*Mary Hrones Parsons*

## INTRODUCTION

A LARGE number of Aztec figurine fragments were picked up on the surface survey portion of the Teotihuacán Valley Project. An additional sample was recovered from the excavation of three rural Aztec sites (see Table 11 and Map 1 for provenience). Of a thousand or more fragments recovered, 755 were usable for analysis. The others were too samll or too badly weathered to be of use. Their fragmentary nature and the fact that they were surface finds, or found in unstratified excavations, makes it difficult to do much more than describe them now. Since the Teotihuacán Valley was a politically marginal area during Aztec times, it will be interesting to see whether the figurines here differ from those from other areas of the Valley of Mexico, especially Tenochtitlán, the Aztec capital. Present excavations at Tlatelolco in Mexico City should provide excellent comparative data. If these figurines were being mass produced by specialists at certain centers in the Valley of Mexico and distributed throughout the valley by periodic markets, as J. R. Parsons (1966) believes some of the Aztec pottery was, then we would expect the figurines from Tlatelolco, the Teotihuacán Valley, and other subvalleys to look much the same. If they were not being produced by specialists in particular centers, then the figurines should vary noticeably. A survey covering the major portion of the Texcoco Valley was undertaken by J. R. Parsons and several field crews in 1967 (see Map 3). A figurine sample comparable to the Teotihuacán sample was obtained through similar surface survey of the Texcoco Region and will be discussed at the end of this paper. TheTexcoco Region was prominent in the Aztec period when the neighboring Teotihuacán Valley was marginal. It is interesting to see whether or not the figurines reflect the differ political importances of the two areas. A comparison of the figurines from the Teotihuacán Valley, the Texcoco Region, and Tlatelolco (3 different sections of the Valley of Mexico) should give us some substantial evidence for or against the idea that in general, Aztec figurines or their molds were mass produced in particular centers in the Valley of Mexico and then distributed through the valley by means of periodic markets.

The Teotihuacán Valley sample consists largely of figurine heads broken at the base of the neck and usually missing the headdress top projections. There are also numerous assorted body fragments. On survey, figurines were picked up when seen, but not actively searched for. Because our sample lacked unbroken figurines (only one was complete), a rather comprehensive study was made of the Aztec figurine collections at the Museo de Antropologiá in Mexico City and at the American Museum of Natural History in New York. I have also examined the University of Michigan Museum of Anthropology's collection. Dr. Gordon Ekholm was especially helpful in my work with the Vaillant collections from Nonoalco and Chiconautla in the American Museum. He directed me to a Master's thesis written by Florence Kaplan at Columbia University, which deals with Vaillant's Aztec and Mazapan figurines. Kaplan has made a very detailed classification, and what I had done on my own with the fragmentary Teotihuacán Valley sample seemed to corollate quite well with her work. I would reject several of her subtypes in the light of data from Barlow and Lehmann (1955). Other subtypes seem to overlap, but this is perhaps a function of working with broken, rather than complete specimens. Each one of Kaplan's major types represents a different god or goddess. Her subtypes define the range of different poses and costumes in which each god or goddess appears. Her thesis is a very good synthesis of a vast amount of material. It was extremely helpful to me, since she worked with many nearly complete figurines as well as fragments, while I had basically only small fragments to work with.

My classification is based on what appear to be different functional attributes. All Aztec figurines are mold-made and, I believe, mass produced. They can be divided into three basic categories according to possible function – hollow rattles, slab-jointed figurines, and solid standing figurines. The classification can be broken down further according to which god or goddess is represented. It should be remembered that my categories, while used to describe the Teotihuacán Valley figurines, were formulated only after examining a large number of complete or nearly complete figurines from collections in Mexico and this country.

## TYPE I: HOLLOW RATTLE FIGURINES

These figurines have hollow bodies and solid, relatively thick heads. They appear to have been used as rattles, since unbroken specimens contain one or two small pottery balls. One broken fragment recovered from excavations at the Maquisco site (T-A-23) still contained a clay ball. The ball was 9-10 mm in diameter and had been shaped prior to placement inside the body. It is clear that the rattling noise of these figurines is caused by the intentional placement of round balls inside the hollow body before firing, and not by unshaped scraps of clay that accidentally crumble off and rattle around inside the body. The face of the figurine is oval, contrasting with the more angular face of the

Type III solid figurines (Pl. 17). The eyes are always incised and usually ringed with a ridge of clay, rather than molded in relief as in Type III figurines. The mouth is open and rimmed. There is a vent hole in the base or side of each figurine to aid in the firing of the hollow body. The surface has a smooth burnished appearance. Facial details are sharp and clear, noticeably more so than in Type III figurines which lack a burnished appearance. This may be because the burnishing acts as a protective coating against erosion and weathering. The figurines fire to a reddish orange color and do not appear to have been painted.

### Type I-A – Coatlicue-Cihuacoatl earth goddess (46 body fragments and 50 head fragments)

This is by far the most common rattle form (Pl. 19). It is the figure of a woman wearing a looped headdress with two top projections. She stands 3-6 inches high, and has a very large projecting nose. She wears an incised or molded necklace and circular ear plugs. The vent hole in the rattle is in the base of the figurine. Most specimens have holes punched through or partially through the solid shoulder region or under the arms (Fig. 14). The earspools are sometimes incised or molded, but more often they, like the shoulders, are completely or partially perforated. In a number of the specimens that I examined, one earspool or shoulder would be completely perforated and the other only partially so. In many cases the holes are deep, but do not quite pierce the figurines, so that they could not have been used for suspension. Perhaps they were used for inserting small pieces of obsidian, feathers, or some other additive decorative element as Nuttall suggests (1886:163).

The figurine may be wearing a diamond-patterned skirt (Pl. 19*d, e, f*), a plain skirt, or a plain skirt with two copal bags hanging from the waist (Pl. 19*g*).[1] She may also have a completely plain body with no indications of waist or legs (Pl. 19*a, b, c*). In all cases she is naked from the waist up. It is the plain form that is most common in our sample. Of forty-six body fragments, twenty-nine clearly belonged to this plain body category. Two, and a possible third, wore a diamond-patterned skirt. The rest were indeterminant. The diamond pattern takes a number of basically similar forms. It usually encloses a dot, a circle, or a smaller diamond. One of our examples is rather exotic, consisting of large diamonds enclosing a nest of five smaller ones. Kaplan and others suggest that this diamond skirt pattern is the stylization of intertwining snakes, a characteristic of the goddess Coatlicue, Serpent Skirt. Kaplan therefore feels this figurine represents Coatlicue, an earth goddess associated with spring. At the American Museum of Natural History, I found a Mazapan (Late Toltec) figurine from San Juan Teotihuacán wearing a diamond pattern skirt in which the snake's head and tail are clearly visible (Fig. 15). The diamond-

[1] Kaplan and others have identified these objects attached to the belt as copal bags.

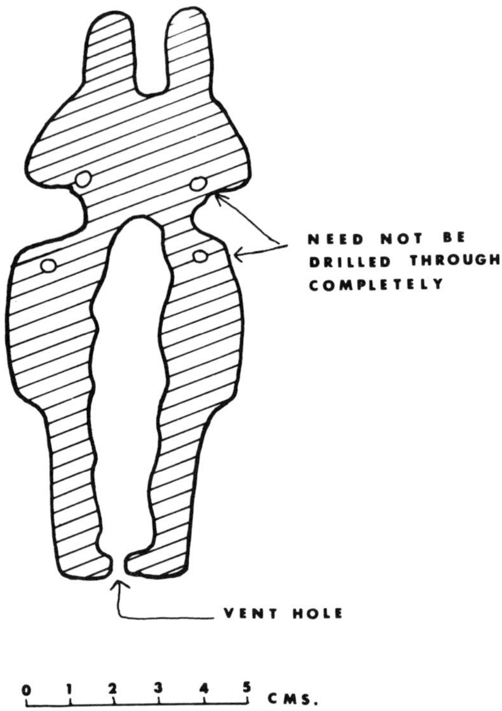


Fig. 14. Type 1-A, hollow rattle figurine.

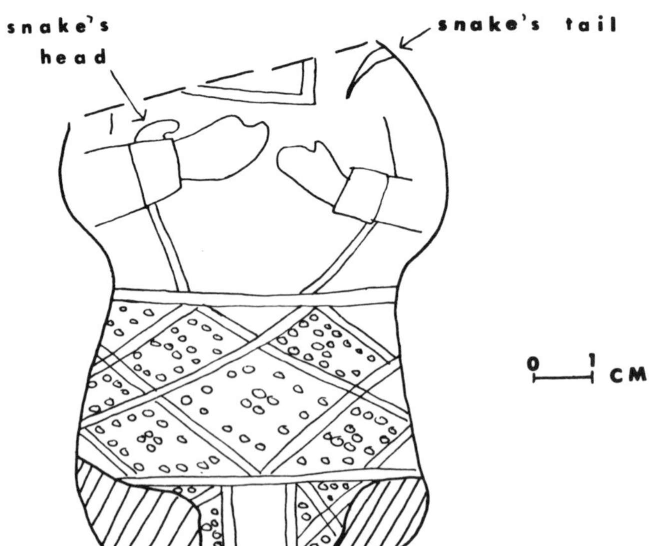


Fig. 15. Mazapan figurine with entwining snake.

pattern skirt does indeed seem to be a stylization of Coatlicue's serpent skirt. But I think it is necessary to see this Type I-A figurine as a composite goddess. She also has features of Cihuacoatl (called Tonantzin by some) and even of Xochiquetzal as Barlow and Lehmann (1955) point out. Both Cook and Seler see this figurine as Cihuacoatl, the goddess invoked in childbirth and the first woman to have children. Cook (1950) refers to her headdress as having a double deer's head profile. Type I-A figurines are sometimes pregnant or holding a child, and each half of the headdress does, to some extent, resemble a deer's head in profile (Pl. 19*i*). The Xochiquetzal traits are the clearly delineated plumes on several specimens, and the twisted headdress that is sometimes present.[2] The diamond-shape pattern of the skirt, while it clearly originated as a highly stylized twining serpent, may also represent elaborate embroidery of which Xochiquetzal is the patroness. The problem of pinning a name on this goddess is extremely complex, and she is probably best referred to as a composite earth goddess – Coatlicue-Cihuacoatl. Her Xochiquetzal aspect is perhaps less apparent.

Type I-A is composed of a number of variables – skirt type, body posture, headdress and plume type – all of which seem to be randomly combined. As mentioned earlier, the skirt may be plain, decorated with a diamond pattern, not indicated, or plain with two copal bags in the front. The goddess may be standing, kneeling, or sitting. She may be carrying a child in her left arm (Pl. 19*g*), in her right arm, (Pl. 19*e*) or one in each (Pl. 19*f*). She may also be holding it in front of her with both hands (Pl. 19*a*). She may be a hunchback or represented as pregnant. These elements are combined in various ways (see Kaplan, 1958 and Barlow and Lehmann, 1955), but the most common in our survey collection was the standing plain body (neither hunchbacked nor pregnant) with the arms held beneath the breasts (Pl. 19*b*, *c*). There is variety in the headdress, although all have the basic looped form with two top projections. The four major headdress forms are:

1) The most frequent type has a double looped headdress with two plain rectangular to trapezoidal top projections (Pl. 19*b*, *c*, *h*). We had 25 of these, only 4 with the top projections intact. But my work at the American Museum and the Museo Nacional showed a large number of complete specimens with similar projections.

2) In the second group, the headdress is double looped with the upper loop twisted (Pl. 18*a*). There are 7 of these – 2 with the top projections incised to represent a plume.

3) This type is a double-looped headdress which encloses the face in a trapezoidal outline, rather than the semicircular outline of

[2] Barlow and Lehmann feel that the two plain top projections frequently found are highly stylized representations of Xochiquetzal's plumes.

headdress variety 1. The top projections in all examples of this type that I have seen are incised plumes (Pl. 18*b, c*). There are 6 of these.

4) This type of headdress is the most unusual. The headdress is that of a single twisted loop with hair delineated underneath the headdress by fine parallel lines. Hair does not usually show below the headdress on any of the other types. The top projections may be either plain or incised to represent plumes (Pl. 19*j*). Occasionally there are flopped over as in Plate 19*k*. There are only 2 examples of this fourth variety of headdress.

All Type I-A figurines wear a necklace. From our sample, 19 have an incised necklace and 7 have a necklace molded in relief. All examples also have circular earspools, three examples have earspools molded in relief, while 42 have punched or partially punched holes. It is interesting that 5 of these are punched through completely while 3 examples have 1 earspool punched through completely and the other only partially punched. The holes were clearly made prior to firing, so that complete piercing would have been a relatively easy matter if so desired. As mentioned earlier, these holes may have been used to hold feathers or other decorative ornaments.

In order to see whether there is a meaningful correlation of any of the variables (skirt type, body position, hunched back or pregnant conditions, headdress type, earspool treatment, etc.) a large sample of unbroken figurines will be needed. As far as I can tell, all possible combinations of the variables seem to exist except when the copal bag element is present. This copal bag element invariably occurs on a plain-skirted standing figure carrying in its left arm a child dressed in a distinctive triangular poncho (quechquemitl) (Pl. 19*g*). She usually wears the fourth type of headdress.

### Type I-B – Macuiloxchitl
### (one of Xochipilli's aspects; god of song, often appearing in monkey form)

This type of rattle figurine is a good deal less frequent in our sample and in all the collections I have studied. We have 10 heads and 3 body fragments. The body position is always the same. The figure is seated on the ground with his legs drawn up to his chest. His arms are flung around his extremely large protruding stomach, grasping his head and shoulders or gripping his knees. The stomach is often so large and protruding that it rests on the ground between the feet (Pl. 20*a, b, c*). The figurine is approximately two and one-half to four inches tall. All examples wear a necklace like that in Type I-A figurines. On the basis of head type, two distinct categories emerge.

1) (Five head fragments)
This type wears a crest-shaped headdress extending forward over the face about 3-8 mm. It has round, ringed eyes (occa-

sionally slit, rimmed eyes), a small short nose, a prognathic jaw, and wears complex earspools composed of a spiral element or a spiral and tear-shaped element (Pl. 20*b, e*).[3] The result is that the figure may have a conventional monkey face or a definitely human face with simian features. In some cases it is difficult to say whether it is more monkey (Pl. 20*b*) or more human (Pl. 20*a*), but in all cases there seems to be evidence of a long thick tail extending up the back and past the top of the head. It is often broken off leaving a stub at the back of the neck (Pl. 20*e*). The presence or absence of the tail seems to be one important way of distinguishing Type I-B1 body fragments from Type I-B2 fragments which lack a tail.

2) (Four head fragments)

The heads of this type closely resemble Type I-A faces in detail, differing only in the headdress form, which in this case forms a single central top projection (Pl. 20*f, g*). This is merely a guess, but the Type I-B2 headdress may be a conventionalization of the Type I-B1 crest-shaped headdress with the tail extending from behind above the top of the crest (see Barlow and Lehmann, 1955: Fig. 22, p. 17). I have never seen evidence of a tail on any of these Type I-B2 figurines, although occasionally they are hunchbacked. If it is true that the Type I-B2 headdress is a conventionalization and combination of two elements (tail and crest headdress) that were separate in Type I-B1 figurines, this distinction may be chronologically important.

3) (One head fragment)

This specimen is a head fragment that clearly belonged on a hollow rattle body, as a portion of the hollow shoulder region is still intact. The head is that of a coyote with a long thin snout and round rimmed eyes. A hand or paw fragment is resting against the ear (Pl. 20*d*). We have no body fragments of this type, nor have I ever seen a similar rattle head in my work at the museums. If Peterson is right about the coyote association with Macuilxochitl, this head may belong on a Type I-B sitting body. The hand or paw position suggests that this is probably so.

## Type I-C – Huehueteol
## (the old god, the god of fire)

We found none of these in our survey collection, but I have seen several examples of this type in the Museo Nacional's collections. The figurine depicts a bald old man in a sitting position. His face is creased with wrinkles, and the mouth forms a toothless grin.

[3]Peterson (1962:136) says that this teardrop-shaped element represents a coyote ear and is worn by Macuilxochitl. The spiral-shaped element is thought to be a conch shell in cross section, often associated with Ehecatl-Quetzacoatl, but also found on Macuilxochitl figurines.

In extremely rare cases one will find a solid slab figurine that in all other aspects resembles the hollow Type I-A or -B figurines. I have seen only 2 of these in my examination of over 150 Type I-A and -B figurines in various museums.

## TYPE II: JOINTED FIGURINES

Jointed figurines have a flat and slablike body measuring 4-6 cm long and only 5-10 mm thick. It is rectangular or trapezoidal in shape with a hole punched completely through each of the four corners (Pl. 21*a*). In most examples the head has been broken off, but I have seen at least four with heads intact. In all cases the head was covered with a mass of curls, characteristic of the god Xochipilli (Pl. 21*b, f*). Since most of these figurines are clearly feminine (breasts are represented or the figurine wears a skirt and carries an infant), they probably represent Xochiquetzal, the female counterpart of Xochipilli. As has been pointed out, all four holes on each figurine have completely punctured the corners, presumably for some functional purpose. Small limbs have been found which could have been attached with twine, resulting in a jointed figurine.

In the Xolalpan phase of the Classic Teotihuacán sequence, we have abundant jointed figurines. The body and head were made in one piece as in the Aztec figurines, and the limbs made separately and attached. In the Xolalpan examples, two holes were laterally drilled for the attachment of limbs, one through the shoulders and the others through the base of the figurines, so that neither can be seen in a front view of the figurine. Wardle (1902) shows a clear transition from two lateral holes in Xolalpan times to one lateral and two dorsal-ventral holes in Aztec times, and then to four dorsal-ventral holes. The jointed limbs of these Aztec figurines are seldom found. The reason for this may be that they are small and easily broken. The Xolalpan jointed figurines are a good deal more abundant than Aztec ones. The limbs of these Xolalpan figurines are much thicker and more muscular, and have a slightly bent elbow (Pl. 21*i*). The Aztec limbs are merely narrow rolled appendages. The arm is straight and unflexed (Pl. 21*j*).

All these jointed figurines wear a necklace incised or raised in relief. The earspools are elaborate, always consisting of two elements: (1) a normal circular earspool and (2) a spiral, thought to represent a conch shell in cross section (Pl. 21*c*).

Type II jointed figurines can be divided into two groups on the basis of the presence or absence of a distinctive polished red slip.

### Type II-A
(4 body fragments, 5 heads, 1 jointed arm)

This jointed figurine does not have a slip. All four body specimens have breasts represented. One appears to be Post-Contact from the type of neckline.

The heads may be covered by a tightly-fitting helmet-like cap (3 examples) (Pl. 21*c, d*), or a mass of curls (3 examples) (Pl. 21*b*). There seems to be a clear transition from massive curls to the helmeted cap which may be a stylization of the curls. The faces in this group are short, thick, and angular. Eyes are incised.

### Type II-B
(2 heads, 6 body fragments)

The front and sides of these figurines are covered with a distinctive polished red slip, but the back is not. As far as I know, these are the only type of Aztec figurine with a red slip. Both our examples of heads in this type have the helmented caps (Pl. 21*g*). A specimen from the American Museum, however, has a mass of curls (Pl. 21*f*). They have long narrow oval faces, in contrast to the thick angular faces of Type II-A. The body may be completely plain with no indication of breasts (2 examples), wearing a very fancy diamond-motif skirt (1 example), or wearing a plain diamond-patterned skirt and carrying an infant in front of her (2 examples) (Pl. 21*e*).

## TYPE III: SOLID FIGURINES

Type III figurines are solid with a flat back and a flat base. The face is generally wide and angular, and the eyes are molded in round relief. This figurine type comes in a wide range of forms which will be described below.

### Type III-A
(62 head fragments, 107 body fragments)

There are six different subdivisions within this type, each having a different headdress treatment. But all Type III-A figurine faces are the same. The face is short, thick, and angular (Pl. 17*b*). The mouth is open and rimmed. The nose is large and protruding. The eyes are round orbs molded in low relief. In cases where the figurine has been badly weathered, the eyes may be worn to an even surface with the rest of the face, and therefore appear absent. The head is that of a female deity with a plumed headdress that varies from subtype to subtype. The body postures of many of the subtypes are much the same, so that it is impossible to say from a body piece what sort of head it originally had. Type III-A body poses will be discussed after each of the Type III-A head categories has been described.

#### 1). Type III-A1
(23 head fragments)

The diagnostic trait of this type is the beaded or sectioned headband from which one or two clearly delineated and rather elaborate plumes arise (Pl. 22*a-d*).

The size range of the headband varies from 8 by 30 mm to 29 by 80 mm, most commonly being about 14 by 40 mm. Sometimes there are elaborate side fans enclosing the face (Pl. 22*c*). Beneath the sectioned headband the face is outlined by a square cap or haircut which ends just above the tip of the circular earspools if they are present. Twelve of our specimens clearly had a single top projection above the sectioned headband; five of these have the entire top projection intact with individual plumes clearly delineated. Two of our figurines had a pair of top projections above the sectioned headband. It is impossible to say in seven other cases whether there had been one or two top projections. The beaded headdress and clearly delineated top plumes are characteristic of Xochiquetzal, goddess of flowers, love, and embroidery.

The body position associated with this figurine type varies a good deal. She may be sitting with her legs at her sides (Pl. 22*e-g*), or she may be standing with her hands in a number of different positions. She may be wearing a fancy necklace or none at all. Her clothing is quite often completely plain, although when she is represented with side fans, she often wears a very elaborately embroidered skirt made of clover leaf flowers enclosed in a diamond-shaped pattern (Fig. 16).

Fig. 16. Type II-A1, Xochiquetzal with eleborate skirt. Drawn from specimen at the Museo Nacional de Antropologia in Mexico City.

2). Type III-A2
(4 head fragments)

This type of head is like Type III-A1 except that the headband is composed of a solid band with three decorative rosettes (Pl. 23*a*). The headband may be topped by one or two top projections as in Type III-A1. The most frequent body position is a standing one with the hands at the sides or bent upward at the elbow.

3). Type III-A3
(4 head fragments)

This type of head is framed by a square haircut – the hair extending below the ear region to the top of the neck. The headdress is composed of a thin, narrow band 4-6 mm wide, above which extend two clearly delineated plumed top projections (Pl. 23*b*). No earspools are discernible. There are traces of white paint on all of these fragments. No definite body form other than the standing slab body can be associated with this type.

4). Type III-A4
(26 head fragments)

The face of this type is like that of Type III-A1, although one is frequently able to see teeth or a tongue visible in the open mouth. All specimens wear circular earspools. A square-shaped hairstyle or cap outlines the face down to the tip of the earspool as in Type III-A1. The headdress consists of a single twisted piece of material looped around the head from the base of one earspool to the base of the other (Pl. 23*c*). Atop this part of the headdress are two small narrow top projections. They are completely plain, lacking any indication of individual plumes. The top projections extend vertically from the top of the headdress (4 examples) or diagonally (5 examples) (Pl. 23*e*) or they may slope to fit the curve of the headdress (2 examples). Eight heads of this type have traces of white paint. This type appears to represent the same earth goddess as Type-IA. Compare Type-IA, headdress variety 4 (Pl. 23*d*) with this Type III-A4 (Pl. 23*c*).

5). Type III-A5
(2 head fragments)

This type is much like Type III-A4. It lacks the twisted piece of material looped around the head. It has only a short squarish cap or haircut extending down to the tip of the circular earspool. A single spindle-like projection rests directly on top of this and extends horizontally at right angles to the side of the face on either side. There appears to be a small twisted piece of material or fiber mass wrapped around the center of the "spindle" (Pl. 23*f*). A stylized spindle is an appropriate headdress for Xochiquetzal, patroness of embroidery and weaving.

6). Type III-A6
(2 head fragments)

A squarish cap or haircut outlines the face and extends to the tip of the circular earspools or down to the top of the neck. Above this is a thick piece of twisted cloth looped around the head from earspool to earspool. There are no top projections (Pl. 23*g*, *h*).

*Body Positions of Type III-A Figurines*

*a*). Sitting female figurine with knees bent at sides and hands resting on top the thighs (27 examples) (Pl. 22*e*-*g*).

These figurine bodies are flat-backed with the mold line clearly visible. They range from 29-60 mm in height from unbroken base to the shoulders. The base area is large, but the figurine rapidly thins out so that it is only 8-12 mm thick in the shoulder region. Nine examples have three or more strings of large beads around the neck, and two wear large circular pendants. This body type is most commonly associated with Type III-A1 heads, although occasionally found with other Type III-A heads.

We have nine other examples of seated female figurines with knees bent at the sides. Breasts are represented on all of these, and none wear a necklace or any other sort of decoration. Five have complete puncture holes drilled under the arms. One holds a child wearing a fancy pendant in front of her. The child wears earspools and a caplike headdress. A second example holds a child, but the child's head is broken off. Another has the hands resting on the waist and the figure is pigeon-breasted in addition to having two normal breasts. Two others are completely plain with the hands at the sides in one case and broken off in the other. Four additional examples had pot attachments on the flat back of the figurine. All four had breasts represented, lacked any sort of decorative element (necklace), and had hands at the sides or broken off.

*b*). Sitting female with the feet extended straight out in front (2 examples) (Pl. 24*a*).

One fragment is dressed in a plain skirt, but is broken off at the waist with no arms indicated. The second example is a nearly complete figurine. The figure sits with bare, clearly delineated legs extending in front. There is no indication of a skirt. Breasts are represented, and the figure holds its hands bent at its sides. The face and headdress are like those of Type III-A4 except that the headdress is made of an untwisted material. The bare legs and child like position of the hands may indicate that the figurine is supposed to represent a child. (Female children in Aztec figurines are often shown with fully developed breasts.) The figurine is 65 mm tall.

*c*). Standing, plain-skirted female with the arms bent at the elbows and raised (7 examples) (Pl. 24*b, c*).

All have clearly represented breasts and lack any sort of necklace. Five have a waistband indicated, and two of these wear a tasseled belt. Three of the figurines bear traces of white paint. Fingers are incised on the one unbroken hand we have. The front part of the foot is broken off on all our examples. The size ranges from 49-80 mm from the base of the foot to the shoulder. They are from 9-18 mm thick, generally being on the thinner side.

*d*). Standing, plain-skirted female with hands resting on hips (22 examples) (Pl. 24*e, f*).

These range in height from 42-95 mm and are from 7-10 mm thick. All are wearing a completely plain skirt, but one does have a tasseled belt. Two wear large elaborate necklaces, but all other examples lack them. Six have traces of white paint on the surface. Elaborate Type III-A1 and -A2 heads with side fans are usually associated with body fragments with elaborate large necklaces such as the two mentioned above.

*e*). Standing, plain-skirted female holding a dog to her chin or ear (2 examples) (Pl. 24*g, h*).

Both of our fragments show small dogs being held to the chin of the figurine. Holes are punched through beneath the arms of the figurine. I have seen both Type III-A3 and -A6 heads on this type of body. We have a third example that is merely the fragment of a small dog that was probably being held up to the face of a figurine.

*f*). Standing, plain-skirted female holding an infant in front of her (3 examples) (Pl. 24*i*).

These figurines also have holes punched through beneath the arms. The child wears earspools and has in one case a caped headdress with a round ball projection on top of each side of the headdress. These are thin slab figurines like the others described above.

Miscellaneous body fragments (47 examples)

There are twenty-six chest area fragments with the arms broken off so that it is impossible to determine their position. Twenty-one are feet and skirt fragments. One of these is an elaborate embroidered skirt fragment which probably belonged with a Type III-A1 head with side fans and an elaborate necklace.

Type III-A1 heads seem to consistently appear on Type III-A1 bodies, but other than that, it is difficult to corollate any body form with any specific head type. I have seen Type III-A1 heads occur on other body forms, but not Type III-A1 bodies with other head forms. We will have to wait until more data are available on unbroken figurines before we can determine how Type III-A1 – A6 heads corollate with Type III-A*a* – A*f* bodies.

Type III-B1, Xochiquetzal
(3 head fragments, 13 body fragments) (Pl. 25*a-d*, Fig. 17)

This figurine is a flat, slablike figurine with the mold line clearly visible on the back. It stands about 15 mm high, and is 7-8 mm thick. The feet and face protrude, but all else is in very low relief. The figure wears a huipilli with a V-shaped neck and sleeves that extend half way down to the elbow. The arms hang straight by the sides. There is no attempt to break the straight line of the

Fig. 17. Type III-B1, Xochiquetzal. Drawn to scale (AMNH Cat. No. 30.1/6402).

arm to indicate wrists and hands, but there are incisions at the base of these rectangular limbs which represent fingers. On the chest there is an elaborate conch shell ornament. The breasts are indicated by a very slight rise beneath the shell ornament on either side of the chest. There is a twisted belt about the waist, and the figure usually wears a distinctively patterned skirt. (We have two examples with a plain skirt and eleven examples with a patterned skirt.) The skirt pattern is composed of rows of squares, each square enclosing two or three smaller squares. The feet extend out from the figurine and are over twice as long as the figurine is wide, thus giving it a stable base to stand on. The head is flat backed, but the features are molded out in the correct proportion of relief for a normal human face. The eyes are deep slits, the mouth is rimmed and open, and the nose is large. The face shape is basically angular and is enclosed by three layers of thick curls. The earspools are circular.

The Xochipilli-like mass of curls would indicate that this female figurine represents Xochiquetzal, Xochipilli's female counterpart. The elaborate square-patterned skirt may symbolize the goddess' role as patroness of embroidery.

### Type III-B2, Xochiquetzal
### (3 body fragments) (Pl. 25*e, f*)

These figurines closely resemble Type III-B1, but are smaller, 6-8 mm tall. They wear square-patterned skirts and no blouse. The breasts are more prominent and protruding, and the figure wears an elaborate string and loop necklace. The arms may hang slablike by the sides or be bent at the elbow forming a right angle with the lower arms, hands resting against the waist. Only one example wears a twisted belt. I have never seen one of these with a head attached, but imagine from the similarity of the skirt, arms, and body position that it would also have had massive curly hair.

Three larger upper body fragments should perhaps be included in this type. They are 45-54 mm in size from the waist to the base of the neck. The necklace, bare breasts, and arm position are just like that of Type III-B2 (Pl. 25*g*). None of these specimens had skirt fragments attached. It seems likely that the skirt would be square patterned.

### Type III-B3
### (5 examples)

We have only waist to shoulder fragments of this type. The arms are bent and held in front of the waist, and fingers are incised on the stump-ended arms as in Type III-B1 and -B2. The one fragment with a piece of skirt attached wears a square-patterned skirt. No breasts are indicated. The figure wears an extremely elaborate fringed quechquemitl which does not reach the waist (Pl. 25*h, i*). We have no heads for this type, but again one might expect a curly Xochiquetzal head.

It is interesting that I did not see any examples of these Type III-B figurines with their diagnostic square-patterned skirt in Vaillant's large collections from Nonoalco or Chicanotla. In all the collections that I have examined, I found only one other example of this square-patterned skirt figurine, and that was from the site of Talhuac. Whether this square-patterned Xochiquetzal was more important in the Teotihuacán Valley than other areas of the Valley of Mexico remains to be seen. But its absence from Nonoalco and Chicanotla is striking. Spindle whorl evidence from our survey indicates that cotton was probably imported and spun as a tribute service in Teotihuacán. These figurines which depict the goddess of weaving and embroidery may indicate that Teotihuacán was weaving and embroidering cotton as well as spinning it as a tribute service.

Type III-C, Quetzalcoatl as Ehecatl, god of the wind
(11 head fragments, 7 possible body fragments) (Pl. 26*a*)

The distinctive feature of this type is the headdress. It consists of a row of vertically placed, oblong units usually 4 by 13 mm in size. (The heads range from 13-25 mm from chin to forehead.) Often in the center of the row is a decorative knot (Pl. 25*b*). Above this part of the headdress is a conical cap once or twice as high as the other part of the headdress and sometimes topped with decorative tassels and fans. A square under-cap or hairline frames the face down to the tip of the circular earspools. The figure may be wearing a lip plug or nose plug, but more frequently wears neither. The features of the face vary a good deal from those of an angular-faced human to those of a narrow-faced simian with a long snout.

1). (7 examples) The face is human just like the Type III-A faces – angular with a large nose, open rimmed mouth, and round eyes molded in relief (Pl. 26*b*).

2). (4 examples) These faces are quite different. They are simian with a long and narrow face and a protruding snout. In some cases the distance of protrusion almost equals the height of the face (Pl. 26*f*). Whiskers are sometimes indicated, and the eyes appear smaller than in those above. There is a large range of variation in this simian group and some merge very closely with the human category (Pl. 26*c-f*).

All face types wear the same headdress and have the same body forms whether the face is human or simian. The figure is usually sitting on a stool or chair, but occasionally it is standing, with a shield held at the right or left side. In all cases the figure wears a large conch shell pendant (Pl. 26*g*). Since Xochipilli figurines also sometimes wear this conch shell pendant, we cannot be sure whether body fragments with a conch shell pendant belong with the Type III-C Ehecatl heads in all cases. One example definitely does not belong to Ehecatl – the mass of curls incised on the head of this fragment indicates that Xochipilli is represented.

### Type III-D, Chalchuitlicue
(4 head fragments, 2 body fragments) (Pl. 27*a-c*)

The figure wears a beaded quechquemitl or a beaded necklace, and can either be kneeling with her hands resting on her thighs (1 example) or standing in much the same position as Type III-A. We have one example of a standing figure with arms bent at the elbow and hands upraised. She wears two strings of large round beads (Pl. 27*c*). The headdress is again the diagnostic feature of this type. It is composed of long horizontal bands enclosed on the top and bottom with a row of beads (Pl. 27*a*). Underneath the headdress is the square cap or hair element we have frequently found in Type III-A. The face is like that of Type III-A – open rimmed mouth with tongue showing, large nose, and round eyes molded in relief. The headdress may be topped with a plume and decorated with side fans and shoulder flaps. The earspools are circular. The skirt is usually plain with no belt present.

### Type III-E, corn goddess
(Centeocihuatl-Chicomecoatl-Cozcamiauh)

Joyce (1920) says that both Chicomecoatl and Centeocihuatl are characterized by wearing a square crown with rosettes and by carrying a double ear of corn in each hand. Chicomecoatl was honored with human sacrifice so that she is sometimes represented as wearing the flayed skin. Joyce also says that the name Cozcamiauh (Ilamatecutli) translates as "maize necklace."

1) (2 body fragments)

A plain-skirted female figure is seated on a chair or stool. Both arms are bent at the elbow and each of the upraised hands holds two ears of corn or a "double ear of corn" (Pl. 27*d*, Fig. 18). Individual corn kernels are discernible on some specimens. Breasts are present on one example; the other lacks them. I have examined examples from the Museo Nacional de Antropología in Mexico City which had the head still intact (Fig. 18). In these cases the face was angular with almond-shaped eyes. The nose is relatively flat, and the mouth is double lipped. Both the almond eyes and the double-lipped mouth indicate that the goddess is wearing a flayed skin. The headdress consists of a rectangular band decorated with four circular elements, perhaps stylized rosettes as Joyce suggests. Broken edges along the top of the headdress suggest that it may have had two top projections. Both of our examples were pot attachments, with the stump of the attachment clearly visible on the back side.

2) (2 examples) (Pl. 27*e, f*).

A plain-skirted female is standing with her hands clasped in front of her waist. In her hands she carries two ears of corn or one "double ear of corn."

Fig. 18. Type III-E1, Corn Goddess. Drawn to scale from a specimen at the Museo de Antropología in Mexico City.

Individual corn kernels are discernible on the cobs. One example is a pot attachment; the other is not. No breasts are represented. We do not know what type of head characterizes this type.

3) (6 examples) (Pl. 27*g*).

A seated female figure is represented. She sits on a stool or chair. Her hands are grasping her knees. She wears a necklace strung with three ears of corn. (Examples in the Museo Nacional have both corn and squash strung on the necklace.) In specimens that are not too badly weathered, one can discern the individual kernels of corn. Three of our samples have breasts well delineated. Five examples from our sample were pot attachments. One of the pot attachments had holes punched under the arms, but they were not punched through completely. The one specimen that was not a pot attachment had holes punched through completely under the arms. We have no examples with the head intact.

Miscellaneous corn fragments (6 examples) (Pl. 27*h*)

These range in size from 47 to over 100 mm in length. The individual kernels of corn are very realistically placed on the cob in a random, not completely regular pattern.

## Type III-F, drummers (19 examples)

1) (8 body fragments)

A standing or sitting figure is playing a tall drum which rests on the ground. The standing figures (6 examples) have their knees slightly bent and their hands resting on the top of the drum. The seated figures (2 examples) also have their hands resting on the top of the drum. There is a band around the top and middle of the drum. The drum has what Kaplan (1958) has referred to as a "terraced bottom," a step design cut into the drum (Pl. 28*a*). Two examples have holes drilled completely through under the arms. One of these wears a necklace with three large balls (Pl. 28*b*). The others have all been broken off at the waist and do not show the neck area. I have seen pigeon-breasted examples of this type.

2) (2 body fragments) (Pl. 28*c, d*)

In these figurines the figure is seated, holding a short cylindrical drum between his legs. The hands rest upon the top of the drum. Both our examples are broken just above the waist. The University of Michigan Museum of Anthropology collection, however, has one with the head intact (Pl. 28*c*).

3) (9 body fragments)

The figure is sitting and playing a small vase-shaped drum which is held between the knees on a drum rest (Pl. 28*e*) or else rests on the ground (Pl. 28*f*). (We have one exception in which the drum is held horizontally, one hand cradling the base of the drum while the other rests on the top of the drum.) The drum resembles a circular bowl with a long neck and flaring rim. This may be the type of drum that Vaillant (1950) describes as made of an inverted gourd in a large bowl of water. Four of our figurines have holes completely piercing the body underneath the shoulder. Three of these also wear necklaces with three large balls attached. The other six examples are broken so that one cannot tell whether or not they wore this type of necklace. We have no complete figurines with the head intact.

4) (2 body fragments) (Pl. 28*g, h*)

Both examples show the lower third of a figure which is either standing or sitting, and plays a conical drum. The pointed end of the drum rests on the ground between the legs of the figure.

Type III-G, Xipe, wearing a flayed skin
(2 body fragments, 1 with part of a head)

In both cases Xipe is standing with slightly flexed knees. He carries a shield in his left hand, and a spear or elaborate rattle in his right hand. He wears a fleck-marked garment representing a flayed human skin. In one example we have half of the face, but none of the headdress. The face has a double mouth outline and partially closed, flap eyes (Pl. 29*a*). Typically, Xipe wears a flaring headdress (Pl. 29*b, c*) or one that is noticeably higher on one side than the other. The diagnostic Xipe features are the headdress and the flayed skin costume with the double mouth and flap eyes. One of our specimens is covered with traces of white paint. The height from feet to base of the neck is 50-65 mm.

Type III-H, Xochipilli
(5 head fragments)

All fragments are head fragments and wear a high peaked cap headdress which represents bird plumage as in Type I-B1. Three have angular faces like Type III-A. Two have narrow oblong faces with a large prominent nose, an open mouth, and round eyes molded in relief. Earspools are circular, sometimes with an added leaf-shaped element which Peterson (1962) suggests represents a coyote ear. The faces range from 22-32 mm long.

The Museo Nacional and the American Museum have several complete specimens of this type (Pl. 29*d*). Some are seated on top of a pyramid holding a shield in the left hand (Fig. 19). They may be wearing a conch shell pendant or a necklace with three balls. One example is of a standing Xochipilli playing a floor drum.

Type III-I, Macuilxochitl
(5 body fragments, 1 with the head attached)

This type is a standing male figure with his hands on his hips. The diagnostic element is the necklace that he wears. On it are strung leaf-shaped objects which Peterson (1962) has called coyote ears (Pl. 29*e*). Two holes are drilled completely through under the shoulders. Two of our examples are pigeon-breasted. One fragment has the head attached, but the headdress has been broken off. The head is long and oval. The nose is normal size, the oval eyes are molded in relief. The mouth is rimmed and open with the tongue or teeth showing. The figure wears large round earspools and a tight-fitting cap. The necklace of three "coyote ears" is characteristic of the god Macuilxochitl according to Kaplan (1958) and Peterson (1962).

### Type III-J
(13 head fragments)

This category consists of head fragments with a distinctive necklace and/or headdress. The necklace which three of our specimens wear consists of three large round balls evenly spaced and tied around the neck (Pl. 29*f*). The face is wide and angular like that of Type III-A figurines. The headdress consists of a rectangular cap. The top two corners of the cap are decorated with a relatively large round ball (5-10 mm in diameter) (Pl. 29*f-h*). In eight of our specimens there is also a trapezoidal decorative flap in the center which rests on the top of the forehead (Pl. 29*f*). The earspools are circular.

There is a problem as to identification. We have examples of both males and females with this same headdress and necklace. These heads often appear on bodies similar to Type III-H and III-I. The headdress with the two decorative top balls occurs on bodies wearing a necklace of three "coyote ears" or three circular balls. Kaplan says that this two-knob headdress is characteristic of the god Xochipilli (also called Macuilxochitl). The female knob headdress figurines would then represent Xochiquetzal, Xochipilli's counterpart. We do have one example wearing a twisted Xochiquetzal headdress topped by two round knobs rather than plumes (Pl. 29*g*).

### Type III-K
(2 body fragments) (Pl. 30)

A male figure is lying on his stomach or kneeling forward on his knees with his feet together. His arms are stretched out in front of him. The back and buttocks are shown in relief while the whole front side on which the figure lies is a flat unmolded surface. The figure wears only a breechcloth. The hair is cut into square bangs with a length of hair cut off at ear level, and a long square shock of hair flows down the back. The eyes are round and molded in relief; the nose is small but relatively long; the mouth is rimmed and open; and the ears are clearly indicated.

### Type III-L
(12 head fragments) (Pl. 31*a, b*)

These are flat slab heads with a squarish appearance. The hair, which completely frames the face to the chin, is square in outline, and makes the face appear as a square or rectangle. The nose is large and protruding, but the open mouth and chin are very flat, molded in very low relief. The eyes are not visible in most specimens although there is a slight depression below the eyebrow area. Occasionally a rounded orb is suggested in extremely low relief. The face is wide and would probably be polygonal if the haircut did not obscure the sides of the face. Three examples show indications of some sort of top headdress or projection, while eight others clearly do not. Two have traces of white paint. The diagnostic features are the flat slab face, the prominent nose, the eyes absent or only slightly suggested, the lack of any headdress, and the haircut which makes the face appear square or rectangular. I have never seen any body fragments which I can associate with this head type.

There are two variations in hair representation. In eight examples the hair is square or rectangular without any indication of individual strands of hair or curls. However, in four other examples a mass of curls is clearly delineated within the square outline of the hair. As mentioned earlier, this mass of curls is characteristic of Macuilxochitl.

### Type III-M, jaguar and eagle warriors
(1 head fragment, 1 body fragment)

In unbroken museum specimens that I have examined, the warrior is standing with slightly bent knees holding a shield and weapons in his two hands. The left hand is by his side holding a shield, while the right hand is upraised carrying a weapon. The warrior wears a jaguar skin (Pl. 31*c*) or an eagle-feather costume. His face sometimes shows only partially through the open jaws of the animal whose skin he wears.

The head fragment from our sample has an angular face with an open rimmed mouth and a large nose. There are traces of white paint on the head. Because of its fragmentary nature it is hard to say whether our specimen is that of an eagle or a jaguar warrior. Our one body fragment is that of an eagle warrior. He is covered with eagle feathers down to his feet.

### Type III-N, Tlaloc
(4 head fragments) (Pl. 31*d, e*)

Each one of these examples is rather different, but all have the same characteristic circular ringed Tlaloc eyes and fanglike mouth. One is covered with white paint and wears a striped headdress. Two others wear peaked headdresses. Two of our specimens look more like fierce animals than humans. They are all 35-40 mm long from chin to top of headdress.

### Type III-O
(3 body fragments) (Pl. 31*f, g*)

These are solid heavy fragments of a crouching body. We have only fragments from the chest down. The figure squats with the weight on the front half of the feet. One fragment has part of a scalloped edge pendant and some traces of white paint. The stomachs of all examples are tremendously enlarged as in advanced pregnancy. The figure is in the Aztec childbirth position, and may illustrate childbirth. Another and perhaps more likely possibility is that this represents a Macuilxochitl, much like Type I-B1 only not hollow. If so, we have one head fragment that would very likely belong to this type. It is much like Type I-B1 heads; it only lacks the burnished appearance and did not fit on a hollow body. The face is oval with a markedly prognathic jaw, small round eyes, small round nose, and small open mouth with teeth showing (Pl. 31*h*). The figure wears large round earspools and a crescent headdress with two decorative round knobs, one at either side of the crest headdress. I have seen similar examples in other collections (Pl. 31*i*).

### Type III-P, warrior
(6 body fragments) (Pl. 32*a, b*)

The warrior is standing with flexed knees and carrying a shield in his left hand and a rattle or short spear in his right hand. He wears only a short loincloth with a knotted belt. Two examples have traces of white paint. The size range is great, varying from 45-110 mm tall from foot to shoulder.

Our sample lacked any fragments with the head still intact. But in museum collections I have seen examples with the complete head, and both Xipe and Macuilxochitl are represented. In the Macuilxochitl examples, the headdress is a high, crested one and the figure usually wears a conch shell pendant or a necklace of three balls. The Xipe examples have the characteristic slit eyes and double mouth to indicate the wearing of a flayed skin. The flayed skin may also be represented by small dots or incisions on the chest of the figure. A typical conical Xipe headdress is usually worn.

### Type III-Q, "cradle figurines"
(8 examples) (Pl. 32*c, d*)

Although these figurines are commonly called "cradle figurines," they actually resemble a child in a highchair or in a carrying frame rather than a cradle. The child in each case is sitting in what appears to be a wooden carrying frame. There is a horizontal crossbar above the knees, two vertical ones on the sides, and one in the center between the child's legs which are bent at the knees with the feet apparently resting on some sort of a footboard. The figurine would be lying flat on its back were it not for a footlike support attached to the center of the figurine which elevates the child to a sitting position. The arms rest on the bar above the knees. On the five fragments that are complete enough, we find two puncture holes in the shoulder or upper arm region. Some of these holes do not penetrate completely through the figurine. On only two of our examples do we have heads – both wear circular earplugs. The face on one is quite childlike; the other has a more adult face and wears two strings of large beads. One example appears to have been a pot attachment.

An example from the Museo Nacional shows a child with the mass of curls characteristic of Xochipilli.

Lehmann (1953) and Morss (1952 and 1954) have discussed these cradle figurines and similar ones that appear to be adults strapped on a frame. In the latter, the arms are strapped down by the sides, and the legs are bent at the knee and extend beyond the frame which encases the rest of the body. Morss suggests that this type of figurine represents a demented or delirious individual. The figure lies flat on his back, and not in the sitting position of the "cradle figurines."

### Type III-R
(1 head fragment) (Pl. 33*a*)

This is a male figure wearing a scallop-edge collar. The face is oval with a nose of normal proportions, eyes molded in relief, and an open rimmed mouth with teeth or tongue showing. The earspools are circular, and there may have been a single central top projection. The hair is concealed under a tight-fitting cap. The Field Museum in Chicago has a nearly complete specimen of this type. The figure is standing and playing a drum which is resting on the floor. He is playing the drum with his right hand. The left hand is bent and holds a mirror or shield at shoulder height (Pl. 33*b*).

### Type III-S
(4 body fragments) (Pl. 34*a*)

The figurine is that of a woman standing with her hands resting on the sides of her abdomen. Breasts are prominent on all four examples, and the fingers are clearly delineated on the hands. The woman wears a plain skirt and no necklace. In two cases the figure appears to be pregnant; the third is a very large woman, but not noticeably pregnant. I have never seen this type of figurine with the head intact.

### Type III-T, figure seated on a chair or stool
(9 examples)

1) Female seated figures (7 examples) (Pl. 34*b, c*)

All examples were a plain skirt and no belt. Breasts are indicated. Three examples have holes punched completely or partially through underneath the shoulders. Two others have pot attachment stubs. Traces of white paint appear on two specimens. The figure is either holding a child or resting both hands on its thighs. The child is held on the right side of the lap in one case, with the left hand resting on the left thigh. Or the child may be carried in a sling resting on the left side with the right hand resting on the thigh (Pl. 34*b*). Figures not carrying a child have both hands resting on the thighs.

2) Male seated figures (2 body fragments) (Pl. 34*d*)

In one example the hands rest on the thighs. The figure is pigeon-brested and has two holes punched completely through under his arms. The second example has his hands grasping his knees. He does not have holes punched under the arms, but he is wearing what appears to be a circular pendant. Both examples are wearing loincloths knotted in front.

We do not have any head fragments for either the male or female seated figurines.

Type III-U
(4 body fragments) (Pl. 34*e, f*)

These figurines portray standing females dressed in plain skirts with the arms bent at the elbow and the hands resting under the breasts. Breasts are clearly delineated. There is no necklace, but two examples show indications of shoulder flaps.

Type III-V
(4 body fragments)

These figurines are quite small, only approximately 47 mm from feet to base of neck. They all wear diamond-patterned skirts with feet and legs clearly delineated below the skirt (Pl. 34*g*). Breasts are represented on all examples. The figure stands with her arms bent at the elbow and her hands placed just below her breasts. On one figurine there is a necklace consisting of a solid band and below that a band of small punctates. One cannot tell whether or not a necklace was present on the other three examples. This type of figurine is probably the same goddess as is represented in Type I-A.

Type III-W, pyramid and temple models
(27 fragments)

These figurines are small models of pyramids approximately 4-6 mm tall. On top of each pyramid there is either a temple structure or a seated figurine.

1) Pyramids topped with temples (8 pyramid step fragments, 5 temple fragments, and 9 roof comb fragments)

These pyramid models are topped with temple structures and often elaborate roof combs (Pl. 35*a*). The temples and their roof combs add a good 8-10 mm more to the height of the pyramid figurine. The roof comb consists of a vertical or horizontal panel filled with a waffle-like pattern and in some cases topped by a wedge or circular pattern (Pl. 35*b*). In five of our specimens, the roof comb has been pierced through with a rather sloppily placed puncture.

The hole does pierce completely through the roof comb, but the off-center and sloppy nature of the hole would make it doubtful that it was used for suspension. Several of the temple structures also have puncture holes, perhaps to hold decorative feathers. Two of these temples are rectangular buildings with a central T-shaped door (Pl. 35*c-e*). They have large overhanging roofs which may have been topped with a roof comb. One small temple is round. Round temples were built in honor of Ehecatl, the wind god.

2). Pyramids topped with a seated human figure (5 examples)

In most cases the figure is Xipe, Xochipilli, or Quetzalcoatl as Ehecatl (Fig. 19, Pl. 35*f*). I have never seen any goddess represented on these pyramids. We have one example of a figurine head resting on the top of a pyramid platform. No body is represented. The face is thick and angular with a large prominent nose. The head wears earspools and a tight-fitting cap that rises to a peak 20 mm above the forehead. This, like Type III-H, is probably Xochipilli in his Macuixochitl form, the headdress representing the crest of a bird. I have seen a complete pyramid model with this type of head resting on top of it at the Museo Nacional (Fig. 20). In our four other examples only the feet of the figurines are present. The rest is broken off. By the feet of one of these and resting on top of the pyramid is a circular shield (Pl. 35*g*). It is impossible to say from our fragments which gods were represented.

### Type III-X, pleated skirt figurines
### (2 body fragments)

Both examples are males wearing full, pleated skirts with the arms resting in front on the figure's abdomen. One of the figures has a concavity under the skirt so that the figure can stand up. There are no feet indicated below the skirt (Pl. 36*a*). This figure is similar to the earlier full-skirted Teotihuacán figurines that also lacked feet and represented priests (Gamio, 1922:Lam. 86, Tomo I). The second figurine may well be Post-Contact (Pl. 36*b*). The pleated skirt is not so full and there appear to be indications of feet. The figure is solid with no concavity under the skirt. Holes have been drilled under the arms. In his left hand the figure carries a cane or baton.

### Type III Miscellaneous

1) Huehueteol (1 head fragment)

The head is angular in shape and lacks any hair or headdress. The eyes are made by concentric circular incisions (Pl. 36*c*). The mouth is open, and the forehead and cheeks are scoured with wrinkles. The head is approximately 31 mm high. Huehueteol is the "old god," the god associated with fire.

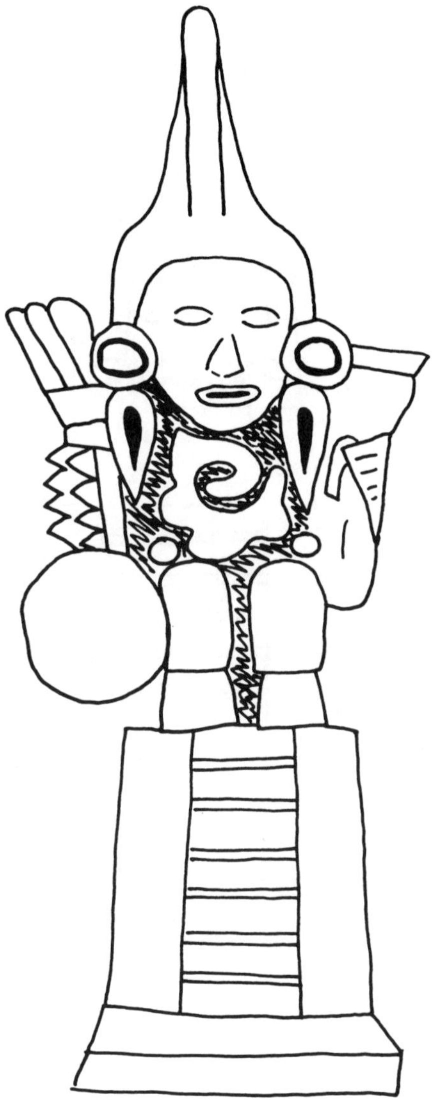

Fig. 19. Type III-W2, Xochipilli on top of a pyramid. Drawn to scale (MNA Cat. No. 11-1990 5145).

Fig. 20. Type III-W2, Macuixochitl head on top of a pyramid. Drawn to scale (MNA Cat. No. DI.3731 11-1371).

2) Huehueteol (1 head fragment)

The head is large and asymmetrical with a long narrow face. Eyes are incised as in Type I figurines. The earspools are punched holes. The mouth is large and opened in a grin. The chin and nose are prominent. Most of the headdress is broken off (Pl. 36*d*).

3) Miniature head (1 head fragment)

This is an extremely small and unique specimen. The head is only 9 mm long, but the facial detail is remarkable (Pl. 37). The figurine is broken just below the neck with a portion of the shoulder left intact. The figure appears to be wearing a necklace of beads and the earspools are leaf-shaped. The eyes are incised at a slant; the nose is large and flat; the mouth is open. There is no headdress.

4) Head fragment (1 example)

The face is thick and angular. The mouth is rimmed and open, the eyes are molded in low relief, and the nose is not prominent. The headdress is double looped with one loop twisted (Pl. 38*a*). There are no top projections.

5) Head fragment (1 example)

The eyes are incised and rimmed, the mouth is open but markedly turned down on the ends. The figure wears spiral earplugs, a lip plug, and a protruding headdress which is largely broken off. The face is polygonal with soft contours (Pl. 38*b*).

6) Head fragment (1 example)

This piece is badly weathered. The face is oval, and an open mouth and large earspools are clearly visible. The eyes are large circles with a horizontal incision across them, which probably means that the figure is wearing a flayed skin. The nose has been badly worn away, as has the headdress if there was one. The figure does wear a tight cap of some sort. This may well represent Xipe (Pl. 38*c*).

7) Wheeled toy fragment (1 example)

We have one wheeled toy fragment which is split in half. The head is broken off at the upper neck (Pl. 38*d*). Our fragment closely resembles the wheeled toy, a dog, found by Charney on the slopes of Popocatepetl near Tenenepango. Charney's example was unbroken.

8) Jaw fragment (1 example)

This is the fragment of a right mandible with three molars, broken immediately anterior of the first molar. It is about seven-eighths life size. See comparison with actual human mandible in Plate 38*e, f.* A small hole is drilled at the base of the coronoid process in both the pottery model (Pl. 38*f*) and the real human jaw (Pl. 38*e*). There is also a hole drilled lengthwise through the mandible, perhaps to make it a whistle. The hole through the base of the coronoid process may be for suspension. The mandible and teeth are covered with a layer of white paint, and were shaped with considerable care.

9) Skeletons (3 head fragments, 1 body fragment)

On all three skulls the eyes and teeth are very prominent (Pl. 38*g*). All appear to have been pot attachments. I have seen rows of three or four skulls attached as decoration to censers. The body fragment is the rib cage and upper leg area of a skeleton. It appears to have been a hollow figurine.

10) Head fragments (62 examples)

These are badly broken and weathered fragments with faces like Type III-A. They could belong to several other types, but one would need more complete examples in order to know in which category to put them. There are two distinct size ranges – those between 32 and 48 mm in length (Pl. 39*a-e*) and those between 20 and 23 mm in length (Pl. 39*f-i*). There are 39 of the former and 15 of the latter.

In addition to these miscellaneous fragments, we also have 11 fragments of top projections (Pl. 40*a*), and plumes, 6 decorative side fan fragments (Pl. 40*b, c*), 4 flower fragments which were either pot attachments or attached to figurines (Pl. 40*d, e*), and 6 leaf fragments that were probably vessel decorations.

## POST-CONTACT FIGURINES (21 examples)

### Type 1
### (6 head fragments)

These are all head fragments that resemble European china doll heads (Pl. 41*a*). The hair is parted in the middle and swept behind the ears in a bun. Individual strands of hair are incised on the head. Earspools are absent. Often a hand-rolled piece of clay is looped around the head to form a simple hat. The face is angular and full with noticeably puffy cheeks. The mouth is small and closed. The nose is not overly large. The brow ridge protrudes over the eye socket where we have faint indications of round eyes. Two of our examples have traces of white paint. Four of the six examples have the hand-rolled additive element, while the other two have nothing resting on top of the hair. In both of the latter cases the figurine has a circular jewel (or decorative element) attached to the area where the hair is parted on the forehead.

### Type 2
(10 body fragments)

These are fragments of robed figures resembling European religious figures. Both hands are held against the chest or abdomen. The hands do not meet and are not clapsed. All figures wear long, sweeping (pleated) robes that reach the ground. The face appears to have been covered with part of the robe in our single preserved facial fragment (Pl. 41*b*). Two examples are wearing particularly richly decorated garments under the robe (Pl. 41*c*). Another clasps in his right hand part of what appears to be a large key (Pl. 41*d*).

### Type 3
(1 head fragment)

This fragment has an oval face with a pageboy haircut. The figure is wearing a small, high bell-shaped hat. The face has a very large, prominent nose, no eyes, and a small mouth. The diagnostic trait is the unusual hat (Pl. 42*a*).

### Type 4
(2 head fragments)

The face is angular with a square pageboy haircut reaching just past the base of the ear. The nose is prominent, the eyes are not indicated, and the mouth is open with teeth showing. One example wears an additive, hand-rolled hat as in Type 1 above (Pl. 42*b*). The other example has a similar hat but it is mold-made in one piece with the head itself.

### Miscellaneous
(3 body fragments)

These figures do not form a type, but are all definitely Post-Contact. Two are fragments of a Spanish soldier wearing a short pleated skirt. The American Museum of Natural History has several much better preserved specimens of Spanish soldiers (Pl. 42*c. d*). The other figurine in this miscellaneous group is our only complete and unbroken figurine. It represents a female wearing a rectangular-patterned skirt such as is associated with Type III-B figurines. The woman is standing with her hands under her breasts. The breasts are clearly delineated under the blouse. The blouse appears to be of Spanish style with a high ruffled collar and pleated sleeves. The hair reaches just below the ears and individual hair strands are clearly delineated. The mouth and eyes are incised, and the nose is small. The fluffy character of the hair outline and the rectangular patterned skirt hint at a possible Post-Contact Xochiquetzal representation.

## ANIMAL FIGURINES

### Monkey Figurines
(2 head fragments)

The first example is small (9 mm high) and solid. It has large, round molded eyes, a prognathic jaw, and a short round nose. The second example is partially hollowed out. Large circular eyes are incised. The jaw is prognathic and the mouth is open showing two teeth. The nose is small and round, and there is a small ornament beneath the mouth.

### Rabbit Figurines
(3 head fragments and 1 body fragment) (Pl. 43*a*)

The three head fragments have large, round bulging eyes, and long ears. The fourth example is a body fragment with a large round "cotton" tail. The animal is sitting on its haunches. It is broken just below the upper shoulder. There are two complete holes drilled through the sides of the animal.

### Bird Figurines
(10 head fragments)

One is an eagle with feathers clearly delineated over the entire head. Another is a duck with a hole drilled through its neck. We have a possible turkey and what may be a dove. Six examples are very conventionalized bird heads with no indications of eyes (Pl. 43*b, c*). One of these has part of a body, wing stubs and a back fragment.

### Coyote Figurines
(7 head fragments) (Pl. 43*d, e*)

All examples are shown baring their teeth. The snout is long and ends in a point. The ears are small. Six have large, round protruding eyes, while a seventh has more tear-shaped eyes.

### Toad
(1 example) (Pl. 43*f*)

This example is complete except for a piece of one foot which is missing. It measures 70 mm long and stands 35 mm high. It looks extremely natural. Its webbed feet are incised and its body is covered with fine raised bumps one and one-quarter mm in diameter.

Mountain Lion Figurines
(7 head fragments) (Pl. 44*a, b*)

The snout is short and square. The mouth is open with the teeth and fangs showing. The eyes are molded, large and round. In most cases the lower jaw juts out somewhat farther than the upper jaw.

Miscellaneous

1) (2 head fragments) (Pl. 44*c*)

These are long square-snouted animals with teeth bared and large round eyes. In both cases the ears have been broken off.

2) (2 head fragments)

These are foxlike animals with small, round incised eyes and pointed snouts.

3) (1 head fragment) (Pl. 44*d*)

This is a serpent-like head with a long neck and slit eyes. The distance from snout to ears is 20 mm.

4) (3 body fragments) (Pl. 44*e*)

All are crouched sitting body fragments with indications of a tail that has been broken off. They range from 36-52 mm in length and from 30-40 mm in height.

5) (4 head fragments) (Pl. 44*f, g*)

These are 15-25 mm long. (All other heads range from 35-55 mm long from snout to ears.) Several appear to be rodent-like creatures. One has a hole drilled through its neck.

6) (21 body fragments)

These are all fragments of four-legged animals with tails ranging in size from 45-65 mm in body length from the base of the neck to the stub of the tail. None have heads or tails unbroken. Three examples have a hole drilled completely through the rib cage area from side to side. One might have been hollow, but the rest were definitely solid. Six examples had some sort of object or person mounted on their backs. I have seen examples of Aztec animal figurines in which there are puppies standing on the mother dog's back, and one Post-Contact figurine of a rider mounted on a horse.

7) (11 head fragments) (Pl. 44*h, i*)

These are unidentifiable head fragments of animals.

## SERPENT HEAD INCENSE BURNER HANDLES
(69 examples and 1 mold fragment)

Incense burners have long, round hollow handles (approximately 24 cm long) that terminate in a serpent's head. In most cases there is a bow or double ax-shaped decorative element attached to the handle several inches back from the serpent head (Pl. 45*a, b*). We have eleven of these bow-shaped elements attached to handle fragments. Two have horizontal incisions over the "bow" area, while four have circular lumps or design elements over the central area of the "bow" where the knot would be (Pl. 45*b*). The neck of the flat serpent head slopes up 16-30 degrees to meet with the long handle part of the censer. While there is a great deal of variety in size, shape and detail, the general form of these serpent heads is the same. They are relatively broad and flat with a forked tongue projecting from an open mouth (Fig. 21). Both fangs are often represented. The eyes are on the top of the head and project out in high relief. They are oblong in shape and covered by a thick fleshy fold. The snout is also elevated and molded up from the flat facial surface. The forked tongue can vary in size from a small tongue (Pl. 45*e, f*) to a greatly exaggerated large tongue. These serpent heads range from 35-60 mm in size from the snout to the top of the neck (not including tongue length).

Eleven of our fragments are merely forked tongues that had broken off the heads. The one mold piece that we found has the tongue and about half of the head intact. The remaining forty-five fragments are serpent head fragments with the eyes and snout unbroken.

## CONCLUSION

This paper has been, and must be at this stage, basically descriptive. I have tried to indicate where I feel that variation within a type might be chronologically significant. These are merely hypothetical guesses. We must await good stratified excavations covering the entire Aztec sequence before we can confirm or deny them.

There seem to be two basic groups of figurines. Whether they are chronologically meaningful or not, we cannot yet say for sure. One group consists of the solid Type III figurines. Their general appearance is dull and unburnished. They have wide, angular faces with eyes molded outward in relief. They sometimes retain traces of white paint. This group is by far the most abundant. The second group consists of the hollow and jointed figurines (my Types I and II).

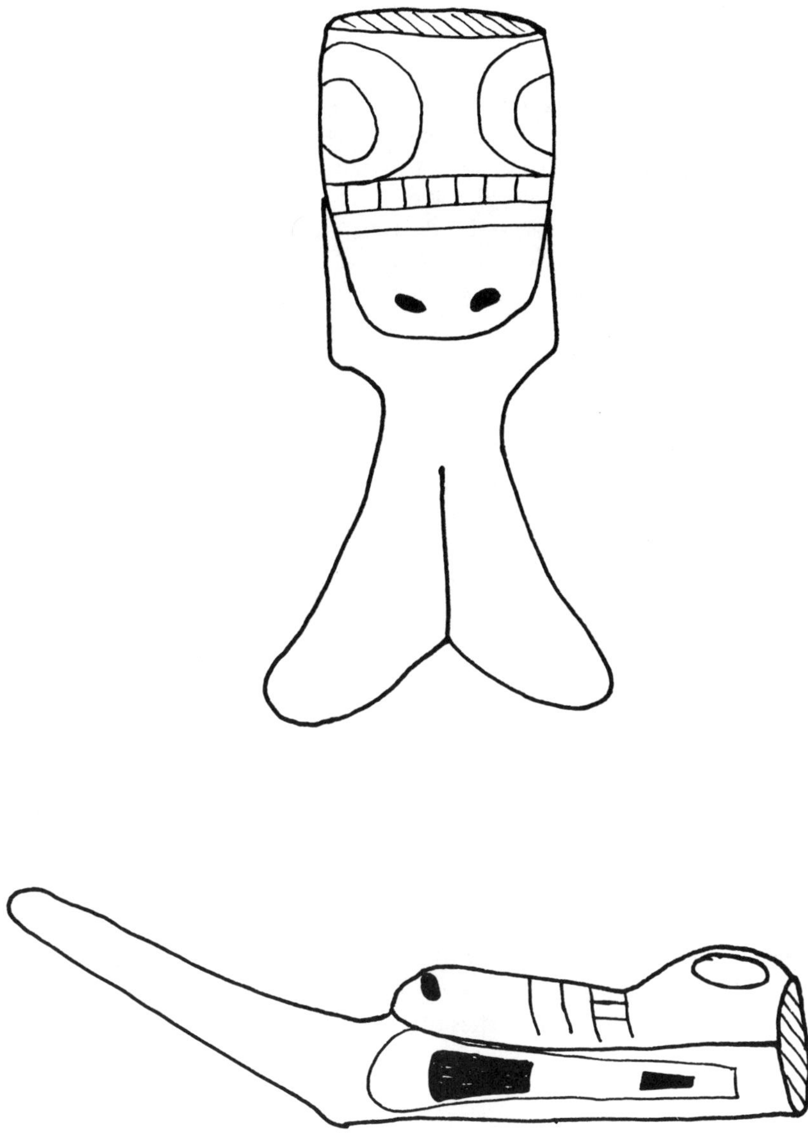

Fig. 21. Serpent head censer handle. Drawn to scale (AMNH Cat. No. 30.1/6072).

They have a burnished orange appearance with details a good deal better preserved. The face is oval, long and narrow in contrast to Type III faces. From our sample we had 122 of these figurines and 633 of the other. (Although an attempt was made to match head fragments with body fragments, it should be remembered that some Type III head fragments were pot attachments and did not have a body.)

There seems to be continuity between the Late Toltec (Mazapan) figurine headdresses and body positions and some of the Aztec Type III figurines. Compare Plate 46*a* and *b* with Plate 22*a* and *g*; Plate 46*c* with Plate 23*a* or Figure 18; and Plate 46*d* body form with Plate 24*e* and *f*. In some cases the rigid stance is nearly identical, and if the head is missing, it may be difficult to say whether the figurine is Aztec or Mazapan. It seems to me that Type III figurines were probably first made in Early Aztec times, but continued to be made until after the Conquest. The large number of these figurines compared with Types I and II argues for their production over a longer period of time *or* indicates that while Type III figurines were mass produced for use by the common people, Types I and II were produced for special ritual or cermonial occasions, perhaps for the use of only a select group. However, the fact that we have Type III figurine bodies almost identical to Mazapan ones, and that we also have Type III figurines in Post-Contact dress, argues strongly for an early Aztec origin of Type III and a progressive evolution of Type III figurines into Post-Contact times. In contrast, Type I and Type II may have been made during only late Aztec times. The form and type of dress are the same – all the figurines are almost identical, varying only in minute details of headdress. Types I and II wear the same diamond-patterned skirt or plain undelineated robe which does not vary in 99 percent of the figurines. The remaining 1 percent have some added Spanish detail of dress (Type II), or have an exotic, wildly moving floral pattern stamped onto the skirt (Type I), in violent contrast to the solemn stately appearance of other Type I figurines. Probably both Types I and II were made for a short time only, and that time was just prior to and shortly after the Conquest, while Type III figurines were made throughout the Aztec period.

Another problem is the identity of these figurines. The exaggerated polytheism among the Aztecs, as Caso (1958) has pointed out, resulted in two aspects of one god sometimes being thought of as two separate gods. Thus one figurine may bear the characteristics of what the present-day observer has been led to believe from his reading are two distinct gods or goddesses.

It is interesting that the deities most commonly represented are not the important state gods (Huitzilopochtli, Tezcatlipoca, and Quetzalcoatl), but rather the deities which Vaillant (1950:187-90) has classified as fertility goddesses and rain and water deities. This should be kept in mind when one tries to determine the function of these figurines. When we have more excavated data we will be able to see where these figurines most commonly occur, whether in burials, household units, etc.

The question of the mass production of these figurines or their molds by specialists was raised earlier. I cannot answer it here. But from my examination of other figurine collections in Mexico and at the American Museum in New York, our sample from the politically marginal Teotihuacán Valley would appear to be representative of Aztec figurines in general, including those from the Texcoco Region (see Appendix) and those from Tlatelolco, part of the old Aztec capital. This similarity between the figurines found in the marginal and dominant areas gives some support to the idea that they were mass produced by specialists in particular centers and distributed throughout the Valley of Mexico, the Aztec stronghold.

# APPENDIX

## AZTEC FIGURINES FROM THE TEXCOCO REGION SURVEY, 1967

A total of 357 Aztec figurine fragments were picked up during the Texcoco Survey. Some came from tlatel ceramic collections and others were picked up when seen in areas where ceramic collections were not made.

The same types of Aztec figurines were found as in the Teotihuacán Valley to the north, and the three major figurine types defined in the Teotihuacán Valley occur in about the same frequencies in both areas. Type III (solid figurines) are the most common and a good deal more abundant than both Type I (hollow rattle figurines) and Type II (jointed slab figurines) combined. Type II figurines are extremely rare as in the Teotihuacán Valley. The fact that the Aztec figurines from Texcoco, a prominent Aztec center, and from Teotihuacán, a marginal area in Aztec times, are identical supports the idea of mass production and distribution of the figurines or their molds.

# BIBLIOGRAPHY


Alva Ixtlilxochital, Fernando de

1952 Obras Historicas, 2 vols. Alfredo Chavero, editor. Editora Nacional. Mexico City.

Anghiera, Petrus Martyr

1628 The Decades of the New World or West India. Second edition. London. On University of Michigan Microfilms, Real 819, Short Title Catalogue No. 652,22208. Ann Arbor.

Barlow, R. H.

1946 Some Mexican Figurines of the Colonial Period. Notes on Middle American Archaeology and Ethnology Vol. III, No. 70. Carnegie Institute of Washington, Division of Historical Research. Washington, D. C.

1949 The Extent of the Empire of the Culhua Mexica. Ibero-Americana Vol. 28. University of California Press. Berkeley.

Barlow, Roberto and Henri Lehmann

1956 Statuettes-Grelots Azteques de la Valle de Mexico. Tribus 4-5:157-76. Stuttgart.

Barnett, Madame

1912 Quelques Observations sur les Petites Têtes de Teotihuacán. El XVIII Congreso Internacional de Americanistas. New York.

Beyer, Herman

1922 Antiguedades Post-Teotihuacanas o Aztecas. *In:* La Población del Valle de Teotihuacán: La Población Prehispánico, by Manuel Gamio. Departmento de Educación Pública. Mexico City.

Biese, Leo

1960 Spindle Whorls from Panama Viejo. Panama Archaeologist Vol. III, No. 1: 35-46. Balboa Heights, Canal Zone.

Caso, Alfonso

1936 La Religión de los Aztecas. Enciclopedian Ilustrada Mexicana, Imprenta Mundial. Mexico City.

1958 The Aztecs: People of the Sun. Translated by Lowell Dunham. University of Oklahoma Press. Norman

Cook de Leonard, Carmen

1950 Figurillas de Barro de Santiago Tlatelolco. Tlatelolco a Traves de los Tiempos Tomo XI, No. 1:93-99. Mexico City.

Cortes, Hernando

1962 Five Letters of Cortes to the Emperor. Translated by J. B. Morris. The Norton Company. New York.

Diaz del Castillo, Bernal

1908 The True History of the Conquest of New Spain. Edited by Genaro Garcia, translated by Alfred Percival Maudslay. The Hakluty Society Series 2, Vols. 23-25, 30 and 40. London.

Duran, Fray Diego

1964 The Aztecs – The History of the Indies of New Spain. Translated by Doris Heyden and Fernando Horcásitas. Orian Press. New York.

Du Solier, Wilfrido

1950 Ancient Mexican Costumes. Ediciones Mexicanas. Mexico City.

Ekholm, Gordon F.

1944*a* Excavations at Guasave, Sinaloa, Mexico. American Museum of Natural History Anthropological Papers Vol. 38, Pt. 2. New York.

1944*b* Excavations at Tampico and Panuco. *In:* The Huasteca, Mexico. American Museum of Natural History Anthropological Papers Vol. 38, Pt. 5. New York.

1946 Wheeled Toys in Mexico. American Antiquity, 11:222-28. Salt Lake City.

Franco C., José Luis

1955 Sobre un Molde para Vasijas con Decoración en Relieve. El México Antiguo, Tomo VII:76-84. Mexico City.

1956 Malacates del Complejo Tula-Mazapan. Estúdios Antropológicos en Homenaje del Dr. Manual Gamio, pp. 201-12. Dirección General de Publicaciones. Mexico City.

1961 Representaciones de la Mariposa en Mesoamerica. El México Antiguo, Tomo IX:195-244. Mexico City.

Gamio, Manuel

1922 La Población del Valle de Teotihuacán: La Población Prehispánico, Tomo I, Vol. I, Departmento de Educación Pública. Mexico City.

Gifford, E. W.

1950 Surface Archaeology of Ixtlan del Río Nayarit. University of California Publication in American Archaeology and Ethnology, Vol. 43, No. 2. Berkeley.

Grollig, Francis X.

1956 Pottery Figurine Heads from the Valley of Mexico. Indiana Academy of Science Proceedings 66:53-54. Indianapolis.

Hooper, Luther

1914 The Loom and Spindle: Past, Present, and Future. Annual Report of the Smithsonian Institution. Washington, D. C.

Joyce, Thomas A.

1920 Mexican Archaeology. Philip Lee Varner. London.

Kaplan, Florence Siegal

1958 The Post-Classic Figurines of Central Mexico. Master's thesis, Columbia University. New York.

Kelly, Isabel

1938 Excavations at Chametla, Sinaloa. Ibero-Americana No. 14. Berkeley.

1945*a* Excavations at Culiacan, Sinaloa. Ibero-Americana No. 25. Berkeley.

1945*b* The Archaeology of the Autlan-Tuxcacuesco Area of Jalisco. Ibero-Americana No. 26. Berkeley.

1947 Excavations at Apatzingan, Michoacan. Viking Fund Publication in Anthropology No. 7. New York.

Kent, Kate Peck
1957 The Cultivation and Weaving of Cotton in the Prehistoric Southwestern U. S. Transactions of the American Philosophical Society Vol. 47, Pt. 3. Philadelphia.

Kidder, Alfred V.
1943 Spindle Whorls from Chichén Itzá, Yucatan. Notes on Middle American Archaeology and Ethnology No. 16. Carnegie Institution of Washington. Washington, D. C.

Krickeberg, Walter
1961 Las Antiguas Culturas Mexicanas. Fondo de Cultura Económica. Mexico City.

Lehmann, Henri
1953 On Noel Morss' "Cradled Infant Figurines." American Antiquity, 19:78-80. Salt Lake City.

Linné, S.
1934 Archaeological Researches at Teotihuacan, Mexico. The Ethnographical Museum of Sweden, n. s., Publication No. 1. Stockholm.

1942 Mexican Highland Cultures: Archaeological Researches at Teotihuacan, Calpulalpan and Chalchicomula in 1934/35. The Ethnographical Museum of Sweden, n. s., Publication No. 7. Stockholm.

1951 A Wheeled Toy from Guerrero, Mexico. Ethnos Vol. 16, No. 3-4:141-52. Lund.

Lister, Robert H.
1947 Additional Evidence of Wheeled Toys in Mexico. American Antiquity 7:184-85. Salt Lake City.

1949 Excavations at Cojumatlan, Michoacan, Mexico. University of New Mexico Publication in Anthropology No. 5. Santa Fe.

Morss, Noel
1952 Cradled Infant Figurines from Tennessee and Mexico. American Antiquity 18:164-166. Salt Lake City.

1954 Clay Figurines of the American Southwest. Papers of the Peabody Museum of American Archaeology and Ethnology Vol. LXIX, No. 1. Cambridge.

Müller, Jacobs
1957 Azcapotzalco: Estudio Tipológico de Su Cerámica. Revista Mexicana de Estudios Antropológicos Tomo 14, Pt. 2. Sociedad Mexicana de Antropología. Mexico.

Noguera, Eduardo
1946 Cultura Azteca, Cihuacoatl, Xochiquetzal, and Chalchuihtlicue. *In:* México Prehispánico – Culturas, Deidades, and Monumentos, edited by Jorge A. Vivó. PP. 312-19; 465-72; 481-84. La Editorial Emma Hurtado. Mexico City.

1954 La Cerámica Arqueológica de Cholula. Editorial Guarania. Mexico City.

1965 La Cerámica Arqueológica de Mesoamerica. Instituto de Investigaciones Históricas, Primera Serie No. 86. Universidad Nacional Autónoma de México. Mexico City.

Noriega, Raul, Carmen Cook de Leonard, et al.
1959 Esplendor del México Antiguo Tomos I and II. Centro de Investigaciones Antropológicas de México. Mexico City.

Nuttall, Zelia
1886 The Terracotta Heads of Teotihuacan. The American Journal of Archaeology and of the History of the Fine Arts 2:157-78 and 318-30. Baltimore.
1926 Translation of the Official Reports of the Towns of Tequizistlan, Tepechpan, Acolman, and San Juan Teotihuacan. Sent by Francisco de Castañeda to His Majesty, Philip II, and the Council of the Indies in 1580. Papers of the Peabody Museum of American Archaeology and Ethnology Vol. II, No. 2. Harvard University. Cambridge.

O'Neale, Lila M.
1945 Textiles of Highland Guatemala. Carnegie Institution of Washington Publication 567. Washington, D. C.

Parker, King Lawrence
1952 A Typological and Distributional Study of a Collection of Ancient Mexican Spindle Whorls. Senior thesis, Yale University. New Haven.

Parsons, Jeffrey R.
1966 The Aztec Ceramic Sequence in the Teotihuacan Valley. Ph.D. thesis, the University of Michigan. Ann Arbor.

Peñafiel, Antonio
1890 Monumentos de Arte Mexicano Antiguo, Ornamentación, Mitología, Tributos, y Monumentos Vols. II and III. Berlin.

Peterson, Frederick
1962 Ancient Mexico: An Introduction to Pre-Hispanic Cultures. Capricorn Press. New York.

Sanders, William T.
1965 The Cultural Ecology of the Teotihuacan Valley, A Preliminary Report of the Results of the Teotihuacan Valley Project. Pennsylvania State University. State College.

Sejourne, Laurette
1960 Burning Water: Thought and Religion in Ancient Mexico. Grove Press. New York.

Stirling, Matthew W.
1962 Wheeled Toys from Tres Zapotes. Amerindia, Prehistoria y Ethnología del Nuevo Mundo 1:43-48. Centro de Estudios Arqueológicas y Antropológicas Americanos. Montevideo.

Thompson, J. Eric
1933 Mexico before Cortez, Chapter 5. Charles Scribner's Sons. New York.

Vaillant, George
1950 The Aztecs of Mexico. Pelican Books, second edition. London.

von Winning, Hasso
1949 Spindle-whorls from Culhuacan, Mexico, Showing Deity Emerging from Conch-Shell. The Masterkey 23:149-52. Los Angeles.
1950 Animal Figurines on Wheels from Ancient Mexico. The Masterkey 24:154-59. Los Angeles.
1951 Another Wheeled Animal Figurine from Mexico. The Masterkey 25:88-89. Los Angeles.
1961 Further Examples of Figurines on Wheels from Mexico. Ethnos 25:63-72. Lund.
1962 Figurillas de Barro Sobre Ruedas Procedentes de México y del Viejo Mundo. Amerinda 1:11-29. Montevideo.

Wardle, H. Newell
1902 Certain Clay Figurines of Teotihuacan. El XIII Congreso Internacional de Americanistas, pp 213-16. New York.

Zorita, Alonso de
1963 Life and Labor in Ancient Mexico: The Brief and Summary Relation of the Lords of New Spain. Translated by Benjamin Keen. Rutgers University Press. New Brunswick.

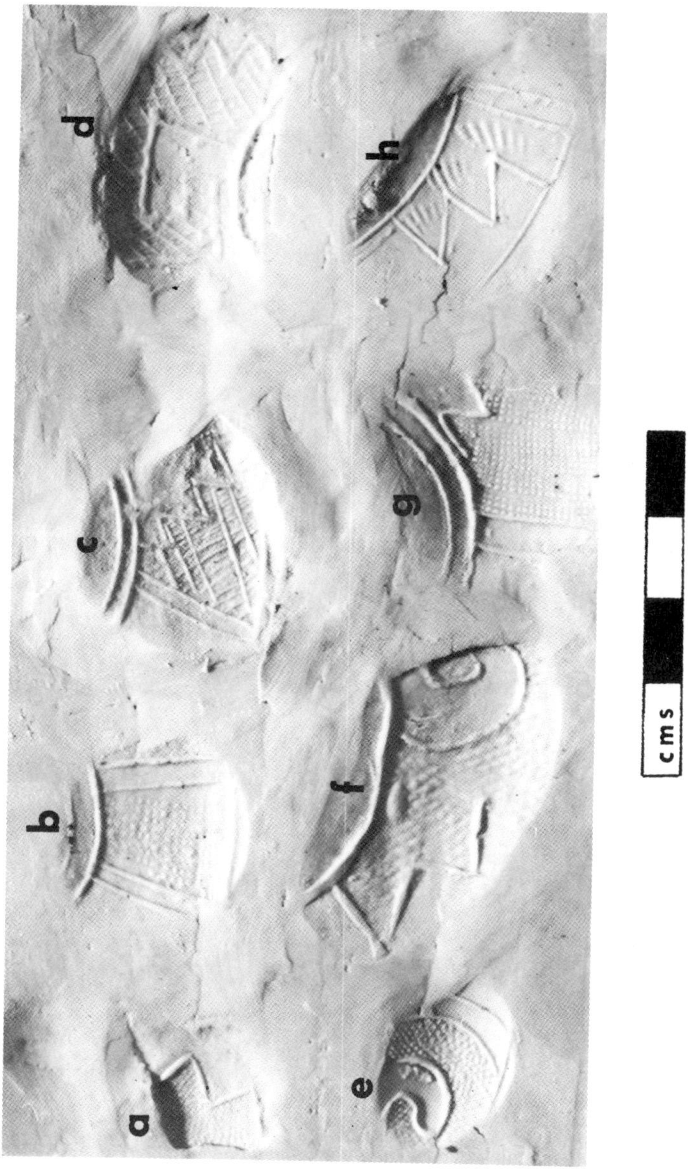


Plate 1. Clay impressions of Type I-A design motifs.

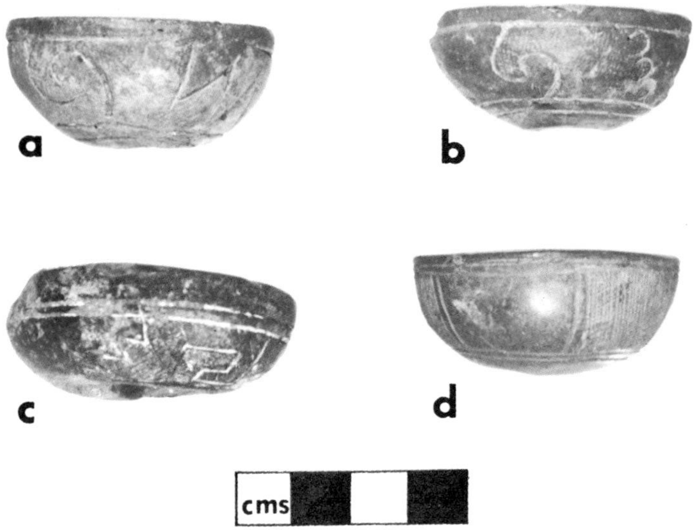


Plate 2. Type I-A spindle whorls.

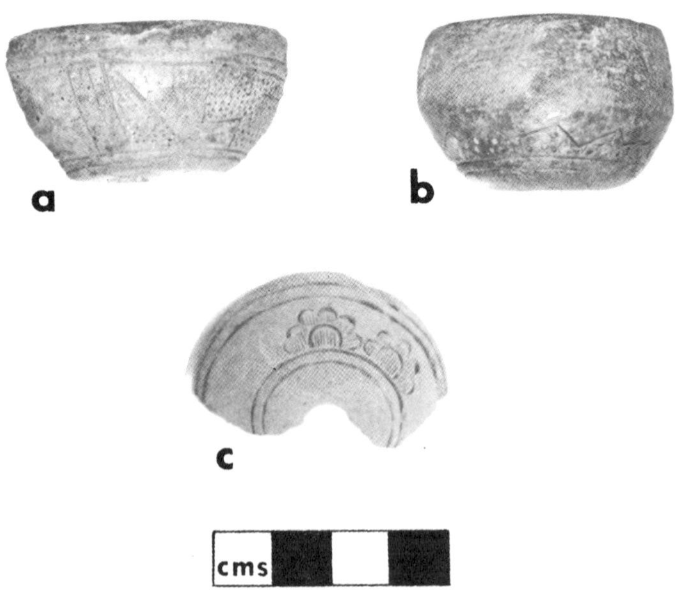


Plate 3. Type I spindle whorls: *a-b*, Type I-C; *c*, Type I-D.

Plate 4. Type I spindle whorls: *a-b*, Type I-E; *c*, Type I-F; *d-e*, Type I-G.

Plate 5. Type II-A spindle whorls.

Plate 6. Type II spindle whorls: *a*, Type II-B; *b-d*, Type II-C.

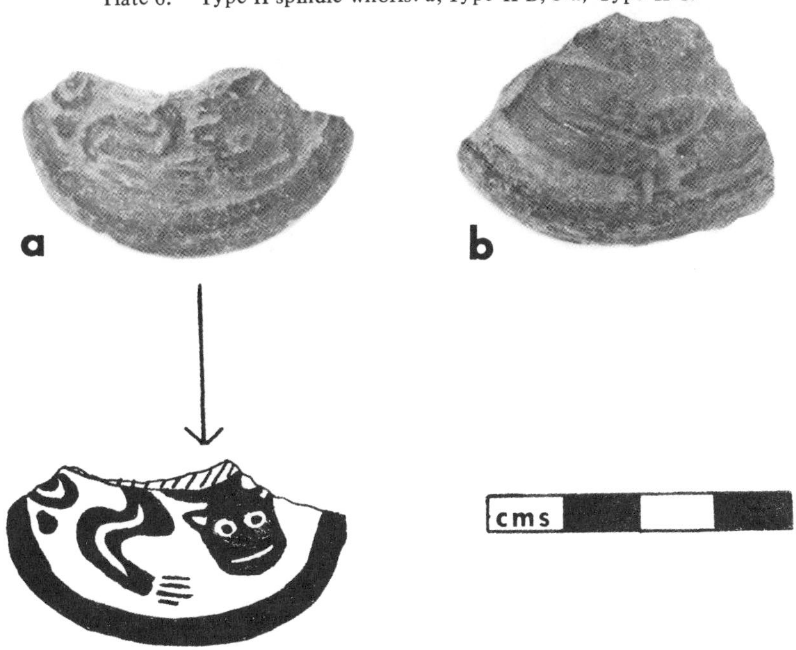


Plate 7. Type II-D spindle whorls.

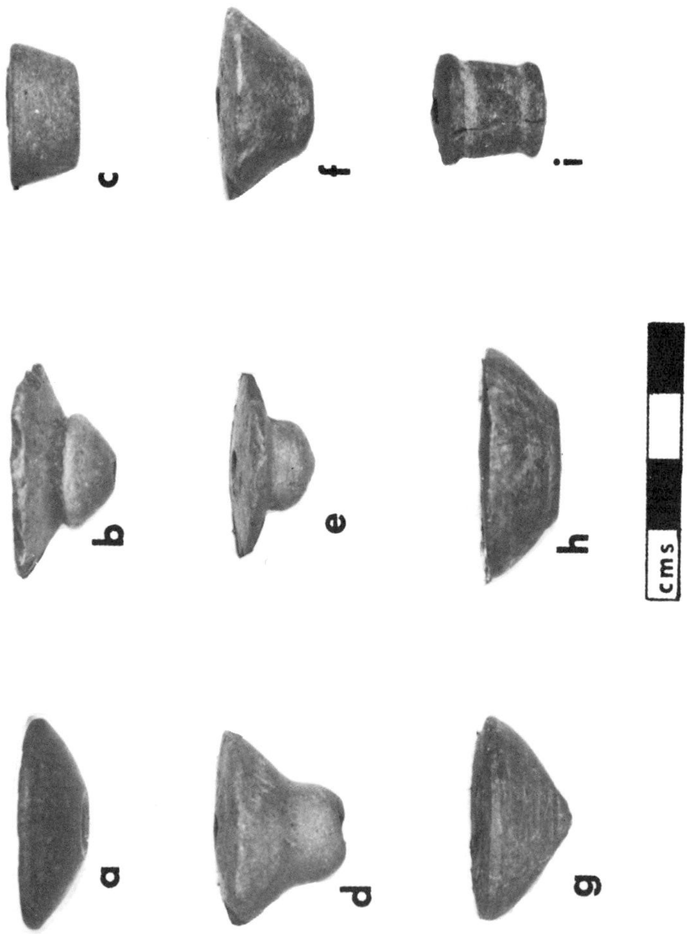


Plate 8. Type III-A spindle whorls.

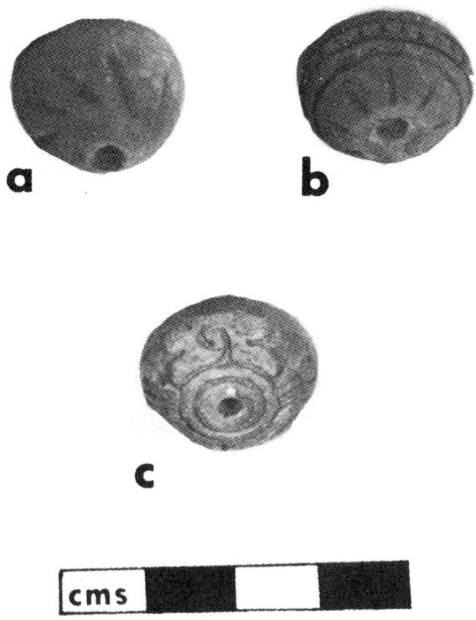


Plate 9. Type III spindle whorls: *a-b*, Type III-B; *c*, Type III-D.

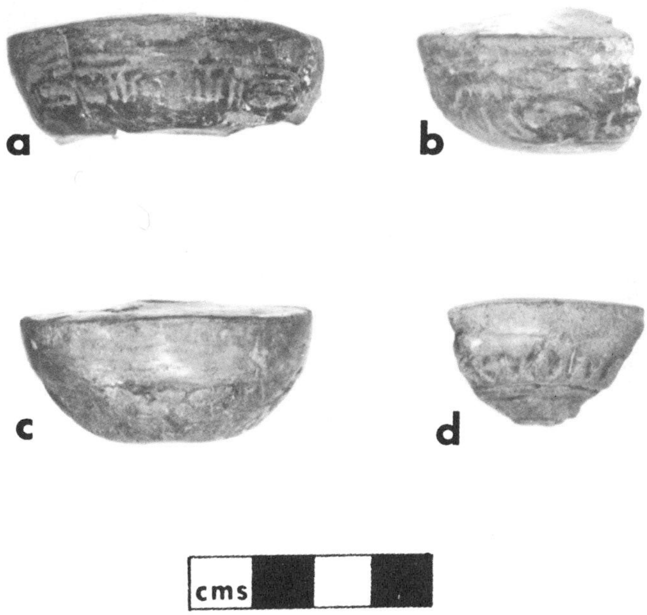


Plate 10. *a*, Type IV; *b-d*, Type V.

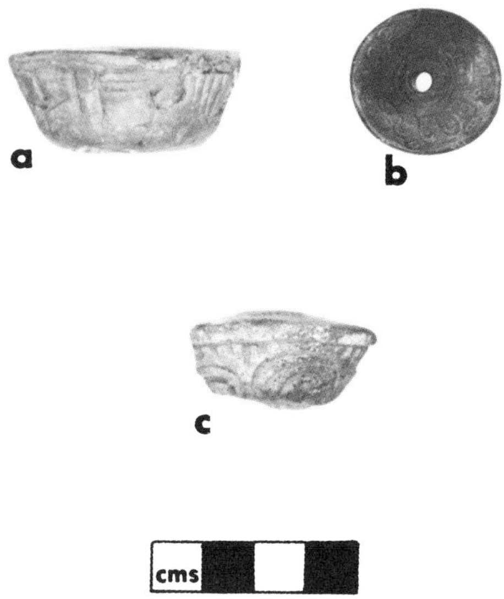


Plate 11. *a*, Type VI; *b*, Type VIII; *c*, Type IX.

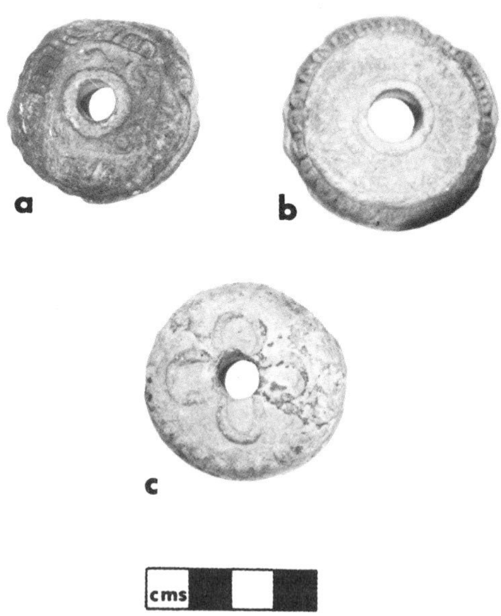


Plate 12. Miscleeaneous spindle whorl types: *a*, Mis. A; *b*, Mis. b; *c*, Mis.C.

Plate 13. Miscellaneous spindle whorl types: *a*, D; *b*, Mis. E.

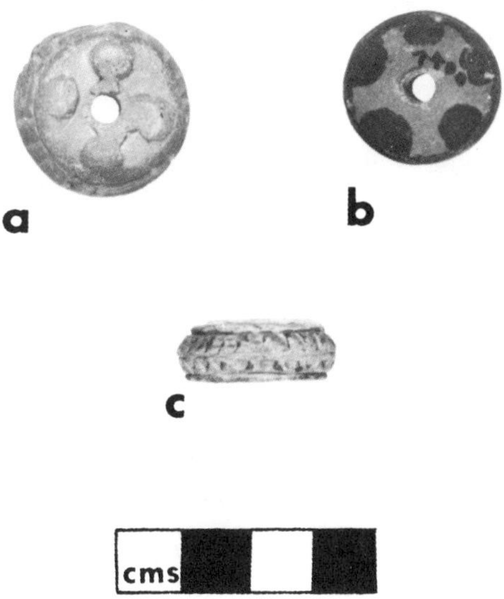


Plate 14. Huasteca spindle whorls.

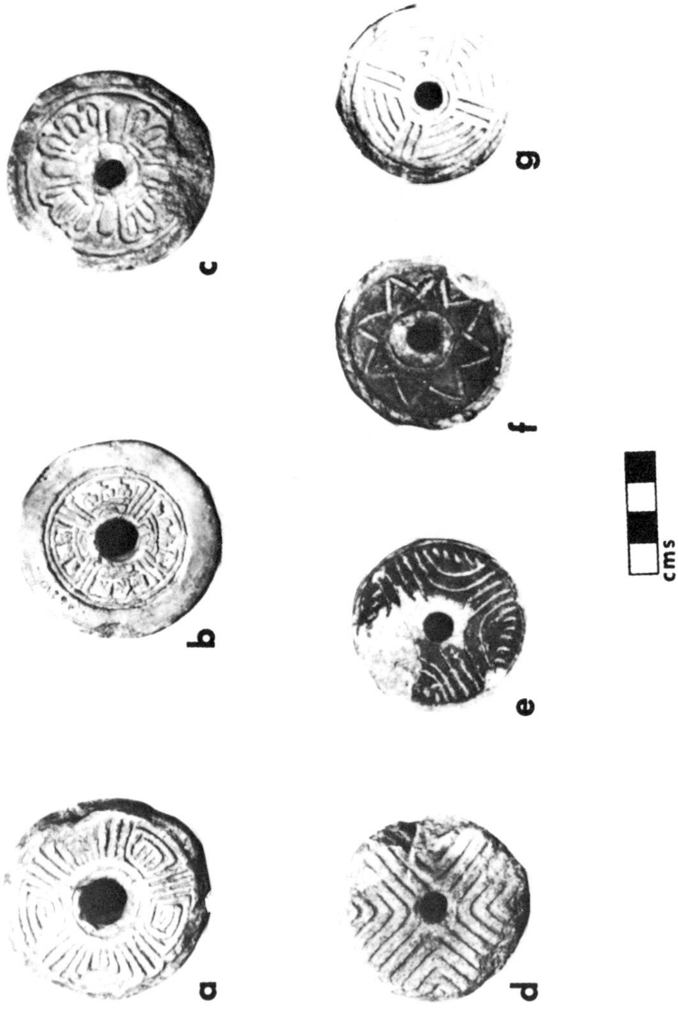


Plate 15. Spindle whorls from the Toluca Basin: *a-c*, Parker's Type 2; *d-g*, Parker's Type 3.

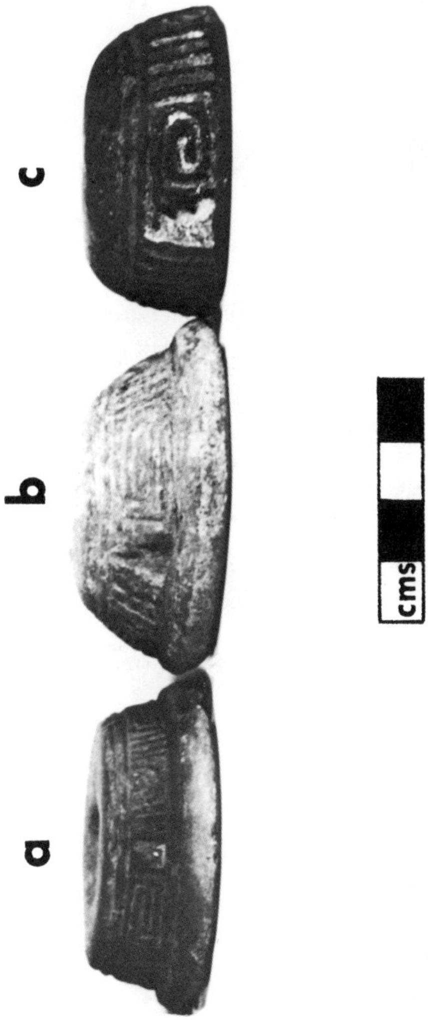


Plate 16. Spindle whorls from the Toluca Basin: *a-c*, Parker's Type 2.

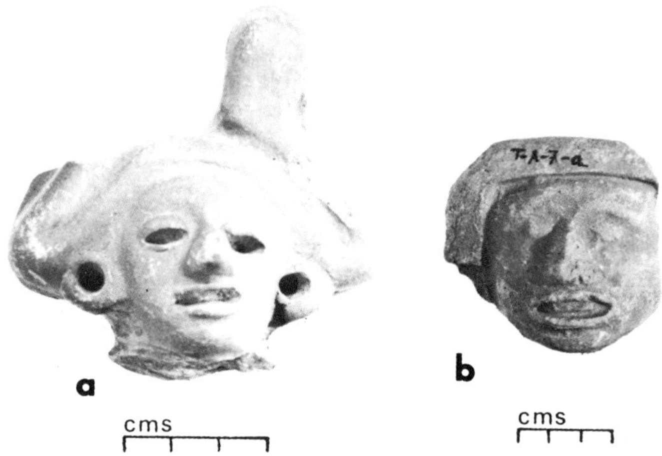


Plate 17. Comparison of Type I and Type III face shapes' *a*, Type I; *b*, Type III.

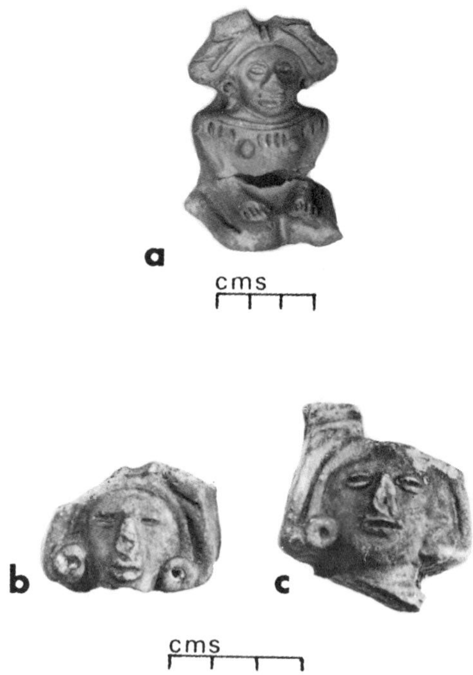


Plate 18. Type I-A: *a*, second variety of headdress; *b-c*, third variety of headdress.

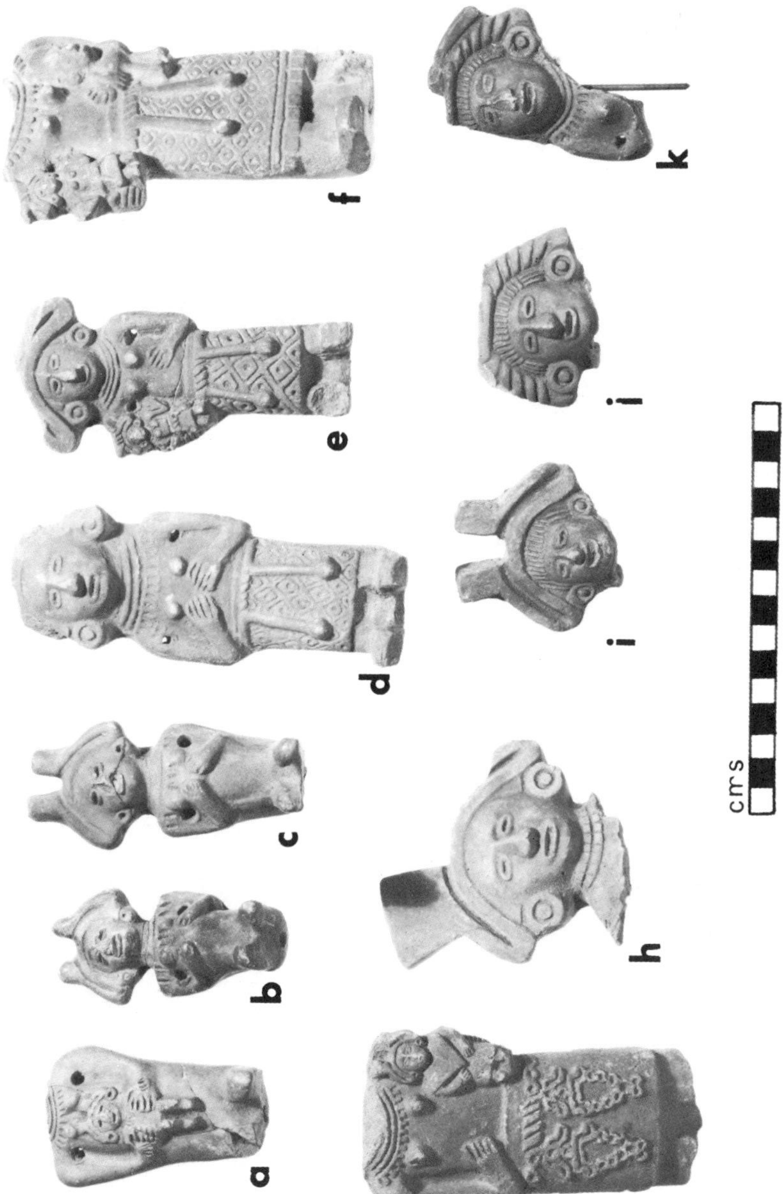


Plate 19. Type I-A variations.

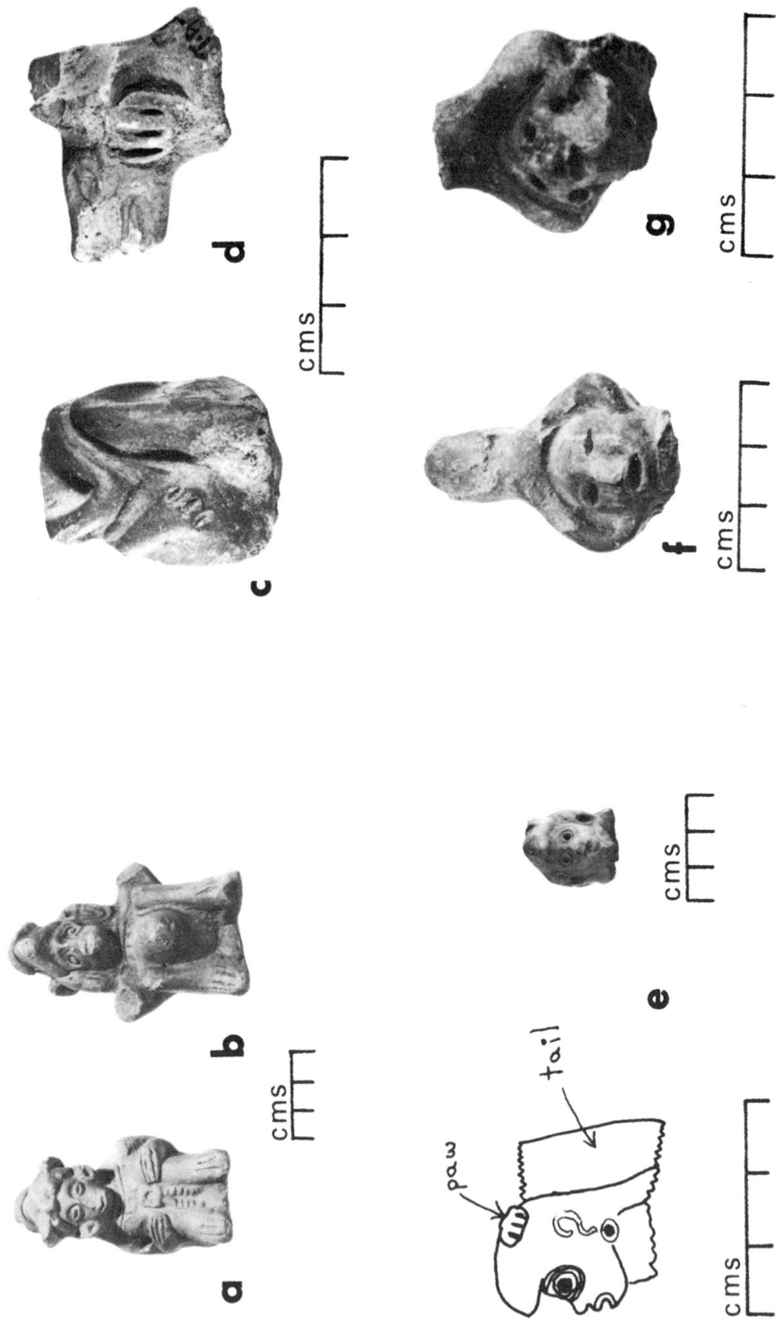


Plate 20. Type I-B: *a-c*, *e*, Type I-B1; *d*, Type I-B3; *f-g*, Type I-B2.

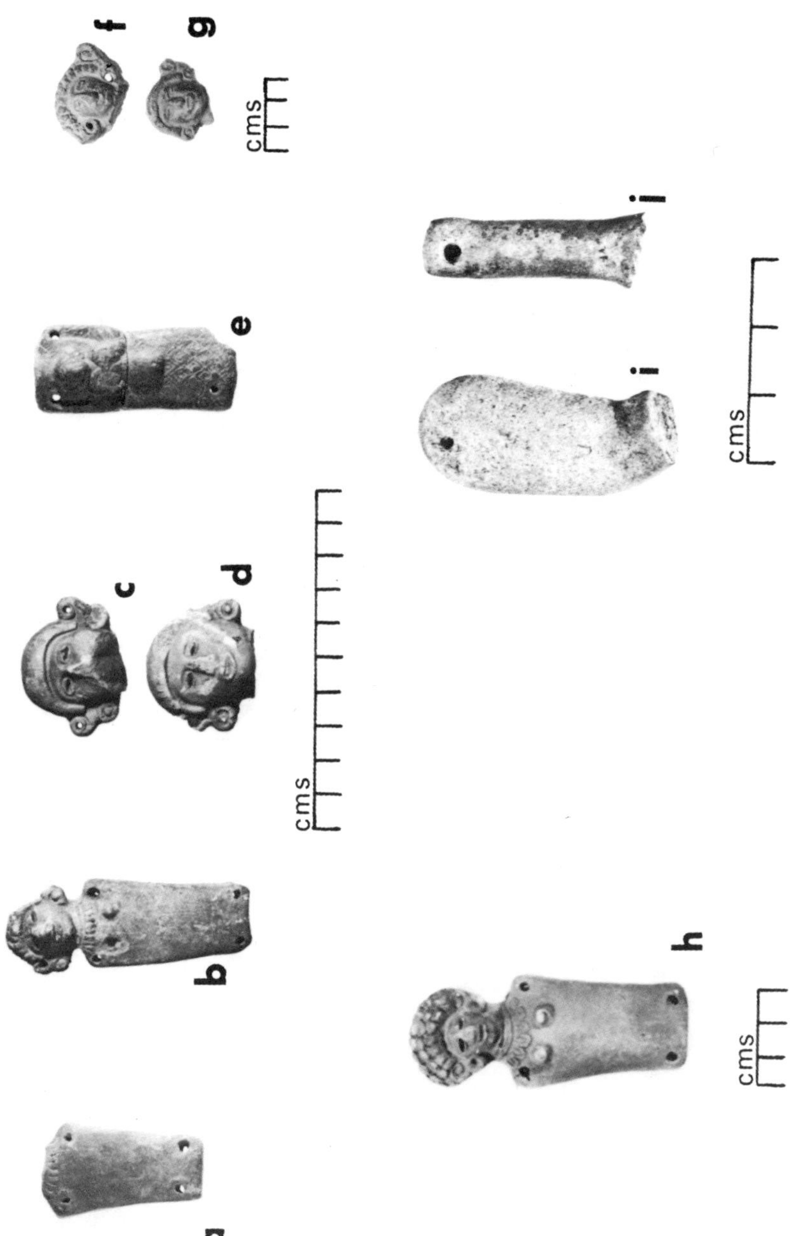


Plate 21. Type II: *a-d*, Type II-A; *e-h*, Type II-B; *i*, Xolalpan figurine limb; *j*, Type II-A limb.

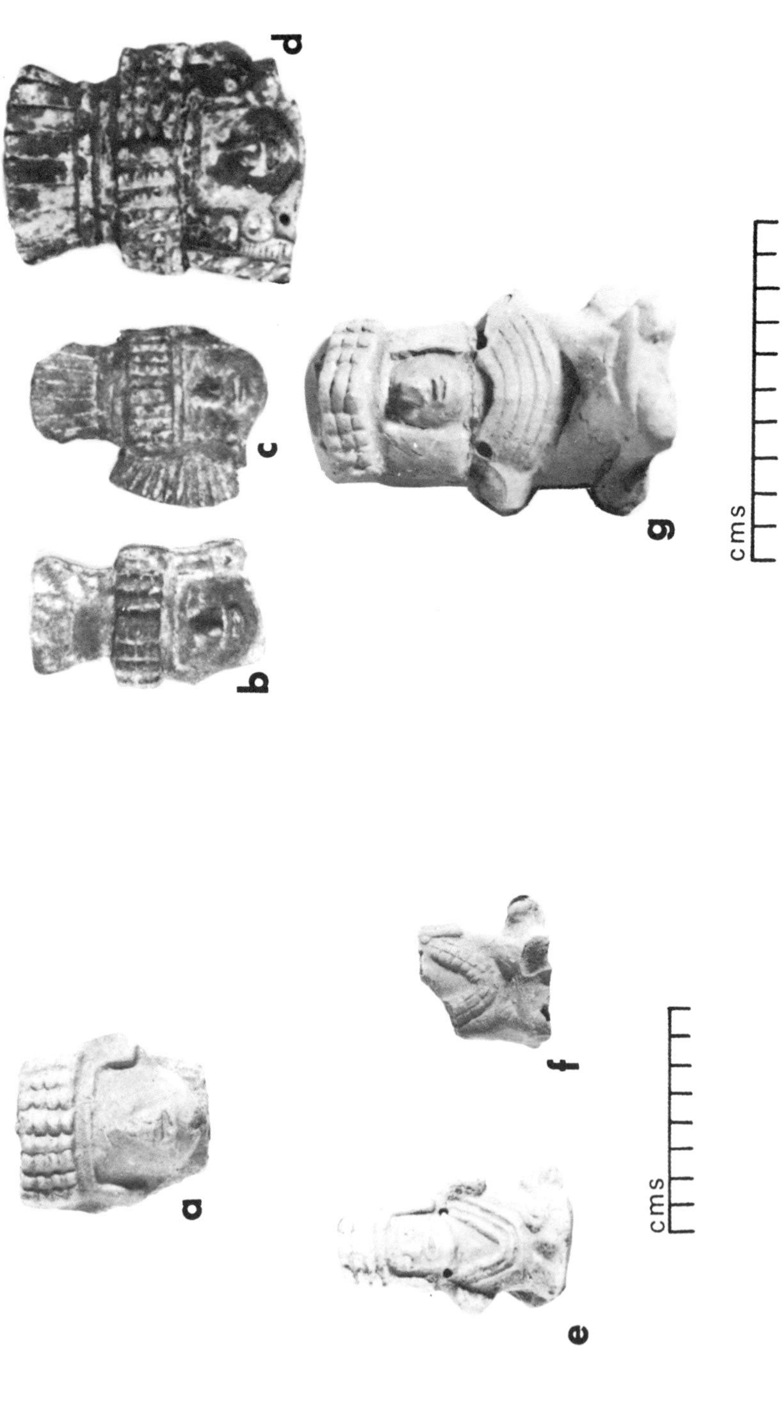


Plate 22. Type III-A1.

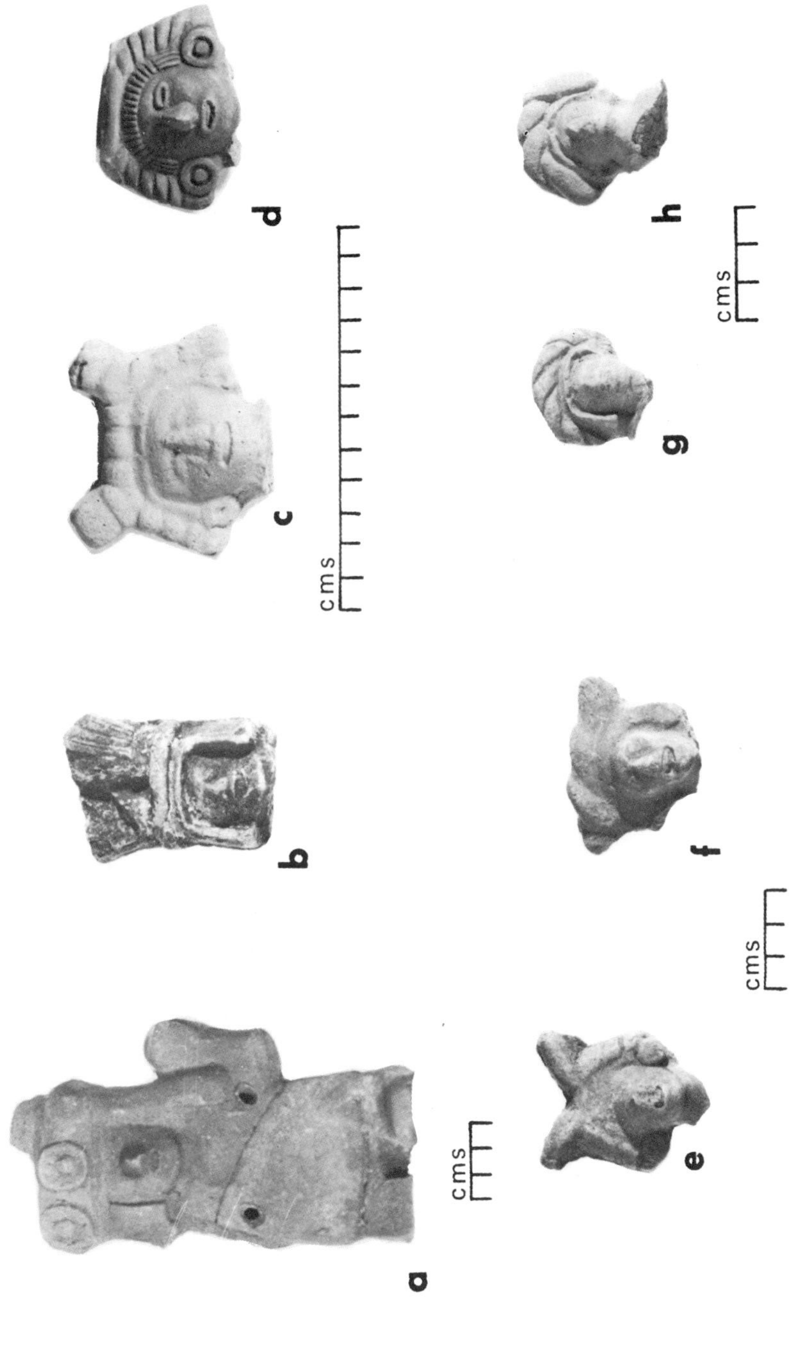


Plate 23. *a*, Type III-A2; *b*, Type III-A3; *c*, *e*, Type III-A4; *d*, Type I-A with headdress variety 4; *f*, Type III-A5; *g-h*, Type III-A6.

Plate 24. Type III-A body positions: *a*, body position b; *b-d*, body position c; *e*, *f*, body position d; *g-h*, body position e; *i*, body position f.

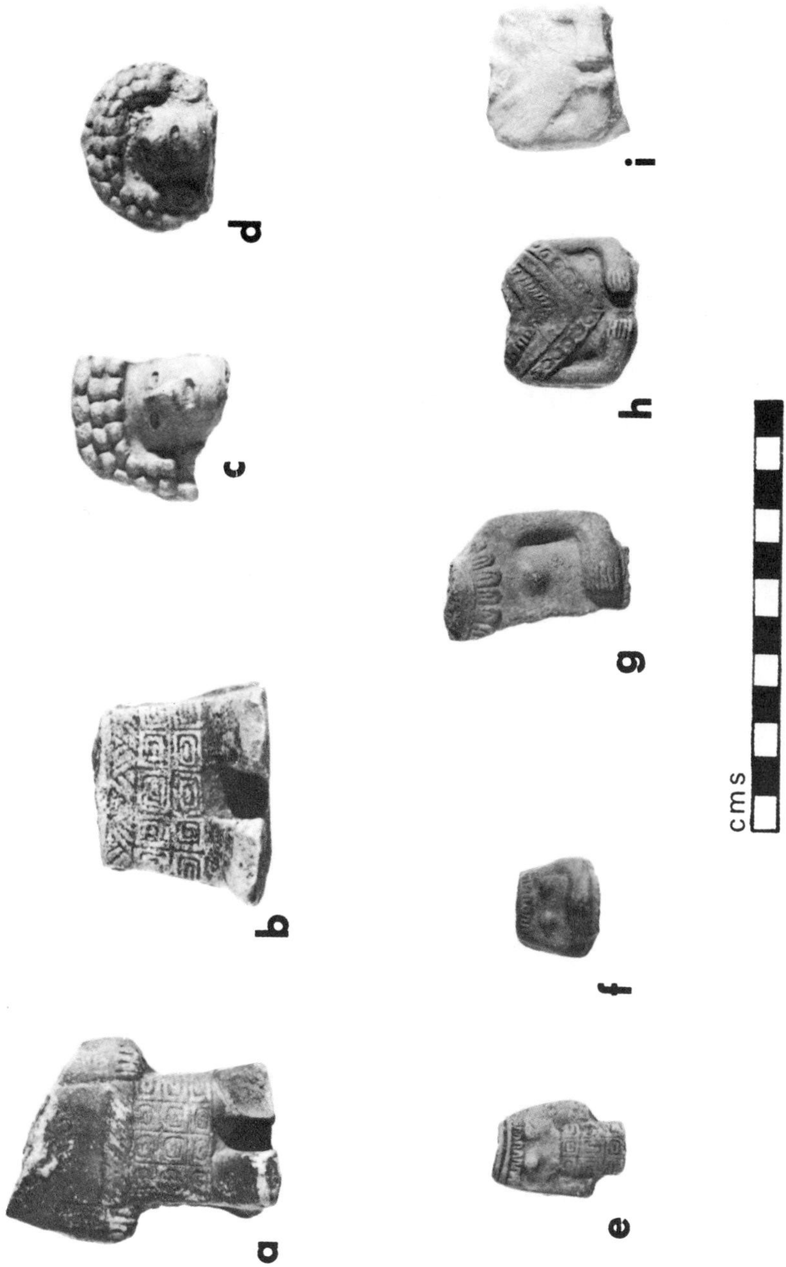


Plate 25. Type III-B: *a-d*, Type III-B1; *e-g*, Type III-B2; *h, i*, Type III-B3.

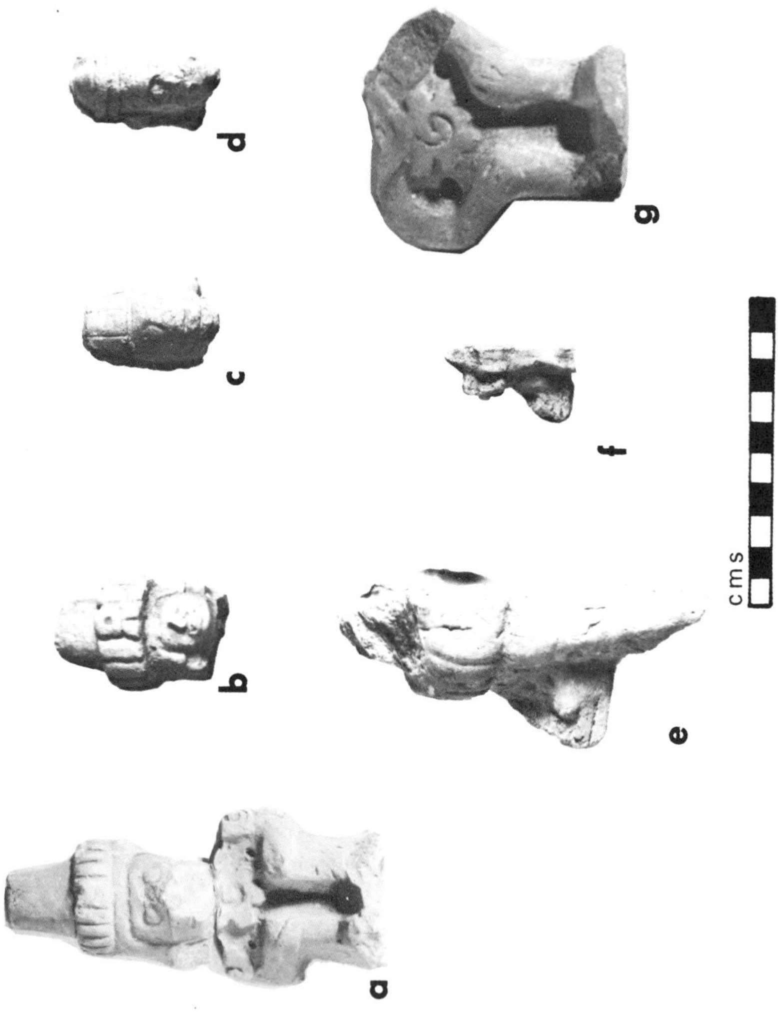

Plate 26. Type III-C: *a*, Type III-C2; *b*, Type III-C1; *c-f*, Type III-C2; *g*, either Type III-C or Type III-H body.

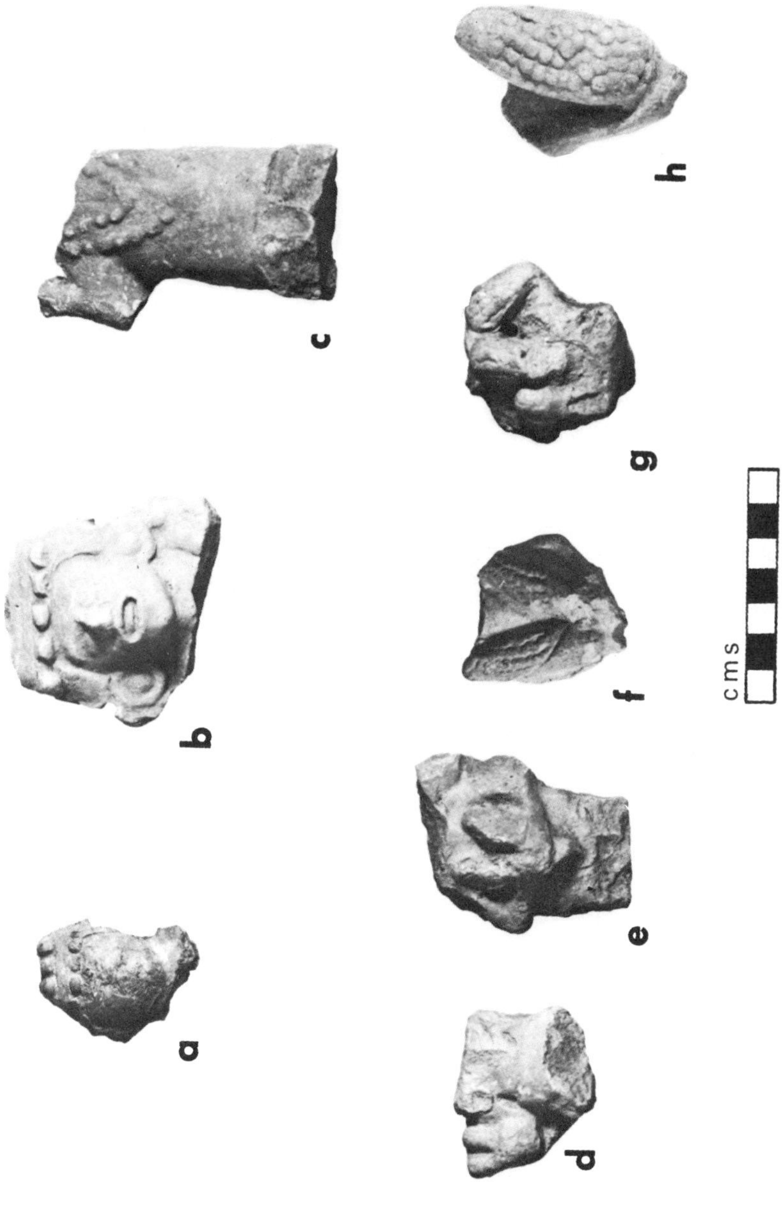

Plate 27. *a-c*, Type III-D; *d*, Type III-E1; *e*, *f*, Type III-E2; *g*, Type III-E3; *h*, miscellaneous corn fragment.

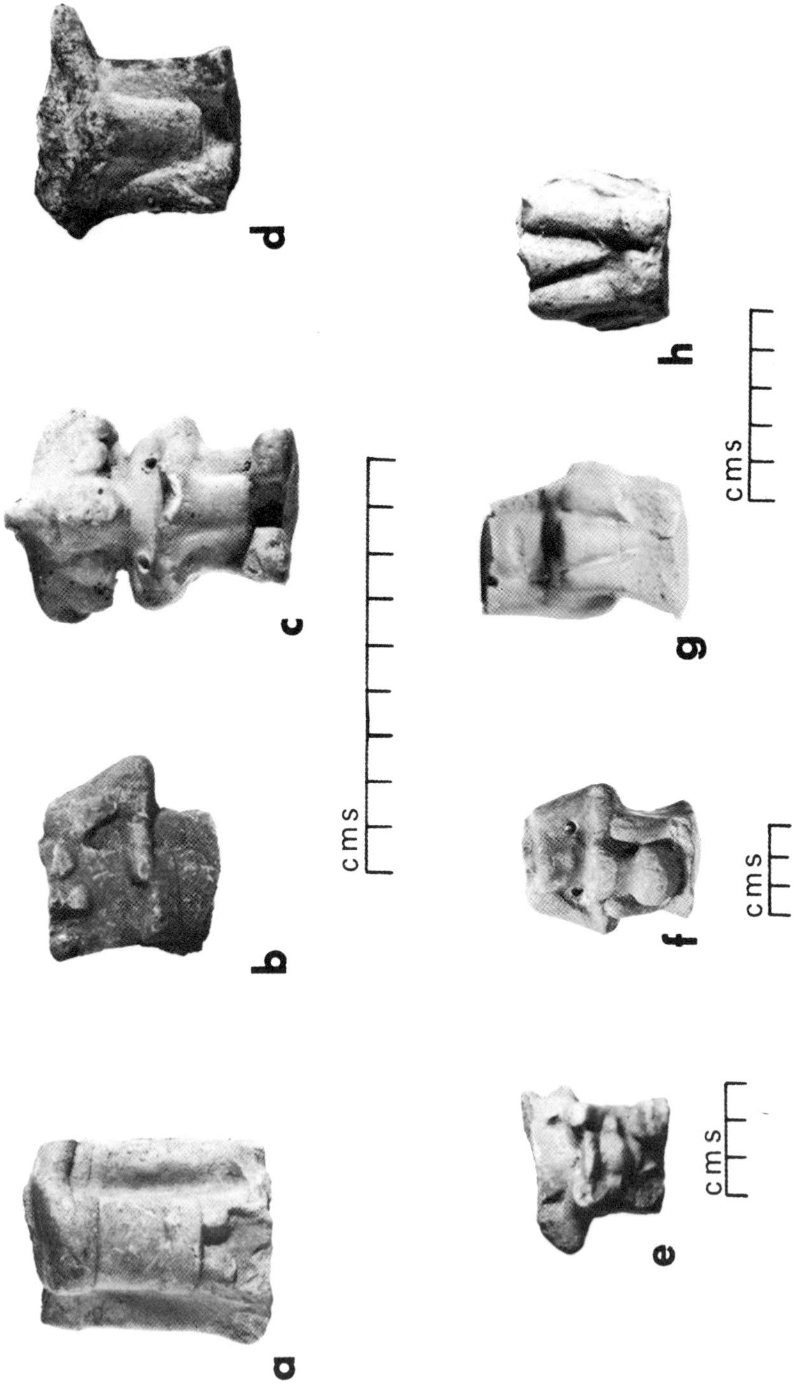


Plate 28. Type III-F: *a*, *b*, Type III-F1; *c*, *d*, Type III-F2; *e*, *f*, Type III-F3; *g*, *h*, Type III-F4.

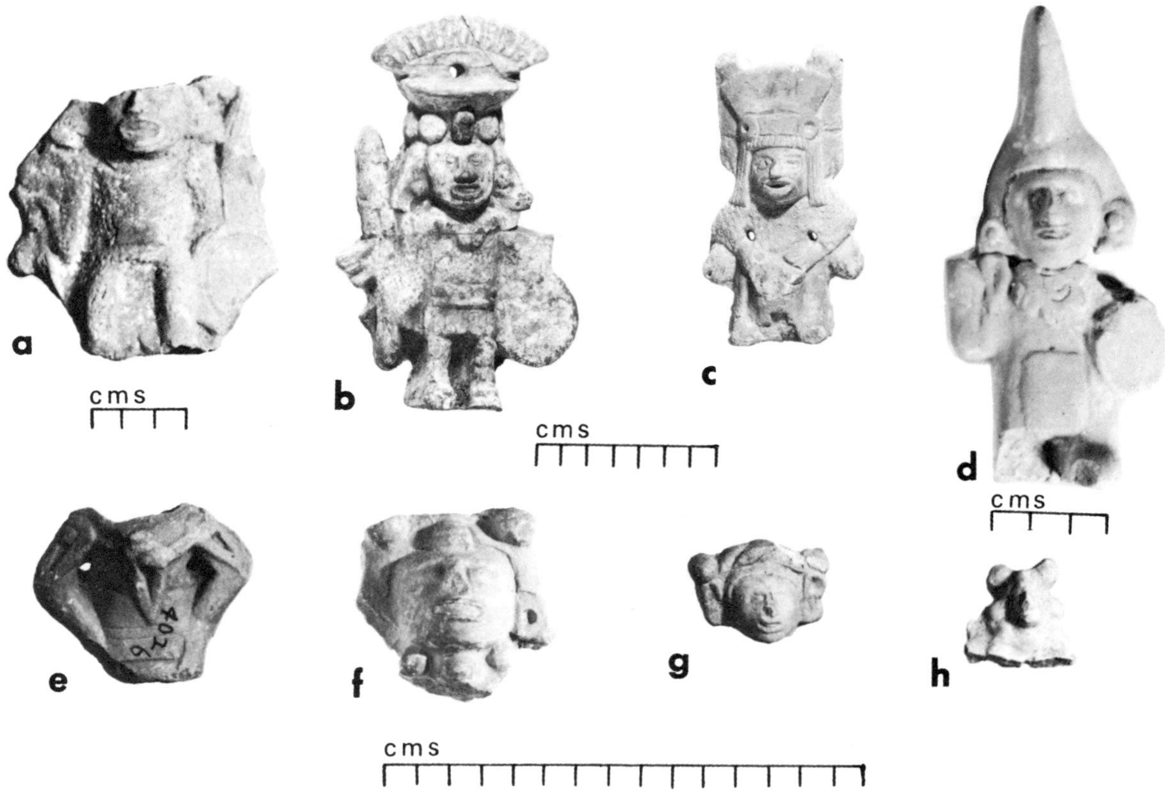


Plate 29. *a-c*, Type III-G; *d*, Type III-H; *e*, Type III-I; *f-h*, Type III-J.

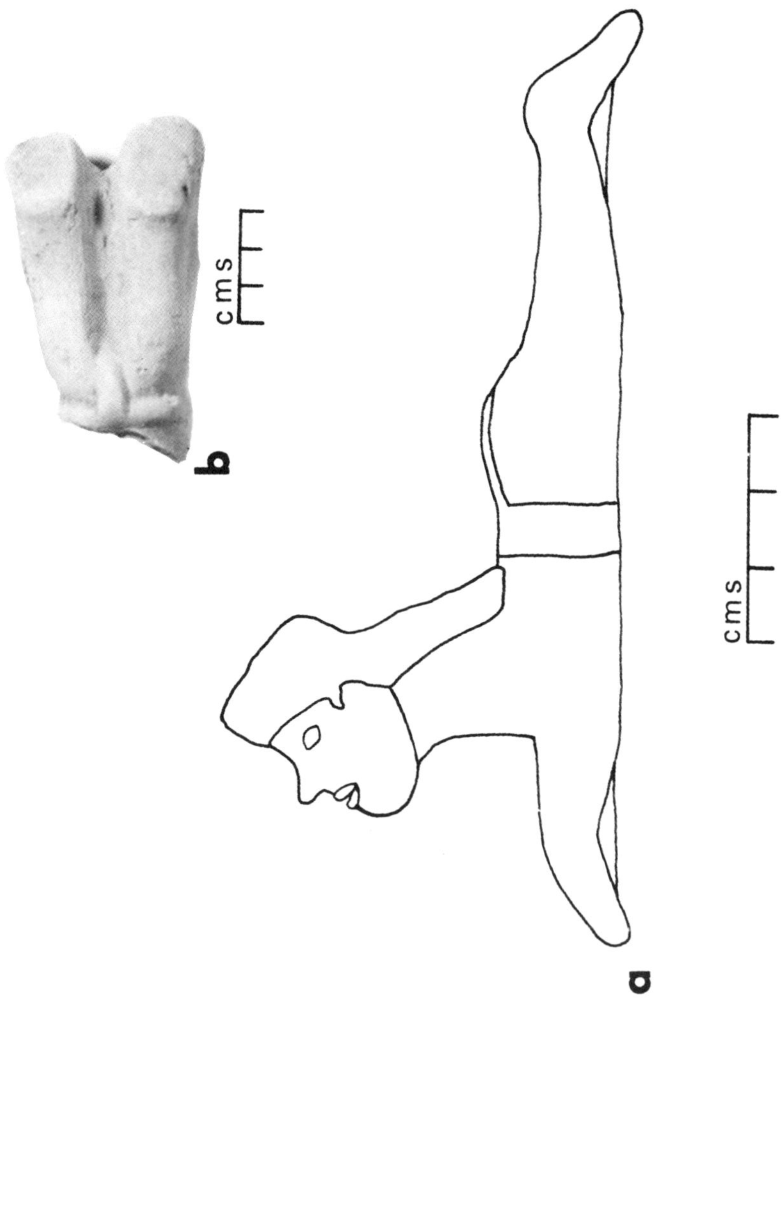


Plate 30. Type III-K.

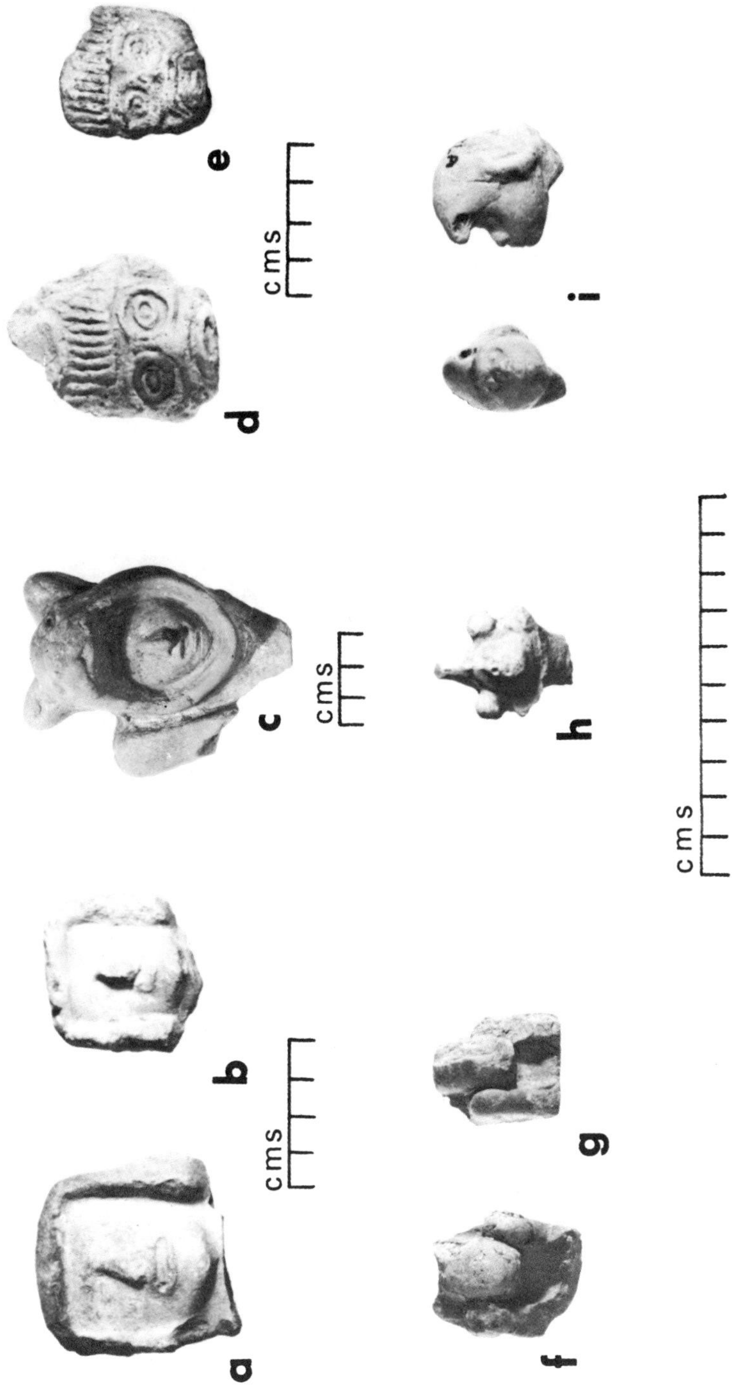


Plate 31. *a*, *b*, Type III-L; *c*, Type III-M; *d*, *e*, Type III-N; *f-i*, Type III-O.

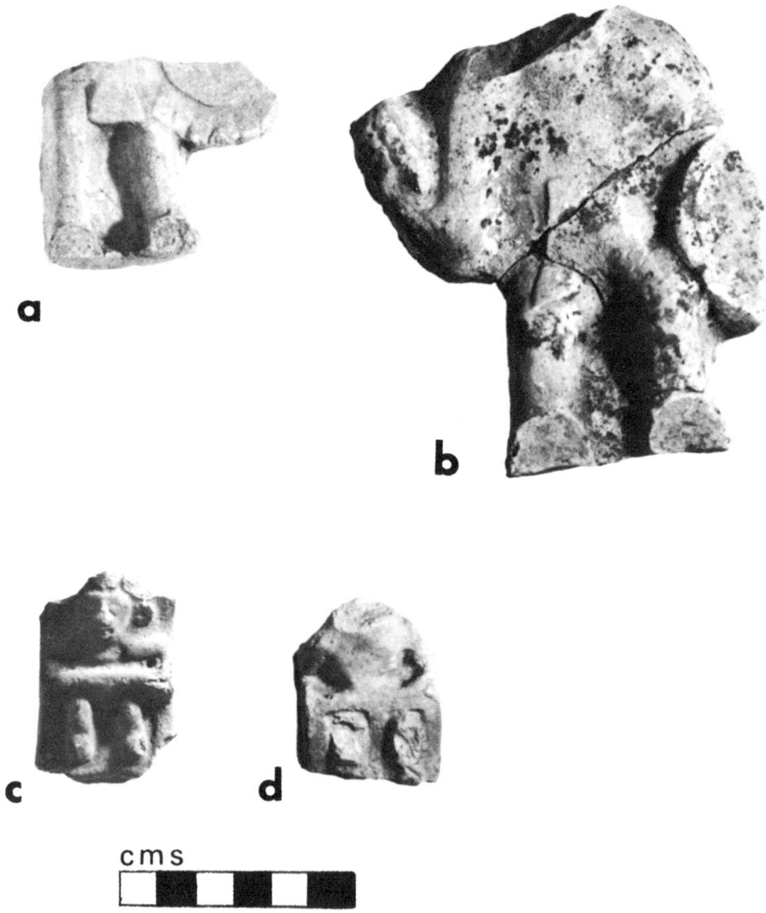


Plate 32. *a, b,* Type III-P; *c, d,* Type III-Q.

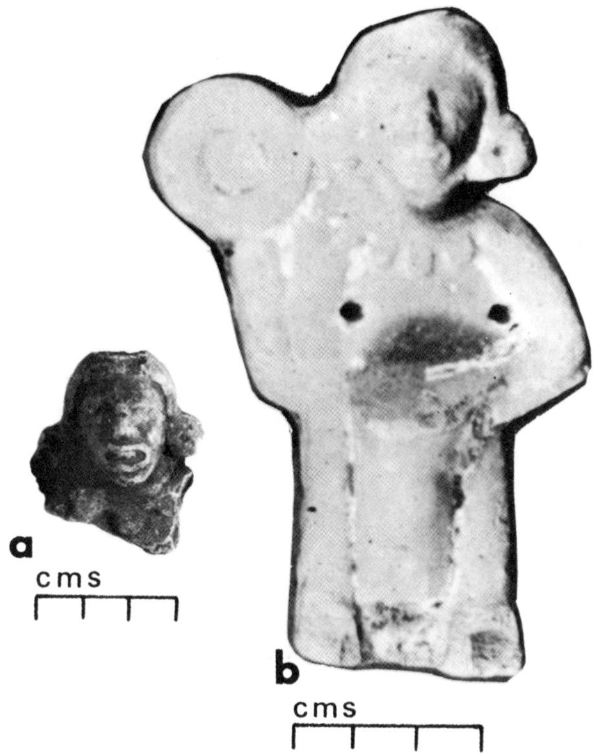


Plate 33. Type III-R.

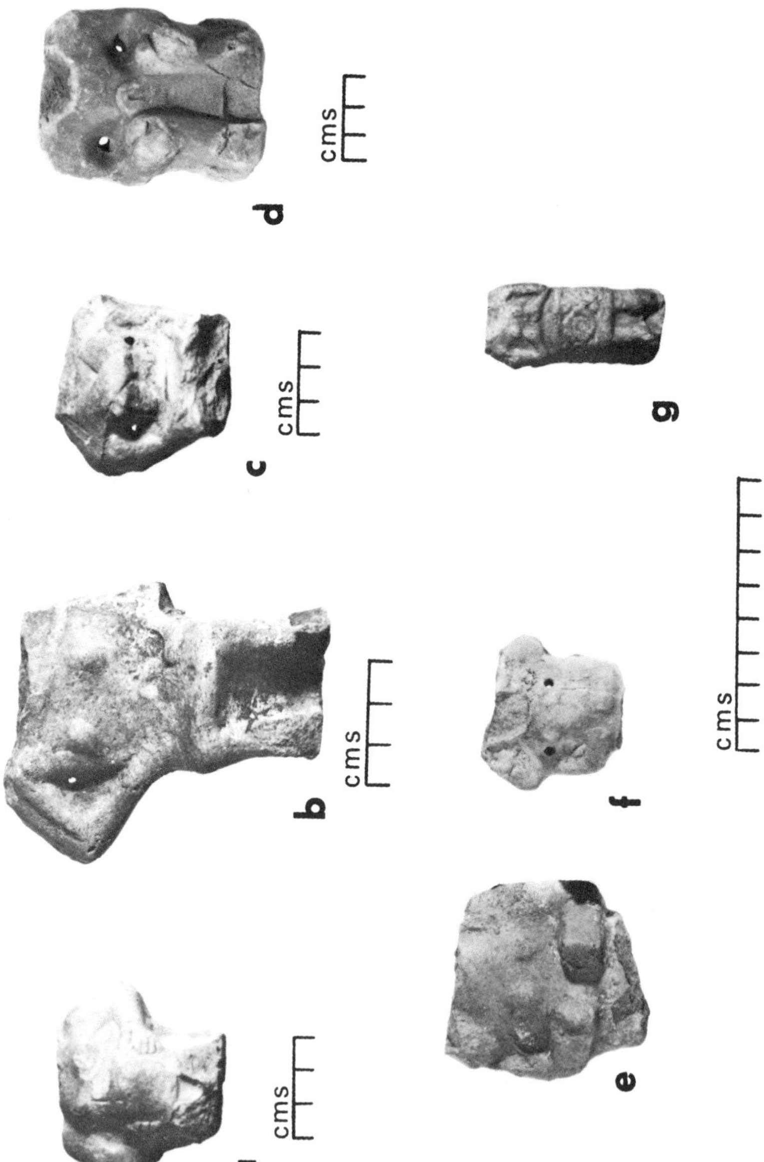


Plate 34. *a*, Type III-S; *b*, *c*, Type III-T1; *d*, Type III-T2; *e*, *f*, Type III-U; *g*, Type III-V.

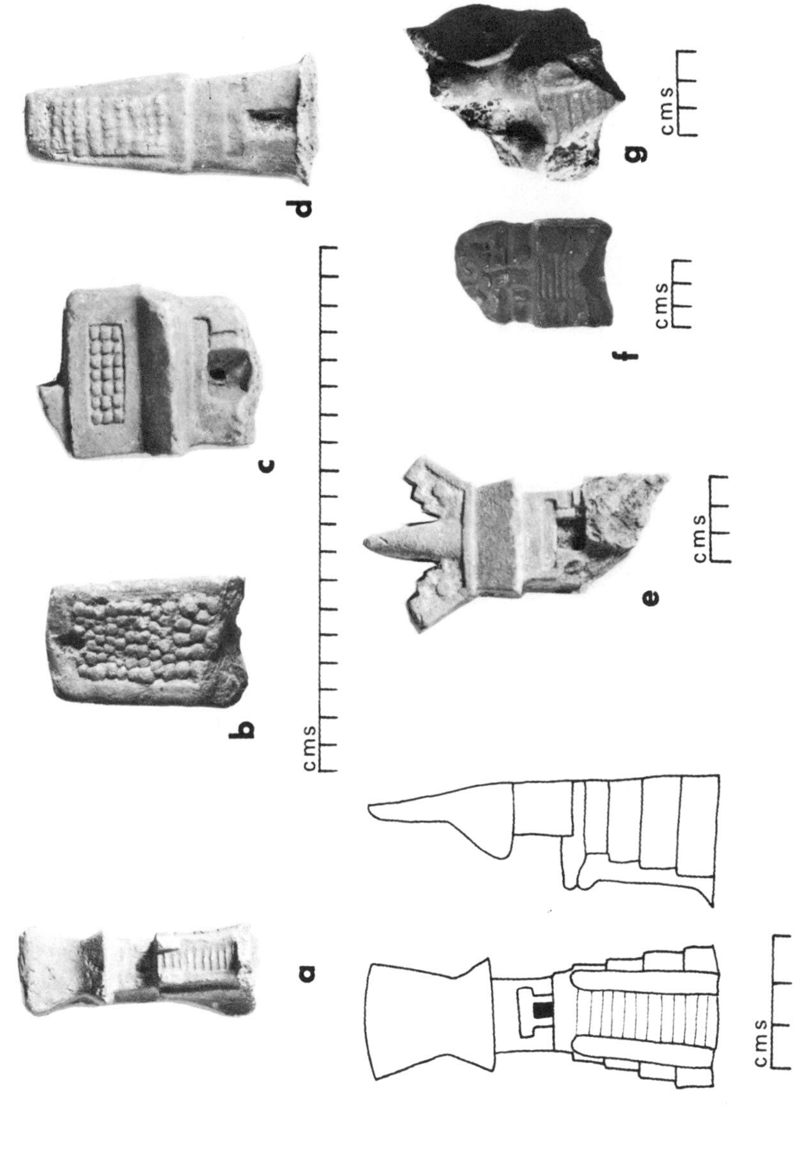


Plate 35. *a-e*, Type III-W1; *f*, *g*, Type III-W2.

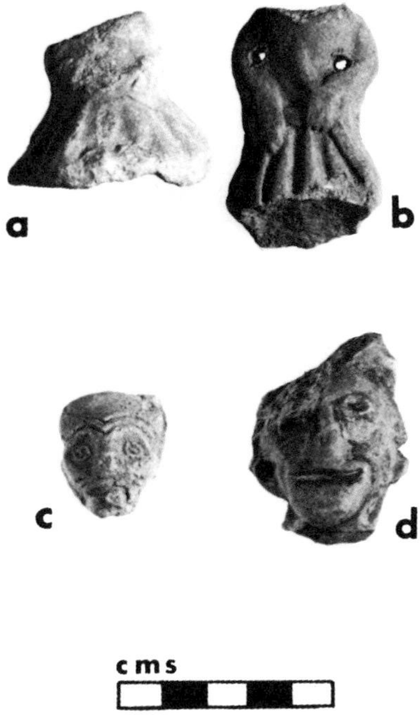


Plate 36. *a, b,* Type III-X; *c,* Mis. 1; *d,* Mis. 2.

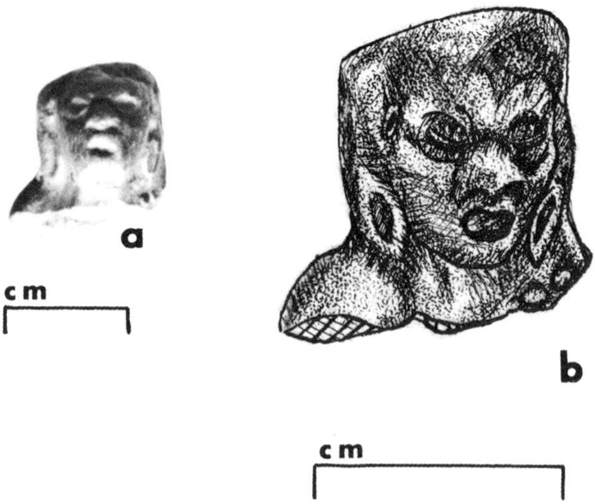


Plate 37. Miniature head, Mis. 3.

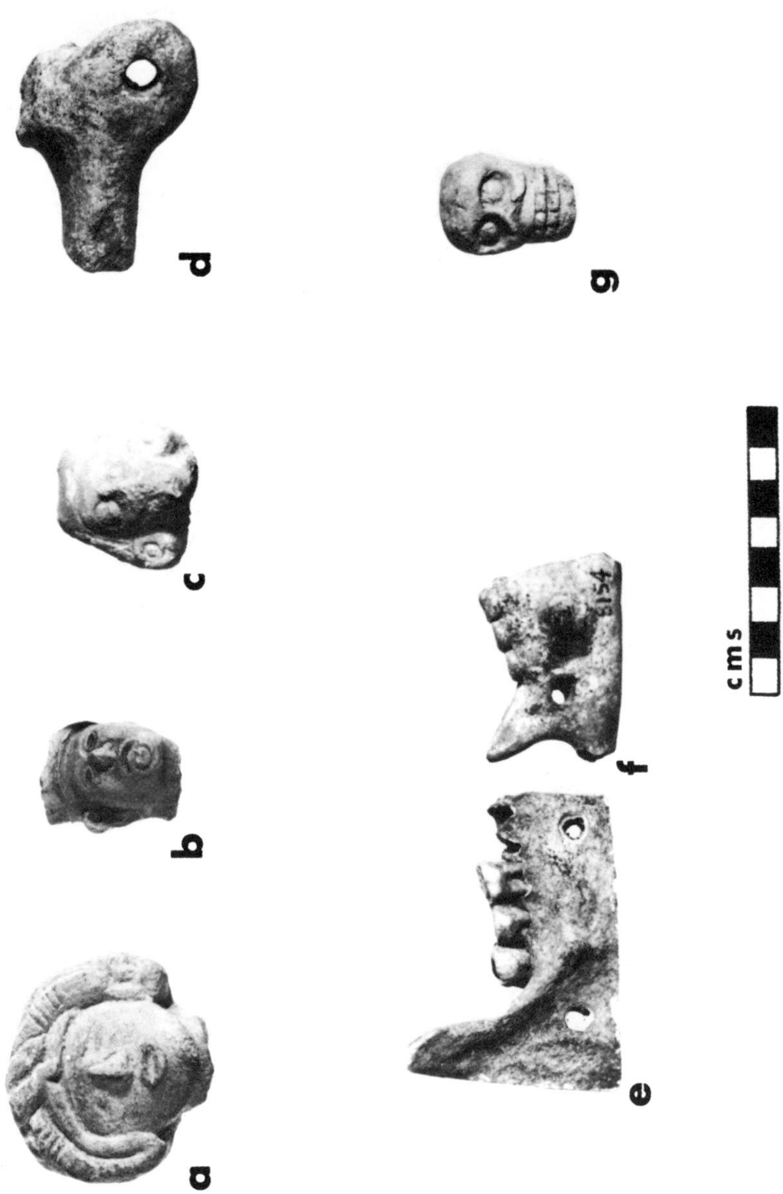


Plate 38. *a*, Mis. 4; *b*, Mis. 5; *c*, Mis. 6; *d*, Mis. 7; *e*, human jaw; *f*, Mis. 8; *g*, Mis. 9.

Plate 39. Miscellaneous broken and unidentified Type III head fragments.

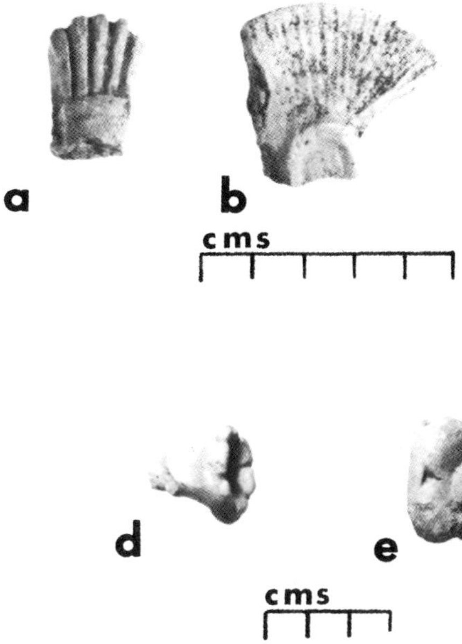


Plate 40. *a*, Top projection fragment; *b, c,* side fan fragments; *d, e,* flower attachments.

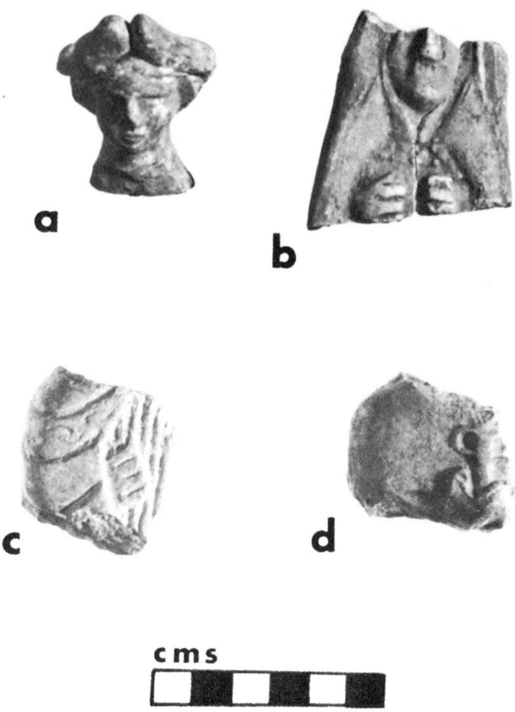


Plate 41. Post-Contact figurines: *a*, Type 1; *b-d*, Type 2.

Plate 42. Post-Contact figurines: *a*, Type 3; *b*, Type 4; *c, d,* miscellaneous.

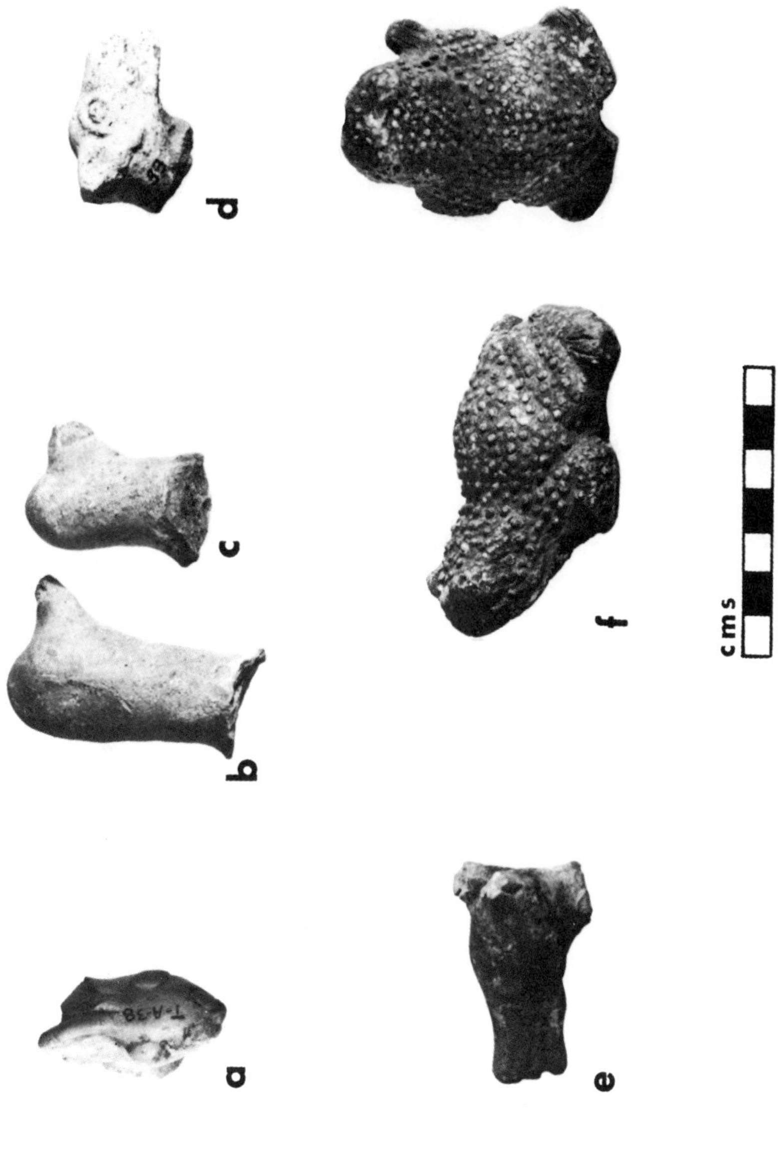


Plate 43. *a*, rabbit; *b*, *c*, birds; *d*, *e*, coyotes; *f*, toad.

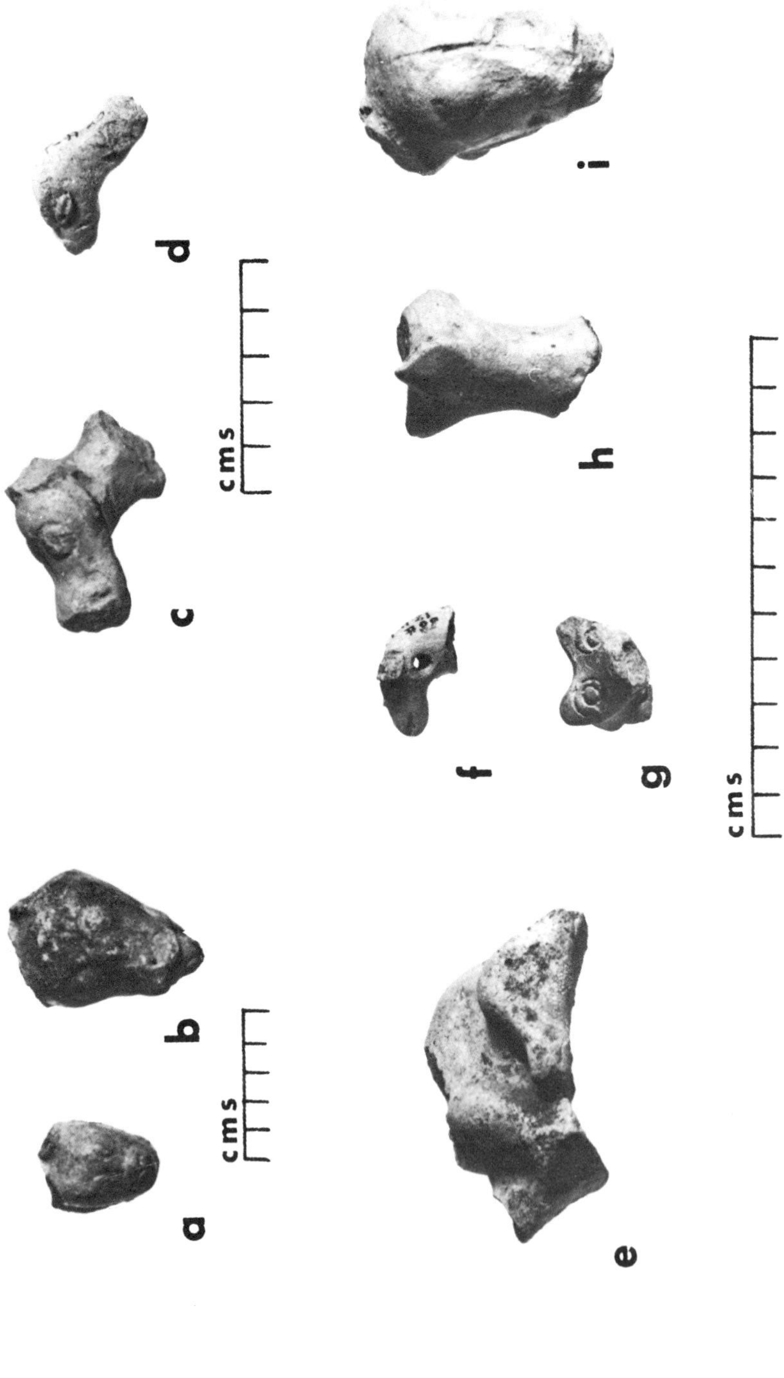


Plate 44. Miscellaneous animal fragments.

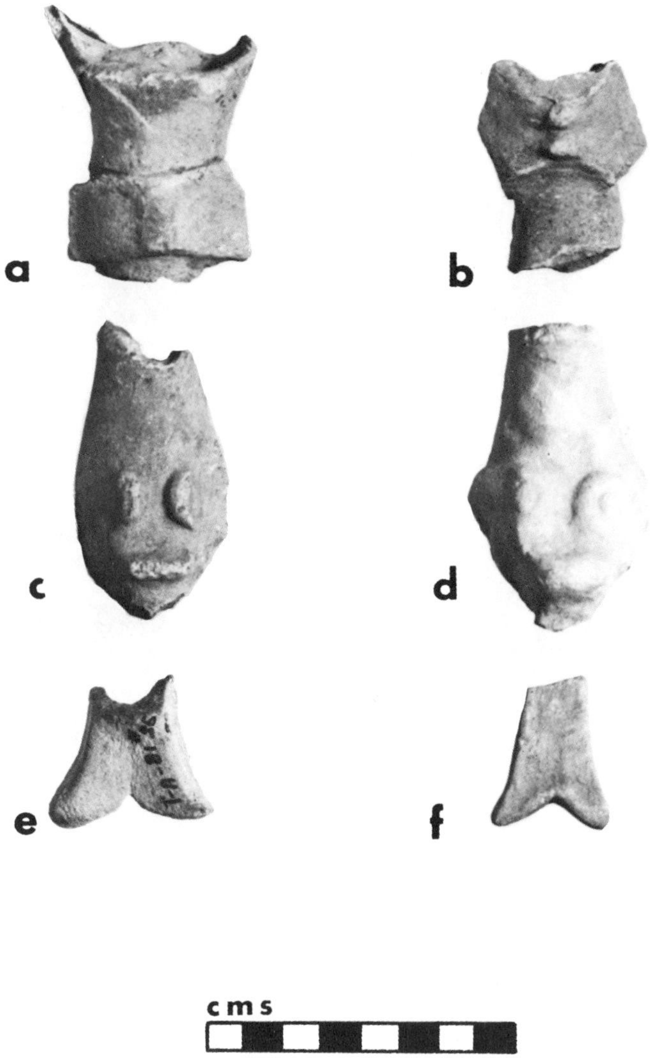


Plate 45. Serpent head censer handle fragments: *a, b,* bow or ax element on handle; *c, d,* serpent head; *e, f,* serpent's tongue.

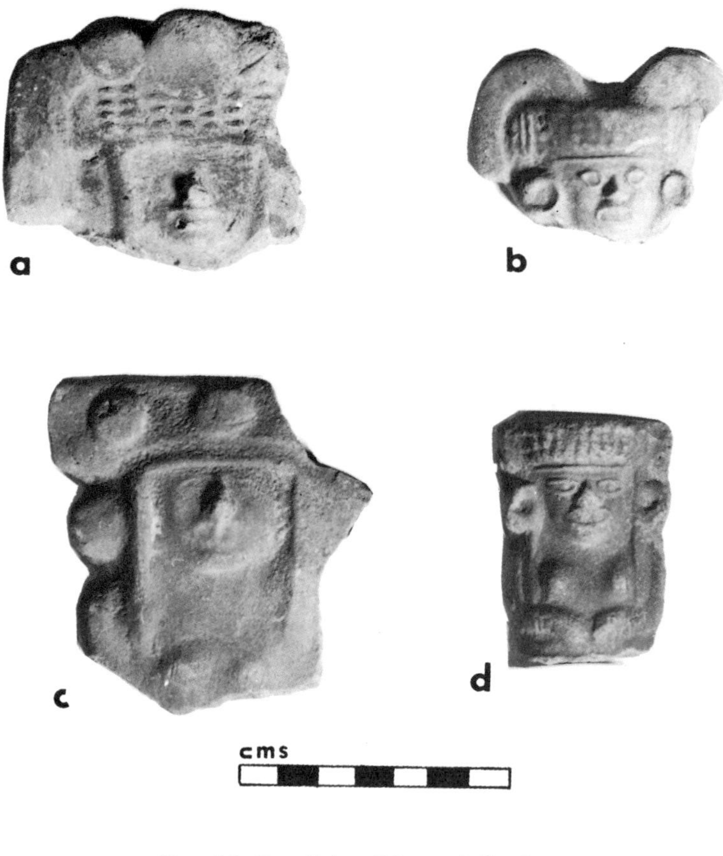


Plate 46. Late Toltec (Mazapan) figurines.

## PROVENIENCE AND NEGATIVE NUMBERS OF PLATES

Abbreviations used:

AMNH – The American Museum of Natural History
FMNH – The Field Museum of Natural History
MNA – Museo Nacional de Antropologia, Mexico City
PSUDA – Pennsylvania State University Department of Anthropology
UMMA – The University of Michigan Museum of Anthropology
YPM – Yale University's Peabody Museum

Plate 1 –– a) PSUDA Cat. No. T-A-239, UMMA Neg. No. 113-4-2; b) PSUDA Cat. No. T-A-80-a, UMMA Neg. No. 113-4-2; c) PSUDA Cat. No. 7645, UMMA Neg. No. 113-4-2; d) PSUDA Cat. No. 8637, UMMA Neg. No. 113-4-2; e) PSUDA Cat. No. T-A-82-b, UMMA Neg. No. 113-4-2; f) PSUDA Cat. No. T-A-239, UMMA Neg. No. 113-4-2; g) PSUDA Cat. No. 4008, UMMA Neg. No. 113-4-2; h) PSUDA Cat. No. 1819, UMMA Neg. No. 113-4-2.

Plate 2 –– a) PSUDA Cat. No. T-A-80-a, UMMA Neg. No. 113-3-4; b) PSUDA Cat. No. T-A-80-a, UMMA Neg. No. 113-3-4; c) PSUDA Cat. No. 8637, UMMA Neg. No. 113-3-4; d) PSUDA Cat. No. T-A-246, UMMA Neg. No. 113-3-4.

Plate 3 –– a) PSUDA Cat. No. T-A-239, UMMA Neg. No. 113-3-4; b) PSUDA Cat. No. T-A-246, UMMA Neg. No. 113-3-4; c) UMMA Tx-A-37, UMMA Neg. No. 120-103-1.

Plate 4 –– a) PSUDA Cat. No. T-A-80-a, UMMA Neg. No. 113-3-3; b) UMMA Texcoco Survey, Strip I (no provenience), UMMA Neg. No. 120-102-5; c) PSUDA Cat. No. 8064, UMMA Neg. No. 113-3-3; d) PSUDA Cat. No. T-A-245, UMMA Neg. No. 113-3-3; e) PSUDA Teotihuacan Valley Project (no provenience), UMMA Neg. No. 113-3-3; f) PSUDA Cat. No. 7615, Neg. No. 113-3-3.

Plate 5 –– a) PSUDA Cat. No. T-A-245, UMMA Neg. No. 113-3-2; b) PSUDA Cat. No. T-A-245, UMMA Neg. No. 113-3-2; c) PSUDA Cat. No. 4001, UMMA Neg. No. 113-3-2; d) PSUDA Teotihuacan Valley Project (no provenience), UMMA Neg. No. 113-3-2; e) PSUDA Cat. No. T-A-246, UMMA Neg. No. 113-3-2; f) PSUDA Cat. No. 8588, UMMA Neg. No. 113-3-2.

Plate 6 — a) PSUDA Cat. No. 9188, UMMA Neg. No. 113-3-2; b) PSUDA Cat. No. 8152, UMMA Neg. No. 113-3-2; c-d) UMMA Texcoco Survey Strip II (no provenience), UMMA Neg. No. 120-104-6.

Plate 7 — a) UMMA Texcoco Survey Strip II (no provenience), UMMA Neg. No. 120-104-1; b) UMMA Tx-A-87 (Texcoco Survey), UMMA Neg. No. 120-104-1.

Plate 8 — a) PSUDA Cat. No. 1630, UMMA Neg. No. 113-3-1; b) PSUDA Cat. No. T-A-80-a, UMMA Neg. No. 113-3-1; c) PSUDA Cat. No. T-A-243, UMMA Neg. No. 113-3-1; d) PSUDA Cat. No. 8556, UMMA Neg. No. 113-3-1; e) PSUDA Cat. No. T-A-80-a, UMMA Neg. No. 113-3-1; f) PSUDA Cat. No. 8061, UMMA Neg. No. 113-3-1; g) PSUDA Cat. No. 8121, UMMA Neg. No. 113-3-1; h) PSUDA Cat. No. 8643, UMMA Neg. No. 113-3-1; i) PSUDA Cat. No. 1631, UMMA Neg. No. 113-3-1.

Plate 9 — a) UMMA Texcoco Survey Strip I (no provenience), UMMA Neg. No. 120-105-3; b) UMMA Texcoco Survey Strip II (no provenience), UMMA Neg. No. 120-105-3; c) PSUDA Cat. No. 8177, UMMA Neg. No. 113-3-1.

Plate 10 — a) PSUDA Cat. Nos. 7648 and 7916, UMMA Neg. No. 113-4-1; b) PSUDA Cat. No. 8265, UMMA Neg. No. 113-4-1; c) PSUDA Cat. No. 8633, UMMA Neg. No.113-4-1; d) PSUDA Teotihuacan Valley Project (no provenience), UMMA Neg. No. 113-4-1.

Plate 11 — a) PSUDA Cat. No. 11, 133, UMMA Neg. No. 113-4-1; b) PSUDA Cat. No. 7015, UMMA Neg. No. 113-3-5; c) PSUDA Cat. No. 8044, UMMA Neg. No. 113-4-1.

Plate 12 — a) PSUDA Cat. No. 3533, UMMA Neg. No. 113-3-5; b) PSUDA Cat. No. 3537, UMMA Neg. No. 113-4-1; c) PSUDA Cat. No. 3565, UMMA Neg. No. 113-3-5.

Plate 13 — a) PSUDA Cat. No. 3565, UMMA Neg. No. 113-4-1; b) PSUDA Cat. No. 7400, UMMA Neg. No. 113-3-5.

Plate 14 — a) PSUDA Cat. 3550, UMMA Neg. No. 113-3-5; b) PSUDA Cat. No. 7400, UMMA Neg. No. 113-3-5; c) PSUDA Cat. No. 3534, UMMA Neg. No. 113-3-5.

Plate 15 — a-c) YPM, UMMA Neg. No. 116-2-4 from Parker Collection; d-g) YPM, UMMA Neg. No. 116-2-6 from Parker Collection.

Plate 16 — a-c) YPM, UMMA Neg. No. 116-2-3 from Parker Collection.

Plate 17 — a) UMMA Cat. No. 56309, UMMA Neg. No. 114-5-1; b) PSUDA Cat. No. T-A-7-a, UMMA Neg. No. 114-4-5.

Plate 18 — a) AMNH, Kaplan Neg.; b) PSUDA Cat. No. T-A-37, UMMA Neg. No. 114-5-4; c) PSUDA Cat. No. T-A-81, UMMA Neg. No. 114-5-4.

Plate 19 –– a) AMNH Cat. No. 30.2/4; b) AMNH Cat. No. 30.0/2191; c) AMNH Cat. No. 30.2/9299; d) AMNH Cat. No. 30.2/1411; e) AMNH Cat. No. 30.2/1394; f) AMNH Cat. No. 30/3683; g) AMNH Cat. No. 30/1942; h) AMNH Cat. No. 30.2/1376; i) AMNH Cat. No. 30.2/1371; j) AMNH Cat. No. 30.2/1377; k) AMNH Cat. No. 30.0/5179.

Plate 20 –– a) AMNH Cat. No. 30.2/1484; b) AMNH Cat. No. 30/2795; c) PSUDA Teotihuacan Valley Project (no provenience), UMMA Neg. No. 118-1-1; d) PSUDA Cat. No. T-A-81, UMMA Neg. No. 118-1-1; e) UMMA Cat. No. 56309, UMMA Neg. No. 114-4-1; f) UMMA Cat. No. 56309, UMMA Neg. No. 114-5-2; g) PSUDA Cat. No. T-A-30-a, UMMA Neg. No. 114-5-6.

Plate 21 –– a) UMMA Cat. No. 56309, UMMA Neg. No. 115-2-6; b) PSUDA Cat. No. T-A-80-a, UMMA Neg. No. 114-2-3; c) PSUDA Cat. No. T-A-80-a, UMMA Neg. No. 114-2-3; d) PSUDA Cat. No. T-A-80-a, UMMA Neg. No. 114-2-3; e) PSUDA Cat. No. T-A-38-a, UMMA Neg. No. 115-2-6; f) AMNH Cat. No. 30/9035; g) AMNH Cat. No. 30/9041; h) AMNH Cat. No. 30.1/9957, Kaplan Neg. 19; i) PSUDA Cat. No. T-A-23, UMMA Neg. No. 118-1-5; j) PSUDA Cat. No. T-A-243, UMMA Neg. No. 118-1-5.

Plate 22 –– a) PSUDA Cat. No. T-A-36, UMMA Neg. No. 115-2-3; b-d) AMNH, Kaplan Neg.; e) UMMA Cat. No. 56330, UMMA Neg. No. 115-3-5; f) PSUDA Cat. No. 11021, UMMA Neg. No. 115-3-5; g) AMNH, Kaplan Neg.

Plate 23 –– a) AMNH, Kaplan Neg.; b) PSUDA Cat. No. T-A-37, UMMA Neg. No. 115-2-4; c) AMNH, Kaplan Neg. 43; d) AMNH, Kaplan Neg. 43; e) PSUDA Teotihuacan Valley Project (no provenience), UMMA Neg. No. 115-3-3; f) UMMA Cat. No. 56318, UMMA Neg. No. 115-3-3; g) PSUDA Cat. No. 11017, UMMA Neg. No. 115-3-2; h) UMMA Cat. No. 9237, UMMA Neg. No. 115-3-2.

Plate 24 –– a) PSUDA Cat. No. 7507, UMMA Neg. No. 114-1-1; b) PSUDA Cat. No. T-A-80-a, UMMA Neg. No. 114-1-6; c) PSUDA Cat. No. T-A-80-a, UMMA Neg. No. 114-1-6; d) PSUDA Cat. No. 8086, UMMA Neg. No. 114-1-6; e) PSUDA Cat. No. 8167, UMMA Neg. No. 114-1-6; f) PSUDA Cat. No. 7635, UMMA Neg. No. 114-1-6; g) PSUDA Cat. No. T-A-80-a, UMMA Neg. No. 114-2-4; h) PSUDA Cat. No. T-A-80-a, UMMA Neg. No. 114-2-4; i) PSUDA Cat. No. 8581, UMMA Neg. No. 114-1-3.

Plate 25 –– a) PSUDA Cat. No. T-A-81, UMMA Neg. No. 115-1-3; b) PSUDA Cat. No. T-A-81, UMMA Neg. No. 115-1-3; c) PSUDA Cat. No. 11018, UMMA Neg. No. 115-3-1; d) PSUDA Cat. No. T-A-38, UMMA Neg. No. 115-3-1; e) PSUDA Teotihuacan Valley Project (no provenience), UMMA Neg. No. 115-1-3; f) PSUDA Cat. No.

T-A-81, UMMA Neg. No. 115-1-3; g) PSUDA Cat. No. T-A-81, UMMA Neg. No. 115-1-3; h) PSUDA Cat. No. T-A-81, UMMA Neg. No. 115-2-1; i) PSUDA Cat. No. T-A-9-j, UMMA Neg. No. 115-2-1.

Plate 26 — a) AMNH, Kaplan Neg. 47; b) PSUDA Cat. No. T-A-80-a, UMMA Neg. No. 114-2-3; c) PSUDA Cat. No. T-A-38, UMMA Neg. No. 114-4-4; d) PSUDA Cat. No. T-A-81, UMMA Neg. No. 114-4-4; e) UMMA Cat. No. 30888; f) UMMA Cat. No. 56309, UMMA Neg. No. 114-2-4; g) AMNH, Kaplan Neg. 22.

Plate 27 — a) PSUDA Cat. No. T-A-38-c, UMMA Neg. No. 121-3-4; b) PSUDA Cat. No. 1505, UMMA Neg. No. 114-1-3; c) PSUDA Cat. No. T-A-80-a, UMMA Neg. No. 114-1-6; d) PSUDA Cat. No. T-A-80-a, UMMA Neg. No. 114-2-2; e) PSUDA Cat. No. T-A-80-a, UMMA Neg. No. 114-2-2; f) PSUDA Cat. No. T-A-80-a, UMMA Neg. No. 114-2-3; g) PSUDA Cat. No. T-A-80-a, UMMA Neg. No. 114-2-2; h) PSUDA Cat. No. T-A-81, UMMA Neg. No. 115-3-4.

Plate 28 — a) PSUDA Cat. No. T-A-81, UMMA Neg. No. 115-3-1; b) PSUDA Cat. No. 8581, UMMA Neg. No. 114-1-2; c) UMMA Cat. No. 56338, UMMA Neg. No. 115-2-6; d) PSUDA Teotihuacan Valley Project (no provenience), UMMA Neg. No. 115-2-6; e) PSUDA Cat. No. 4026; f) AMNH Cat. No. 30/9036; g) AMNH, Kaplan Neg. 49; h) PSUDA Cat. No. 11015.

Plate 29 — a) PSUDA Cat. No. 4032, UMMA Neg. No. 114-1-5; b) AMNH Cat. No. 30/730; c) AMNH Cat. No. 30/1938; d) AMNH Cat. No. 30.2/1735, Kaplan Neg. 50; e) PSUDA Cat. No. 4026, UMMA Neg. No. 114-1-4; f) UMMA Cat. No. 56309, UMMA Neg. No. 114-4-4; g) PSUDA Cat. No. T-A-80-a, UMMA Neg. No. 114-2-2; h) PSUDA Cat. No. 8048, UMMA Neg. No. 114-1-3.

Plate 30 — a) AMNH Cat. No. 30.1/6419; b) AMNH Cat. No. 30.2/1628, Kaplan Neg. 52.

Plate 31 — a) PSUDA Cat. No. T-A-80-a, UMMA Neg. No. 114-2-1; b) PSUDA Cat. No. T-A-80-a, UMMA Neg. No. 114-2-1; c) AMNH Cat. No. 30.2/357; d) UMMA Cat. No. 56309, UMMA Neg. No. 115-3-3; e) PSUDA Cat. No. T-A-80-a; f) PSUDA Cat. No. T-A-81, UMMA Neg. No. 114-4-3; g) PSUDA Teotihuacan Valley Project (no provenience), UMMA Neg. No. 114-4-3; h) PSUDA Cat. No. 1619, UMMA Neg. No. 114-3-1; i-j) UMMA Cat. No. 56309, UMMA Neg. No. 114-4-1.

Plate 32 — a) PSUDA Cat. No. T-A-21-a, UMMA Neg. No. 115-2-1; b) PSUDA Cat. No. 4031, UMMA Neg. No. 114-1-5; c) PSUDA Cat. No. 8569, UMMA Neg. No. 114-3-2; d) PSUDA Cat. No. T-A-80-a, UMMA Neg. No. 114-2-4.

Plate 33 –– a) PSUDA Cat. No. T-A-35-a; b) FMNH, UMMA Neg. No. 121-2-4.

Plate 34 –– a) PSUDA Cat. No. T-A-80-a, UMMA Neg. No. 114-2-4; b) PSUDA Teotihuacan Valley (no provenience); c) PSUDA Cat. No. T-A-80-a, UMMA Neg. No. 114-1-6; d) AMNH Cat. No. 30.2/1726; e) PSUDA Cat. No. T-A-37-d; UMMA Neg. No. 115-3-6; f) PSUDA Cat. No. T-A-81, UMMA Neg. 115-3-6; g) PSUDA Cat. No. T-A-80-a, UMMA Neg. No. 114-1-6.

Plate 35 –– a) AMNH Cat. No. 30.2/1793, Kaplan Neg. 54; b) PSUDA Cat. No. T-A-12; c) AMNH Cat. No. 30.2/1800; d) AMNH Cat. No. 30.2/1803, Kaplan Neg. 54; e) AMNH Cat. No. 30.2/1794, Kaplan Neg. 55; f) AMNH Cat. No. 30.2/9651; g) PSUDA Teotihuacan Valley Project (no provenience).

Plate 36 –– a) PSUDA Cat. No. T-A-9; b) PSUDA Cat. No. 11004; c) PSUDA Cat. No. T-A-27-c, UMMA Neg. No. 115-3-4; d) PSUDA Cat. No. T-A-37-a, UMMA Neg. No. 115-3-6.

Plate 37 –– a) PSUDA Cat. No. T-A-37, UMMA Neg. No. 121-1-2.

Plate 38 –– a) UMMA Cat. No. 56309, UMMA Neg. No. 115-3-1; b) PSUDA Teotihuacan Valley Project (no provenience), UMMA Neg. No. 115-3-4; c) PSUDA Cat. No. T-A-80-a, UMMA Neg. No. 114-2-2; d) PSUDA Cat. No. T-A-81, UMMA Neg. No. 121-3-6; human jaw from Eastern United States, UMMA Neg. No. 114-3-1; f) PSUDA Cat. No. 8154, UMMA Neg. No. 114-3-1; g) PSUDA Cat. No. T-A-80-a, UMMA Neg. No. 114-2-3.

Plate 39 –– a) PSUDA Cat. No. T-A-37, UMMA Neg. No. 114-4-5; b) PSUDA Cat. No. T-A-37, UMMA Neg. No. 114-4-5; c) PSUDA Cat. No. T-A-7-a, UMMA Neg. No. 114-4-5; d) PSUDA Cat. No. T-A-35, UMMA Neg. No. 114-4-5; e) PSUDA Cat. No. 114-4-5; e) PSUDA Cat. No. T-A-81, UMMA Neg. No. 114-4-5; f) PSUDA Cat. No. T-A-36-b, UMMA Neg. No. 114-4-6; g) PSUDA Cat. No. T-A-39, UMMA Neg. No. 114-4-6; h) PSUDA Cat. No. T-A-37-d; UMMA Neg. No. 114-4-6; i) PSUDA Teotihuacan Valley Project (no provenience), UMMA Neg. No. 114-4-6.

Plate 40 –– a) PSUDA Cat. No. T-A-77-a, UMMA Neg. No. 115-3-5; b) PSUDA Cat. No. T-A-38-e, UMMA Neg. No. 115-3-5; c) PSUDA Cat. No. T-A-29-a, UMMA Neg. No. 115-3-5; d) PSUDA Cat. No. T-A-80-a, UMMA Neg. No. 114-2-5; e) PSUDA Teotihuacan Valley Project (no provenience), UMMA Neg. No. 114-2-5.

Plate 41 –– a) PSUDA Cat. No. 7681, UMMA Neg. No. 114-1-1; b) PSUDA Cat. No. 7708, UMMA Neg. No. 114-1-1; c) PSUDA Cat. No. T-A-9-j; d) PSUDA Cat. No. T-A-81.

Plate 42 –– a) PSUDA Cat. No. 7561, UMMA Neg. No. 114-1-1; b) PSUDA Cat. No. T-A-81, UMMA Neg. No. 115-3-4; c) AMNH Cat. No. 30/9095; d) AMNH Cat. No. 30/8222.

Plate 43 — a) PSUDA Cat. No. T-A-38, UMMA Neg. No. 121-3-5; b) PSUDA Cat. No. T-A-81; c) PSUDA Cat. No. T-A-81; d) PSUDA Cat. No. T-A-29-c, UMMA Neg. No. 121-3-5; e) PSUDA Cat. No. T-A-80-a, UMMA Neg. 114-2-1; f) PSUDA Cat. No. T-A-35-a, UMMA Neg. Nos. 114-4-4 and 121-3-6.

Plate 44 — a) PSUDA Cat. No. T-A-80-a, UMMA Neg. No. 114-2-1; b) PSUDA Cat. No. T-A-80-a, UMMA Neg. No. 114-2-1; c) PSUDA Cat. No. T-A-80-a, UMMA Neg. No. 114-2-1; d PSUDA Cat. No. T-A-23; e) PSUDA Teotihuacan Valley Project (no provenience), UMMA Neg. No. 121-3-6; f) PSUDA Cat. No. T-A-81; g) PSUDA Cat. No. T-A-8-f; h) PSUDA Cat. No. T-A-81; i) PSUDA Teotihuacan Valley Project (no provenience), UMMA Neg. 114-2-1.

Plate 45 — a) PSUDA Cat. No. T-A-80-a, UMMA Neg. No. 114-2-5; b) PSUDA Cat. No. 4074, UMMA Neg. No. 114-1-4; c) PSUDA Cat. No. 4012, UMMA Neg. No. 114-1-4; d) PSUDA Cat. No. T-A-80-a, UMMA Neg. No. 114-2-5; e) PSUDA Cat. No. T-A-81, UMMA Neg. No. 121-3-5; f) PSUDA Cat. No. 4032, UMMA Neg. No. 114-1-4.

Plate 46 — a-c) AMNH, Kaplan Neg. 33; d) AMNH, Kaplan Neg. 34.